STUDYING SCOTTISH HISTORY, LITERATURE & CULTURE

Edited by Ian Donnachie

Centre for Scottish Studies

The Open University in Scotland

The Open University

PA734 Project Team

Angus Calder

Ian Donnachie

William Donnelly

George Hewitt

Sheila Lodge

Glenda Norquay

With thanks to:

Averil Gibb

Margery McCulloch

Roderick Watson

Front Cover: First Steamboat on the Clyde by John Knox. Glasgow Museums: Art Gallery & Museum, Kelvingrove.

Back Cover: Robert Burns at an Evening Party at Lord Monboddo's by James Edgar. Scottish National Portrait Gallery

Published by The Open University in Scotland,

Drumsheugh Gardens, Edinburgh EH3 7QJ.

First published 1996

Copyright 1996 The Open University in Scotland

Designed by Scott Ballantyne

Printed in Scotland by Russell Print, Blantyre

ISBN 0 7492 7349 6

CONTENTS

Part I : History Introduction 1

1. SCOTLAND ON THE EVE OF THE REFORMATION 3
2. THE SCOTTISH REFORMATION 7
3. MARY, QUEEN OF SCOTS 10
4. JAMES VI AND I 13
5. THE CROWN AND THE KIRK, 1625-1685 17
6. SCOTLAND ON THE EVE OF THE UNION 21
7. THE UNION OF PARLIAMENTS AND ITS AFTERMATH 25
8. THE LOWLANDS AND THE AGRICULTURAL REVOLUTION 29
9. THE SCOTTISH ENLIGHTENMENT 33
10. THE HIGHLANDS TO 1880 36
11. THE INDUSTRIAL REVOLUTION 40
12. GOVERNMENT AND POLITICS, 1789-1918 44
13. VICTORIAN SCOTLAND: WORKSHOP OF THE EMPIRE? 48
14. PEOPLE, TOWNS AND CITIES 51
15. THE INTER-WAR YEARS 55
16. SCOTLAND SINCE 1945 59

Part II : Literature Introduction 63

1. SOME ASPECTS OF EARLY SCOTTISH LITERATURE 65
2. ROBERT HENRYSON (c1420-1490) 71
3. SCOTTISH LITERATURE IN THE SIXTEENTH CENTURY 76
4. SCOTTISH LITERATURE FROM REFORMATION TO ENLIGHTENMENT 84
5. ROBERT BURNS 90
6. ENLIGHTENMENT AND FEELING 1746-1832 95
7. SCOTT, GALT AND CARLYLE 102
8. JAMES HOGG 110
9. ROBERT LOUIS STEVENSON 115
10. THE KAILYARD AND REACTIONS 119
11. HUGH MACDIARMID 124
12. LEWIS GRASSIC GIBBON 129
13. THE MODERN SCOTTISH NOVEL 134
14. MODERN SCOTTISH POETRY 139
15. GAELIC LITERATURE 143
16. SCOTTISH DRAMA 147

Part III : Culture Introduction 151

1. CULTURE AND HISTORY BEFORE 1560 152
2. REFORMATION AND UNION: SOME CULTURAL EFFECTS 167
3. ENLIGHTENMENT AND ROMANTICISM 1746-1832 173
4. SCOTLAND IN THE MODERN AGE: QUESTIONS OF IDENTITY 182

PART 1:
HISTORY

Glasgow, the industrial city, viewed through clouds of smoke in an early 19th century print.

INTRODUCTION

Working your way through Part I of this volume and following up the associated reading you will obtain a good understanding of some of the major themes in Scottish history since the mid-sixteenth century. Three books, in particular are referred to in some detail:

• G. Donaldson, *Scotland: James V to James VII*, Oliver and Boyd, 1978 (Vol. III, The Edinburgh History of Scotland, paperback ed.) Reprinted by the Mercat Press (James Thin), 1987.

This provides a comprehensive survey of Scotland from the reign of James V to James VII (1513-1688).

• W. Ferguson, *Scotland: 1689 to the Present*, Oliver and Boyd, 1978 (Vol. IV, The Edinburgh History of Scotland, paperback ed.) Reprinted by the Mercat Press (James Thin), 1987.

Another broad survey of Scottish history from 1689 to the present.

• T.C. Smout, A *History of the Scottish People* 1560-1830, Collins/Fontana, 1969 (and subsequent eds.)

A major socio-economic study of Scotland during the period. Page references here are to the paperback edition.

- I. Donnachie and G. Hewitt, A *Companion to Scottish History from the Reformation to the Present*, Batsford, 1989.

A useful reference work covering many aspects of Scottish history in the period.

Your concern will be with broad themes rather than specific details, a concentration on historical problems rather than the personalities and myths which have often clouded the study of Scottish history in the past. With such a wide coverage we have inevitably restricted ourselves to some of the key issues from 1650 to the present and consequently much has had to be omitted, particularly intellectual, educational and cultural developments. This does not mean that one could not pursue such subjects if one wishes.

In each theme you will be given a clear outline of the main issues involved and guidance on recommended reading. This is followed by a discussion of the theme, closely linked to your reading, but incorporating some of our own views and those of recent research. A comprehensive further reading list is provided. The later volumes in the *New History of Scotland* series (Edward Arnold/Edinburgh University Press) provide detailed studies of specific periods while T.C. Smout's A *Century of the Scottish People* (Collins) extends his earlier work. But at the same time we have written this with the four key books firmly in mind.

If you are interested in testing your understanding of each theme we have designed some self-assessment questions which might be used in various contexts, for example as essay topics, or points for further discussion or reflection.

SCOTLAND ON THE EVE OF THE REFORMATION

OBJECTIVES

Your objectives in this section should be to obtain a general understanding of the following:

✪— the structure of Scottish society and politics by the middle of the sixteenth century,

✪— foreign relations 1513-1554.

READING

Donaldson, Chapters 1-5 contains many references, and Smout, Chapter 1, pp. 31-46.

SOME MAJOR THEMES

(i)   The Structure of Scottish Society and Politics by Mid Sixteenth Century

This is best looked at under two main headings:

(a)   Government

"The monarchy gave Scotland most of the institutional unity which it possessed" (Donaldson, p. 4) and clearly, therefore, a powerful king meant strong government. James V (1513-1542) ultimately became such a ruler although at the cost of antagonising many of his most influential subjects. Unfortunately he was succeeded by yet another minor, Mary, queen of Scots, which meant a period of much weaker government in which the crown suffered considerably, particularly from a financial standpoint. Lacking any regular system of taxation, the main sources of royal income were the crown lands, customs, the profits from justice and burghal payments. Responsible for handling these items were two royal officials, the Comptroller and the Treasurer. However, in times of minority rule the crown, in one way or another, tended to receive nothing like what it should have from these sources.

The king was also the head of the judicial system but here a great deal of royal authority had been alienated by the creation of baronies and regalities. Moreover, in many cases the office of Sheriff had become an hereditary appointment. You should also observe the existence of ecclesiastical courts for certain branches of the law. Nonetheless a vigorous king could overcome some of these obstacles although whether James V's establishment of the College of Justice for the administration of civil law strengthened his own position or that of the legal profession is a moot point.

Undoubtedly the most important administrative body within the central government was the privy council. It consisted of the king and, generally, a handful of royal officials, prelates and peers. Parliament, which met only when summoned by the crown, assembled infrequently and normally comprised the lords, spiritual and temporal, and certain burgesses from the towns. By the sixteenth century the task of actually framing policy was being undertaken by a body known as the Committee of Articles. (N.B. Donaldson does not discuss this committee nor the summoning of the less formal Convention until pp. 284-287.)

(b)   Social and Economic Developments

Although there certainly were differences between conditions in the Highlands and Lowlands in sixteenth century Scotland, Donaldson and Smout both stress that these should not be over-emphasised. Thus in both areas there were striking contrasts in wealth between those who were rich and powerful, i.e. the magnates and prelates, and those who were poor and weak i.e. their tenants and followers. Nonetheless there were strong links between the various classes and you should note carefully the ties established by kinship, bonds of manrent and hereditary service. Note also the growing importance of the burghs during the sixteenth century as their trade expanded and some of them, at least, became more prosperous. In this connection pay particular attention to the paramount position occupied by Edinburgh.

(ii) Foreign Relations 1513-1554

(N.B. Donaldson, Ch. 2 gives a broad overview of the period but for the finer details you should also consult Chs. 3-5.)

Broadly speaking Scottish foreign policy in these years was basically pro-French, while another main feature of the period is the growing extent of French hegemony in Scotland. The other principal development is the increasing interaction between events in Scotland and those on the Continent. There are two obvious sub-sections: (a) James V, 1513-1542, and (b) Minority of Mary, 1542-1554.

(a)   James V, 1513-1542

James V did not assume control of Scottish affairs until he freed himself from the clutches of the earl of Angus (1528). Before this, so long as the Duke of Albany was regent (1515-1524) Scotland was Francophil, renewing the "auld alliance" at Rouen in 1517. Once James took over the kingdom, he had several good reasons for continuing Albany's policy e.g. reaction to the Anglophile Angus, the ministerial influence of Gavin Dunbar and financial motivation (the French marriage would bring a profitable dowry). You should observe the prolonged negotiations over this

French marriage in the 1530's and the fact that it was further complicated by the Habsburg-Valois rivalry prevailing in Europe, not to mention the religious ferment created by the reformation. James made two French marriages (his second wife was Mary of Guise) and the importance of this

Anon., James V and Mary of Guise, c1538. From the Blair Castle Collection, Perthshire.

was the gradual deterioration in Anglo-Scottish relations which now ensued. Note the breakdown of friendship between James and Henry VIII which led to hostilities between the two countries and a Scottish defeat at Solway Moss in November 1542. James V died the following month.

(b)   The Minority of Mary, 1542-1554

Scottish affairs were either in the hands of the pro-French archbishop of St. Andrews, David Beaton, or the weak, vacillating James Hamilton, earl of Arran. Initially when Arran's faction accepted Henry VIII's marriage proposals i.e. Mary would ultimately marry Edward (Treaty of Greenwich, 1543) it seemed as if England had scored a notable diplomatic success. But Beaton's party superseded Arran's and repudiated the treaty. Henry VIII's subsequent policy, the "Rough Wooing", 1544-1545, with its devastation of much of lowland Scotland only served to drive Scotland further into the French camp. Beaton's assassination in 1546 made little difference since Henry VIII's successor Edward VI, or at least his guardian, Protector Somerset, pursued the same maladroit tactics towards Scotland as Henry had done. In 1547 there was another English invasion and another Scottish defeat at Pinkie, near Musselburgh. English troops now occupied much of South East Scotland. Arran and other leading Scottish noblemen had little alternative but to look towards France for succour. Hence the Treaty of Haddington (1548) which not only greatly benefited Arran and his family but also by arranging that Mary should marry the French dauphin committed Scotland even further to the cause of France. The treaty also meant more French troops arrived in Scotland although the subsequent English evacuation of

South East Scotland was really a consequence of Continental events. The years 1549-1554 saw a further increase in French control of Scottish affairs culminating in 1554 in the ousting of Arran (now known as the Duke of Chatelherault), with the appropriate compensation of course, and his replacement by Mary of Guise as regent of the country.

You should now have a clear view not only of internal developments within Scotland by mid-century but also of the country's relations with foreign powers. Equipped with this knowledge you are now in a position to tackle one of the main issues of the period, the Reformation.

SAQs

1.   In what ways were Scottish affairs shaped by events and developments in other countries during the reign of James V?

2.   Trace and account for the changes in Anglo-Scottish relations between 1513-1550.

3.   What significance do you attach to the battle of Flodden as a turning point in Scottish history?

4.   What were the main objectives of English governments in their policy towards Scotland between 1542 and 1550 and how far was this policy successful?

FURTHER READING

W. Dickinson, G. Donaldson and E.I. Milne (eds.) (1961) A Source Book of Scottish History, Vol. II, pp. 37-52, 68-73, 125-155, 215-264.

W. Dickinson (1977) Scotland from Earliest Times, Chs. 25 and 26.

G. Donaldson (1967) Scottish Kings, Ch. 8.

W. Ferguson (1977) Scotland's Relations with England to 1707, Ch. 4, pp. 51-64.

N. Macdougall (1989) James IV.

P.G.B. McNeill (1993) An Atlas of Scottish History to 1707.

R. Marshall (1977) Mary of Guise.

M. Sanderson (1986) Cardinal of Scotland: David Beaton, 1494-1546.

THE SCOTTISH REFORMATION

OBJECTIVES

Your objectives in this section should be to study:

✪— the causes of the reformation,

✪— the course of the reformation, 1559-1560.

READING

Donaldson, Chs. 6 and 8 (to p. 144), and Smout, Ch. 2, pp. 49-57.

SOME MAJOR THEMES

(i)   The Causes of the Reformation

The reformation had religious, economic, and political antecedents.

(a)   Religious Causes

You should note here the condition of the pre-reformation church and the impact of the continental reformation.

John Knox

The Scottish church had all the defects to be found on the Continent e.g. a poverty stricken priesthood (here, the great harm done to most parishes by the extensive appropriations of parish revenues by religious houses, cathedral chapters, collegiate chapters and universities is very significant); corruption-immorality, simony, nepotism, pluralism, and non-residence were common features in Scotland; secularisation - observe especially the increasing number of non-churchmen who held high positions in the church, many by grants of commendatorships. However, you should also give some consideration to the attempts at reform within the church undertaken by archbishop Hamilton.

From the 1520's there was increasing signs of Lutheran doctrines in Scotland as well as government action against such heretical opinion e.g. the execution of Patrick Hamilton, 1528. However, by the 1550's it was Calvin who was making the greater appeal and who principally influenced John Knox.

(b)   Economic Causes

Donaldson (pp. 137-139) identifies the motives of the various elements of society (nobility, lairds, burgesses, rank and file). A feature worth noting is the unpopularity of the church's financial demands. These, of course, were considerably increased by the exactions of the crown which, among other things, greatly accelerated the feuing movement within the church.

(c)   Political Causes

The regency of Mary of Guise saw French influence reach its apogee as French officials infiltrated government circles. There was widespread antagonism to this not least because of the financial implications of the French presence e.g. the upkeep of a foreign army resulted in unpopular tax proposals in 1555-1556. The marriage, in 1558, of Mary, queen of Scots, to the dauphin only seemed, in many Scots eyes, to epitomise their country's position as a satellite of France. Nonetheless you should note the considerable diplomatic skill exercised by Mary of Guise although this meant that she did little to hinder the expansion of protestantism between 1554 and 1558.

Thus, in December 1557 a number of Scottish noblemen and lairds signed a bond agreeing to establish the protestant religion in Scotland. The formation of the "Lords of the Congregation", while it should not be over-emphasised too much, is clearly a major step on the road to the protestant revolution.

(ii)   The Reformation, 1559-1560

During 1559 the reformers became a serious threat to the regent, the first notable incident being the disturbances at Perth in May 1559. These were followed by sporadic outbursts of disorder throughout Scotland and numerous towns now declared their protestant affinities. But the forces of the Lords of the Congregation although initially experiencing some success soon found that the regent's professional army was too strong for them. The only remedy was an alliance with England. Note the ensuing Anglo-Scottish negotiations and the eventual Treaty of Berwick, February 1560. This was the turning point in the protestant revolution and shortly after Mary of Guise's death (June, 1560) the hostilities ended with the signing of the Treaty of Edinburgh, July 1560. You should check the details of this agreement noting carefully the various "concessions", one of which permitted a meeting of the Scottish parliament in order to settle the outstanding religious issues. The principal decisions taken by the "Reformation Parliament" in August 1560 were:

(a) the abolition of the jurisdiction and authority of the Pope,

(b) a declaration that the mass was illegal,

(c) the acceptance of a Scots confession of faith.

It is important, from a religious standpoint, that we clear what had been achieved by August 1560. Undoubtedly protestantism had been established by act of parliament (although, strictly speaking, by the terms of the Treaty of Edinburgh, this still required the approval of Mary and her husband). On the other hand, nothing had been done about:

(a) the endowment of the new kirk e.g. how were the stipends of the new clergy to be provided?

(b) the system of government i.e. the "polity" of the reformed church was still undecided, for example, what functions, if any, were the bishops to exercise?

In short, these two issues, endowment and polity, discussed, at great length by the reformers in their first Book of Discipline, were to be the main preoccupations of the kirk for many years to come. In the next section we will examine the policy of Mary's government towards this problem.

SAQs

1.	How far was the progress of the Reformation in Scotland affected by Scotland's relations with England and France?

2.	To what extent does the year 1560 only mark the beginning of religious change in Scotland?

3.	Estimate the importance of religious defects in causing the Scottish reformation.

4.	Was the Scottish reformation movement merely a nationalistic protest against French domination?

FURTHER READING

I. Cowan (1982) The Scottish Reformation.

W. Dickinson, G. Donaldson and E.I. Milne (eds.) (1961) A Source Book of Scottish History, Vol. II, pp. 135-187.

W. Dickinson (1977) Scotland from Earliest Times, Chs. 28-29.

G. Donaldson (1960) The Scottish Reformation, Chs. 1-2.

J. Kirk, (1989) Patterns of Reform: Continuity and Change in the Reformation Kirk.

M. Lynch (1981) Edinburgh and the Reformation.

D. McRoberts (ed.) (1962) Essays on the Scottish Reformation.

J. Wormald (1981) Court, King and Community, Chs. 5-7.

MARY, QUEEN OF SCOTS

OBJECTIVES

Your aims in this section should be an understanding of:

Anon., Mary, Queen of Scots.
Scottish National Portrait Gallery.

❂— Mary's personal rule, 1561-1567,

❂— Mary's subsequent career, 1567-1587.

READING

Donaldson, Chs. 7 and 9 (pp. 157-167).

SOME MAJOR THEMES

(i) Mary's Personal Rule, 1561-1567

(Donaldson, Ch. 7.)

You might wish to check the details of Mary's earlier career, and this can be done via the Index in Donaldson and also Section 1 (The Minority of Mary). The personal reign of Mary is best divided as follows:

(a) Religious Policy

While Mary sometimes upset John Knox, particularly by her insistence on observing mass, the reformers were never united in their opposition to the queen. Thus, generally speaking, although she still refused to ratify the legislation of the reformation parliament, Mary pursued an astute religious policy designed to placate many protestants. Two acts of parliament and one by the privy council serve to illustrate this point:

1562 Thirds of Benefices (for details consult Donaldson, p. 111). But note that the arrangements regarding the thirds, while by no means ideal and nothing like the financial provisions envisaged in the First Book of Discipline, were at least a major step towards providing some kind of regular income for the clergy in the reformed church.

1563 Ministers to be given the use of glebes and manses (another act that year also ordered the repair of churches).

1566 The privy council gave the ministers a definite portion of the thirds and allowed the reformed church the right of collection.

(b)   Political Developments, 1561-1567

Between 1561-1565, Mary gave no indication of that lack of political acumen which was to characterise the final years of her reign. In 1562, for instance, assisted by her brother, the earl of Moray, she dealt effectively with the earl of Huntly, a contumacious catholic nobleman, who was defeated at Corrichie (and conveniently died shortly afterwards). However, Mary's main problem in these years was the question of her remarriage, a matter naturally followed with close attention by the English government. The issue at stake between the two countries was the English succession, i.e. so long as Elizabeth persisted with her policy of refusing to give any guarantees to Mary, the latter, abetted by her principal adviser, Maitland of Lethington, felt no obligation to accede to English directives regarding her choice of husband. You should note the various suitors (not to mention the prevalence of insanity among them!) and pay particular attention to her ultimate, and calamitous. choice, Henry Stewart, Lord Darnley (Donaldson, p.423 gives his genealogical details). The decision to marry her worthless cousin was Mary's first major mistake and, like subsequent errors, it almost immediately had serious consequences by antagonising, in one way or another, Moray, Chatelherault, and Lethington. Some of this hostility to Darnley found expression in the ineffectual "Chaseabout Raid" of September, 1565. But the Darnley marriage also marked the beginning of a series of remarkably violent episodes, e.g. Rizzio's murder (March, 1566); Kirk o' Field affair (February, 1567). Moreover, following the death of Darnley at Kirk o' Field, Mary, by agreeing to marry the earl of Bothwell, now committed her second cardinal mistake. By this union, she not only forfeited the allegiance of many Scotsmen (because of Bothwell's unpopularity) but also, for the time being, lost the support of France, Spain, and the Papacy as well. Thus, her reign virtually ended at Carberry in June, 1567 when she surrendered to her opponents and Bothwell fled the country (ultimately becoming a prisoner of the king of Denmark). The next month, on 24th July, 1567, Mary was forced to abdicate in favour of her infant son, James.

(ii)   Mary's Subsequent Career, 1567-1587

(Donaldson, Ch. 9, pp. 157-167.)

Mary's deposition was largely the work of one faction within Scotland, and her overthrow, unlike the pretty widespread disapproval of Bothwell, was by no means a universally popular action. Evidence of this is provided by the large amount of support which she gathered about her on her escape from Lochleven in May, 1568. (Donaldson gives the figures in p. 159 although he omits to mention that this declaration of allegiance to Mary is usually entitled the "Hamilton Bond".) Mary's defeat at Langside (13th May, 1568) was patently a setback but, as the Hamilton Bond indicates, she still had an impressive body of supporters in Scotland. Indeed, most of the leading Marians, like Argyll, Cassillis, Boyd, and Eglinton continued the struggle on her behalf until the middle of 1571. Nonetheless, it was after her setback at Langside that Mary, by leaving Scotland and putting herself at the mercy of Elizabeth, committed the third major mistake of her career. Clearly the most sensible course would have been to remain in Scotland and continue as the figurehead of the Marian faction rather than risk the uncertainty of exile in a foreign country. The details of Mary's life as a prisoner of the English government can be traced in a standard account of Elizabeth's reign, e.g. J.B. Black (1959), *The Reign of Elizabeth* or, in greater depth, in Antonia Fraser's biography. In Scotland itself, the Pacification of Perth (February, 1573) and the fall of Edinburgh castle, after English assistance, in May, 1573 signalled the collapse, to all intents and purposes, of the Marians as a party of any real consequence.

Mary's personal rule was not one of unmitigated failure and, in the earlier years, she and her advisers showed commendable skill in their handling of the kirk, turbulent noblemen like Huntly and the preliminary marriage negotiations. Her downfall, therefore, was the unfortunate decision to marry Darnley. This, in fact, was the first of three disastrous miscalculations (the others were her marriage to Bothwell and her flight to England) which ensured her reign, and her own life, would end in calamity.

SAQs

1.   Give an outline of Anglo-Scottish relations, 1561-1573.

2.   To what extent did the kirk benefit by having a catholic queen between 1561 and 1567?

3.   "Political ineptitude of staggering proportions". Do you agree with this assessment of Mary's decision to marry Darnley?

4.   Account for the failure of Marian's attempts to restore Mary between 1568 and 1573.

FURTHER READING

J.B. Black (1959) *The Reign of Elizabeth*.

I. Cowan (1971) *The Enigma of Mary Stuart*.

G. Donaldson (1960) *The Scottish Reformation*.
G. Donaldson (1967) *Scottish Kings*. Ch. 9.
G. Donaldson (1974) *Mary Queen of Scots*.
G. Donaldson (1969) *The First Trial of Mary Queen of Scots*.
G. Donaldson (1983) *All the Queen's Men. Power and Politics in Mary Stewart's Scotland*.

A. Fraser (1969) *Mary Queen of Scots*.

M. Lee (1953) *James Stewart, Earl of Moray*.

M. Lynch (ed.) (1988) *Mary Stewart. Queen in Three Kingdoms*.

JAMES VI AND I

OBJECTIVES

Your task in this section is to examine the following aspects of James VI's reign:

❂— the union of the crowns,

❂— the aftermath of the Reformation,

❂— Scotland under James VI and I.

READING

Donaldson, Chs. 8 (pp. 143-153) and 9-13, and Smout, Chs. 2 (pp. 57-61) and 3-4 (pp. 94-106).

SOME MAJOR THEMES

(i)   The Union of the Crowns

(Donaldson, Chs. 9-10.)

The first eighteen years of James VI's reign saw control exercised by various regents or noble factions. The most important of the regents was the earl of Morton (in charge from November, 1572 to December, 1580) who restored a certain amount of stability after the turbulence of the civil war (1568-1573) and whose anglophile policy survived the intrigues of the French and Spanish governments in the 1580's. Ultimately, under James himself, an alliance between England and Scotland was signed at Berwick in July, 1586. James passed the various "tests" to which he was subsequently subjected, e.g. his policy towards Spain in the Anglo-Spanish war, and persisted with his claim to the English throne. By 1600, it was obviously very likely that he would succeed Elizabeth, and his accession in March, 1603 took place without incident. Thus, exactly one hundred years after the marriage of James IV to Henry VII's daughter, Margaret, the crowns of Scotland and England were united under a Stewart king.

(ii)   The Aftermath of the Reformation

(Donaldson, Ch. 11.)

For the sake of convenience, and easier understanding, religious developments are best divided chronologically as follows:

(a)   1567-1585

In the 1570's, we should pay particular attention to the significance of the Leith conference (1572), the oath affecting holders of benefices (1573) and especially the growing controversy over the Second Book of Discipline (1578). Check the similarities between the Second Book and its predecessor but also note the important differences (See Donaldson, pp. 149-150.) Basically what Melville and the more radical churchmen sought was a theocracy but their attempts at establishing such a regime received something of a setback with the passing of the so-called "Black Acts" (1584). These measures, intro-duced just before James

James I and VI, artist unknown. Scottish National Portrait Gallery.

himself took over the reins of government, asserted royal control over general assemblies, confirmed the position of bishops within the church and denounced the presbyterian movement.

(b)   1585-1603

This was a period of fluctuating fortunes for the Melvillians. In the early 1590's, their star was in the ascendant especially with the passing of the "Golden" Act (1592) which, among other things, saw the crown losing ground over the question of holding general assemblies and the erection of presbyteries. These concessions were partly a result of James VI's difficulties with the catholic nobility, notably Huntly, and once these problems were resolved, the king began to take a stronger line with the radicals (note particularly his astute handling of the general assemblies after 1596). Thus, gradually, James retrieved his position and, by 1603, was well on his way to moving over to the offensive against the kirk.

(c)   1603-1625

With Melville imprisoned in 1606 and his leading followers either gaoled or exiled, James VI was able to restore not only bishops but also consider liturgical change within the Scottish church. Consequently, bishops were officially reinstated in 1610 while other alterations, e.g. kneeling at communion, or private baptism were effected by the controversial Five Articles of Perth (1618). The latter were distinctly unpopular and James showed a sagacity subsequently lacking in his son, Charles, by eschewing their effective implementation.

(iii) Scotland under James VI and I

(Donaldson, Chs. 12-13, and Smout, pp. 94-106.)

While James remained in Scotland, he depended on the normal governmental machinery but, on going south (and remember he only returned on one solitary occasion in 1617), he placed greater emphasis on controlling the northern kingdom by the Committee of Articles and the Privy Council. Here his comparative success led him to boast that he governed Scotland "with his pen".

James certainly did not discourage magnates participating in his government but there was a distinct tendency to employ numerous non-aristocratic people. Such ministers or officials, like Lethington's brother, Maitland of Thirlstane, frequently were rewarded with peerages for faithful service, a process accelerated after 1587 by the erection of ecclesiastical properties into hereditary temporal lordships.

Both before and after his ascent to the English throne, James VI's major administrative problem was the establishment of law and order, particularly in the borders and the highlands and islands. His solution for the frontier was Anglo-Scottish co-operation. This was obviously more easily undertaken once the union had taken place and joint action by both governments, in conjunction with the stationing of a small but permanent force in the border area, resulted in a great improvement in conditions. In the highlands and islands, he relied to some extent on traditional expedients such as depending on certain powerful families, like the Campbells, to execute royal policy, but, at times, he adopted other methods such as the appointment of "trouble-shooting" royal officials, e.g. Andrew Knox, bishop of the Isles, and James Law, bishop of Orkney, co-operation with England (especially to cut off links between Ulster and the west of Scotland) and the outlawing of recalcitrant clans like the Macgregors. James, once he had overcome the obstacles presented by the northern catholic earls, not to mention the maverick earl of Bothwell, had less difficulty exerting control over the central part of his kingdom. Perhaps the best evidence of what has been termed the "king's peace" is the way in which the greater stability prevailing in Scotland in the latter part of James VI's reign brought significant social and economic benefits to most of the population. (A good outline of these is given in Donaldson, Ch. 13, and Smout, pp. 99-106.)

James VI, despite the vicissitudes of his earlier career, subsequently pursued a policy towards England which ensured that he would unite the two countries under one monarch; in ecclesiastical matters, he restored episcopacy and effected liturgical change in the kirk yet also showed that "he knew where to stop"; he greatly improved law and order, giving the nation a stability which had beneficial social and economic consequences. It is these achievements which make him one of Scotland's most successful kings.

SAQs

1. With what justification could James VI claim to govern Scotland "with his pen"?

2. To what extent was there social and economic progress between 1567 and 1625?

3. What contribution did Andrew Melville make to religious developments in the reign of James VI?

4. Describe James VI's policies towards the borders and the highlands and islands. Estimate how successful they were.

5. Give an account of Anglo-Scottish relations between 1567 and 1603.

FURTHER READING

W.C. Dickinson and G. Donaldson (1961) A Source Book of Scottish History, Vol. III, pp. 3-65, 227-237, 261-287, 303-315, 426-455.

W.C. Dickinson (1977) Scotland from Earliest Times to 1603, Chs. 31-32.

G. Donaldson (1960) The Scottish Reformation, Chs. 7-9.

W. Ferguson (1977) Scotland's Relations with England, pp. 88-96.

B. Galloway (1986) The Union of England and Scotland 1603-08.

G. Hewitt (1982) Scotland under Morton.

J. Kirk (1981) The Second Book of Discipline (Introduction).

M. Lee (1981) Government by Pen: Scotland under James VI and I.

S.G.E. Lythe (1960) The Economy of Scotland, 1550-1625.

T.I. Rae (1966) The Administration of the Scottish Frontier, 1513-1603.

A.H. Williamson (1974) Scottish National Consciousness in the Age of James VI.

J. Wormald (1981) Court, King and Community, Chs. 8-9.

THE CROWN AND THE KIRK, 1625-1685

OBJECTIVES

Your objectives in this rather wide-ranging section are to examine the period between 1625 and 1685 with particular emphasis on the relations between church and state. This study is best divided into:

- Charles I and the Scottish Revolution,
- Scotland and the English Civil War,
- Scotland under Cromwell,
- The Restoration and its aftermath.

READING

Donaldson, Chs. 16-19, and Smout, Ch. II, pp. 61-65.

SOME MAJOR THEMES

(i) Charles I and the Scottish Revolution

(Donaldson, Chs. 16, and 17 to p. 325.)

The key issue is the growing hostility towards Charles I. The main reasons for this were:

(a) The Act of Revocation

Try to note carefully the implications of this important, if complex, statute and the series of measures which followed it. You should be clear about the well-intentioned motives behind the legislation but, at the same time, aware of how, by its clumsy presentation, it provoked great resentment and feelings of insecurity among most landowners.

(b) The Crown's Financial Demands

James VI had found it necessary to introduce what virtually amounted to a regular system of taxation in Scotland with a larger proportion of the population being liable to contribute. Under Charles I, the burden became even heavier and, with parliamentary requests in 1625, 1630, and 1633 spread over several years, the country was, in effect, being taxed annually. Note other financial grievances, for example, increased customs duties and, in the case of Edinburgh, the catalogue of additional expenses incurred as a result of Charles I's policies.

(c)   Charles I's Religious Policy

You should note the mounting opposition to Charles I's ecclesiastical measures culminating with the introduction of the new prayer book in July, 1637 (the main criticisms against it are given in Donaldson, pp. 309-310).

The series of events leading to the First and Second Bishops' Wars are set out pretty clearly in Donaldson (pp. 311-325). Critical here were the signing of the National Covenant, the actions of the general assembly at Glasgow in November-December, 1638, the pacification of Berwick, the decisions taken by the Scottish parliament at Edinburgh in August, 1639 and the Treaty of Ripon. This latter agreement and the subsequent peace treaty signed by Charles I in June, 1641 underline the sweeping success of the covenanting forces over the crown.

(ii) Scotland and the English Civil War

(Donaldson, Ch. 17, pp. 325-342.)

The major development in the years 1642 to 1649 is the disintegration of the nearly universal support which existed for the covenanters and the emergence of a royalist party in Scotland. Although this was a very gradual transition and only of any real significance after 1646, its origins were present from the start of the civil war. These stemmed partly from the constitutional objections of certain noblemen to the policies of the covenanters, from the unpopularity of the earl of Argyll and from objections to the signing of the Solemn League and Covenant. Regarding the latter, we should note, not only its principal terms but also the fact that the subsequent military pact between the two sides had important consequences for the course of the English Civil War.

Although the Montrose rising (1644-1646) was the first sign of opposition to covenanting policies, it should be noted that it attracted little support in lowland Scotland. Thus the real catalyst was the failure of the English parliamentarians, increasingly dominated by the anti-presbyterian military leaders, to honour the terms of the Solemn League. This led to the agreement with Charles I, known as The Engagement (December, 1647), and ensured the division of Scotland into two factions - the Engagers and Anti-Engagers. The defeat of the former by Cromwell at Preston in August, 1648 gave the presbyterian extremists their opportunity to take over the country and pass swingeing legislation against their opponents, e.g. the Act of Classes (January, 1649).

(iii) Scotland under Cromwell

(Donaldson, Ch. 18.)

The religious and political divisions existing in Scotland between 1649 and 1651 made Cromwell's task of subjugation much easier than it might have been and, from 1652 until 1660, England and Scotland were united. However, although

Scotland did send representatives to the parliament at Westminster, this was essentially a union inflicted on a vanquished foe by a victorious military power. The more important aspects of the Cromwellian interlude include the improvement in the administration of law and order (particularly in the highlands), the considerable deterioration in social and economic conditions, and the distinct religious schism between the more moderate presbyterians ("Resolutioners") and the die-hards ("Protestors"). Initially, Cromwell's government preferred the latter since they were hostile to Charles II but ultimately abandoned this policy in favour of giving some recognition to the resolutioners.

(iv) The Restoration and its Aftermath

(Donaldson, Ch. 19.)

The church settlement, after the restoration of Charles II in 1660, was encompassed in the Act Rescissory (1661) and other legislation the next year by which a moderate episcopalian system was imposed on the country. Our main concern is to examine the reaction to these ecclesiastical arrangements and how the government tackled the problem of religious dissidence.

From 1662 onwards, it was the more extreme presbyterians who were prepared to challenge the government's religious policy, and one of their main grounds for opposition was the vexed question of lay patronage. This led to about one quarter of the clergy being deprived but, despite legislation imposing fines and residential restrictions on such clergymen, they continued to hold their illegal services or conventicles.

From this juncture until the end of Charles II's reign, government tactics alternated between repression and conciliation. Initially, a hard line was taken including the use of troops to break up conventicles, and this produced the small-scale rebellion known as the Pentland Rising (1666). This was followed from about 1667 to 1674 by a more conciliatory governmental attitude largely through the efforts of the royal secretary, the earl of Lauderdale. Thus, between 1669 and 1672, many ministers accepted indulgences, and the presbyterian opposition to the crown was seriously split. There now followed a further period of repressive measures (note the introduction of the intensely unpopular "Highland Host" in 1678) culminating in a more serious rising in 1679 and defeat for the covenanters at Bothwell Bridge. By 1680 the only active opposition to the government came from the Cameronians, a body of fanatical presbyterians with most support in south west Scotland. They fought relentlessly against the government forces commanded by Graham of Claverhouse who, in his efforts to suppress them, often did not bother to distinguish between active Cameronians and those who were simply non-conforming presbyterians. Doubtless, as Donaldson states, "the atrocities of the 'killing time' have been exaggerated" but, by the same token, the callous, vindictive treatment of many of those who were merely presbyterian sympathisers in one way or another has tended to be understated.

Charles I's reign inaugurated a period of bitter religious dissension within Scotland. The restoration of Charles II seemingly established a moderate episcopal polity in the country, although presbyterian opposition was by no means extinguished. The strength of this presbyterian movement was to be revealed in the ecclesiastical developments which followed in the reigns of James VII and William of Orange.

SAQs

1. To what extent was the revolution against Charles I inspired by religious grievances?

2. What were the merits and demerits of the Cromwellian union as far as Scotland was concerned?

3. Why, and with what consequences, did the restoration church settlement experience so much opposition?

4. Discuss the historical importance of two of the following: James Graham, Marquis of Montrose; Scotland's contribution to the English Civil War, 1642-1646; John Maitland, Duke of Lauderdale; John Graham of Claverhouse.

John Graham of Claverhouse, Viscount Dundee, "Bonnie Dundee", An engraving by W. J. Edwards from the original by Sir Peter Lily.

FURTHER READING

J. Buckroyd (1980) *Church and State in Scotland, 1660-8l.*

I Cowan (1976) *The Scottish Covenanters.*

E. Cowan (1977) *Montrose: For Covenant and King.*

F. Dow (1980) *Cromwellian Scotland.*

W. Ferguson (1977) *Scotland's Relations with England,* Chs. 6-8.

M. Lee (1985) *The Road to Revolution. Scotland under Charles I.*

G. Menzies (ed.) (1972) *The Scottish Nation,* Chs. 8-9.

R. Mitchison (1983) *Lordship to Patronage,* Chs 2-4.

D. Stevenson (1973) *The Scottish Revolution, 1637-1644,* Chs. 11-15.

Scotland on the Eve of the Union

OBJECTIVES

Working through this section, you should gain an understanding of:

❂— constitutional and religious developments by the end of the seventeenth century,

❂— social and economic conditions before 1707,

❂— industry and trade prior to the Union.

READING

Donaldson, Chs. 15 and 20, Ferguson, Chs. 1 and 3, and Smout, Chs. 5-8.

SOME MAJOR THEMES

(i)   Constitutional and Religious Developments by the end of the Seventeenth Century

(Donaldson, Ch. 15, and Ferguson, Ch. 1.)

The revolution settlement, accomplished between April, 1689 and June, 1690, brought to an end a century of considerable constitutional and religious change. From a constitutional standpoint, and it would be a good idea to check earlier 16th century developments in Section 1, the main points to observe are:

(a)   the composition of parliament, particularly the addition of shire members,

(b)   crown influence especially the part played by the Committee of the Articles,

(c)   the importance of the privy council both as a legislative and judicial body.

(d)   the introduction into local government of justices of the peace and commissioners of supply.

The outlines of the revolution settlement are to be found in the Claim of Right drawn up by the Scottish convention which met in April, 1689. The two most important constitutional consequences were the abolition not only of the committee of the articles but also of episcopacy (thus denuding parliament of bishops).

As far as religious developments are concerned, the most crucial, apart from the removal of bishops, were:

(a)   the restoration of the presbyterian system on the lines of the 'Golden' Act of 1592,

(b)   the abolition of lay patronage,

(c)   the reinstatement of all ministers ejected in 1662,

(d)   the restoration of the general assembly (it had not met since the Cromwellian union).

While, generally speaking, this was a moderate church settlement, it is worth noting that many episcopalian clergy did not conform, although some rejoined via conciliatory statutes in 1693 and 1695, and that there also remained a small remnant of Cameronian dissenters.

(ii)   Social and Economic Conditions before 1707

(Smout, Chs. 5-7, and Ferguson, Chs. 1 and 3.)

There has been little discussion so far about the social and economic background to the various political and religious events of the sixteenth and seventeenth centuries and this is the point to rectify this omission. Smout provides a sound outline, and the best idea is to work your way systematically through Chapters 5 to 7. Thus, Chapter 5 deals with the farmtoun, its baron courts and the different farming methods in use; Chapter 6 covers both the landowners with their various systems of tenure and rental arrangements, and the peasantry, especially the problems facing this class in the "ill years" of the 1690's; Chapter 7 concentrates on the burghs, their institutional structure, the corrupt nature of municipal government, the numerous social stratifications and the problems arising from population increase and epidemics.

Smout also makes some reference to conditions in the highlands but, for William III's policy towards this region and the events leading to the Massacre of Glencoe, you should consult Ferguson, pp. 15-26. The encouragement given to the Jacobite cause which this episode produced is clearly the most important consequence of the whole unsavoury business.

(iii) Industry and Trade before the Union

(Donaldson, Chs. 15 and 20, and Ferguson, Chs. 1 and 3.)

This topic has had limited coverage, so if you are interested in earlier developments, particularly under James VI, you should read Donaldson, pp. 244-252. What is said there largely holds good for much of the 17th century as well, i.e. Scotland's principal economic disadvantages were that, with the exception of linen, it mainly exported raw materials while, apart from timber, most of its imports were either manufactured items or wine. Similarly, Leith remained the chief port of Scotland, and England the main market for Scottish trade. However, you should note the gradual emergence of Glasgow as a commercial centre and its links, frequently illegal, with the North American colonies.

Scottish governments in the post-restoration period also pursued the policies of earlier administrations regarding the encouragement of native industries, e.g. 1661 establishment of a Council of Trade designed to foster home-based industries and commerce. This eventually led to a plethora of joint-stock companies including the Royal Fishing Company, Glasgow Soap Company, the Linen Company, and the Bank of Scotland. But the protectionist policy of the English parliament, especially the Navigation Act (1661), proved a major obstacle to any expansion in Scotland's trade overseas, and it was a desire to obtain a greater share of colonial wealth and markets which led to the formation of the Company of Scotland. This is given sound coverage in Ferguson, pp. 26-30 but you might like to pay particular attention to the following points:

(a)   the Company of Scotland was initially sanctioned by William III in order to distract attention from the Massacre of Glencoe,

(b)   the so-called Darien Scheme was only adopted because of the withdrawal of English financial backing,

(c)   William III's objections to the Darien venture were originally based not on diplomatic considerations but on pressure from English commercial interests,

(d)   the Darien plan was not necessarily utopian but failed because of inadequate resources and planning plus William III's eventual hostility,

The Arms of "The Company of Scotland Trading to Africa and the Indies" ~ The Darien Scheme.

(e)   the failure of the enterprise underlined the problems surrounding a dual parliamentary system and gave strength to the economic argument for a parliamentary union.

By the beginning of the eighteenth century, although the government's ecclesiastical measures were unpopular in many circles, religious issues were gradually being resolved. But if religion was no longer quite so controversial a topic, the consequence of ill-advised policy towards the highlands and the treatment of Scotland's search for overseas markets was the creation of serious antagonisms between the Scottish and English parliaments. William III's remedy, given shortly before his death in 1702, was to advocate "some happy expedient for making England and Scotland one people".

SAQs

1.   For what reasons was the reign of William III an unpopular one as far as many people in Scotland were concerned?

2.   To what extent were the main religious issues in Scotland resolved by the settlement of 1689-1690?

3.   What were the most important constitutional developments which took place during the course of the seventeenth century?

4.   Give an outline of the organisation of the burghs and their social structure during the seventeenth century.

FURTHER READING

W.C. Dickinson and G. Donaldson (1961) A *Source Book of Scottish History*, Vol. III, pp. 185-260, 303-344, 345-398.

W. Ferguson (1977) *Scotland's Relations with England*, Ch. 9.

P. Hopkins (1986) *Glencoe and the End of the Highland War*.

B. Lenman (1980) *The Jacobite Risings in Britain 1689-1746*.

R. Mitchison (1983) *Lordship to Patronage*, Chs 5-6

P. Riley (1979) *King William and the Scottish Politicians*

T.C. Smout (1963) *Scottish Trade on the Eve of the Union*.

I. Whyte (1979) *Agriculture and Society in Seventeenth Century Scotland*.

THE UNION OF PARLIAMENTS AND ITS AFTERMATH

OBJECTIVES

Once you have worked your way through this section you should have a good grasp of the following:

⚙— the union of parliaments, 1707,

⚙— Scotland after the union, 1707-1750.

READING

Ferguson, Chs. 2 and 4-6 (pp. 180-183), and Smout, Chs. 9-10 (to p. 230).

SOME MAJOR THEMES

(i)   The Union of Parliaments, 1707

(Ferguson, Ch. 2.)

Although William III may have thought parliamentary union was imperative, relations between Scotland and England in the opening years of Queen Anne's reign were so strained that such a possibility seemed increasingly unlikely. Granted, there were abortive discussions about the possibility of union in 1702, but the succession issue soon ensured a worsening in relations already seriously weakened by the Darien affair.

In 1701, by the Act of Settlement, the English parliament had bestowed the succession to the throne upon the electress of Hanover and her descendants. The Scottish assembly, believing, quite rightly, that it should have been consulted, now refused to recognise this legislation by their English counterparts. Thus, since the French, at war with England over the Spanish Succession, had recognised the son of James VII as heir to the British throne, there was the obvious possibility of two candidates for the crown and one of them backed by England's enemy.

The potential danger facing England and the extent of Scottish opposition were underlined by three measures passed by the Scottish parliament in 1703, i.e. the Act of Security, the Wine Act, and the Act Anent Peace and War. In fact, the Act of Security, which laid down very stringent terms regarding the succession, was so controversial that Queensberry, the royal commissioner, refused to give his assent in 1703. But, the following year, by withholding supply at a critical phase in the continental war, the Scottish parliament forced Queensberry's replacement, Tweedale, to accept a Security Act only minimally different from that of 1703.

It was now the turn of the English parliament to retaliate by means of the Alien Act which threatened to treat all Scotsmen as foreigners and place embargoes on all Scottish exports to England until such time as the Act of Security was repealed. The only way Scotland could end this economic blockade, so the Act stipulated, was to arrange a settlement of the succession question or agree to hold discussions about a union of the rival parliaments.

The Alien Act proved to be a trump card for England and, by February, 1706, Scottish commissioners (all but one of them members of the pro-government or Court party) were in London negotiating and incorporating union. It is important you should familiarise yourself with the main details of the subsequent Treaty of Union (Ferguson, p. 48) and the passage, between October, 1706 and January, 1707, of these proposals in the Scottish parliament. Undoubtedly, the proposed union was generally unpopular in Scotland but, although some parliamentarians like Fletcher of Saltoun resisted all blandishments and contested it to the bitter end, the various inducements proferred by the government, not to mention the divisions existing within the opposition or Country party, ensured the safe passage of the bill. Moreover, ecclesiastical criticism was stifled by a separate act guaranteeing the security of the presbyterian system.

(ii)   Scotland after the Union, 1707-1750

(Ferguson, Chs. 4-5, and Smout, Chs. 9-10 (to p. 230).)

This section is best studied under the following headings:

(a)   Anglo-Scottish Relations, 1707-1750

You should distinguish between the period immediately after the union, i.e. 1707-1715 and the later phase from 1715 to 1750. In the early years after the union, there was mounting hostility towards England for reasons which are not difficult to find, e.g. the imposition of the English law of treason; the peerage dispute; the Toleration Act; the Patronage Act. These measures, in conjunction with a new export duty on Scottish linen and the proposal to introduce the detested Malt Tax into Scotland, led to a demand in 1713 by the Scottish M.P.'s at Westminster for the termination of the union. This attempt to end the union was only narrowly defeated and was followed, almost immediately, by another crisis in Anglo-Scottish relations, the 1715 Jacobite rebellion.

Ferguson (pp. 63-69) gives ample coverage of the 1715 rising but it is worth noting the futility of the whole business without French support and the generally poor response in Scotland, despite widespread antagonism towards England, for the Jacobite cause.

The years after 1715 saw a certain amount of anti-Jacobite activity, e.g. the Clan Act, General Wade's road-building and the garrisoning of certain parts of the highlands. However, the social conditions in the highlands remained unaltered and this proved a decisive factor when Charles Edward Stewart, son of the 'Old Pretender' of 1715, decided to raise the clans on his behalf in 1745. Again, the details of the Forty-Five rebellion are very clearly outlined in Ferguson (pp. 149-156) but you should pay particular attention to the main areas of support for the rising and the reasons why it was unsuccessful. Note, also, the subsequent legislation against the Jacobites, in particular the Disarming Act and the abolition of heritable jurisdictions.

Prince Charles Edward Stewart, "Bonnie Prince Charlie" by Antonio David. Scottish National Portrait Gallery.

(b) The Church after the Union, 1707-1750

This topic might seem a rather esoteric one - is it necessary, for instance, to spend a great deal of time on the "Marrow Controversy" of 1719-1720? Possibly not, yet we really do need to understand the consequences for the church of such unpopular governmental statutes as the Toleration Act and the Patronage Act. Similarly, in the latter part of this period, you should also be clear about the issues involved in the dispute which produced the Secessions. Ostensibly, these originated over patronage but, in reality, it emphasised the fact that, in the 18th century Scottish kirk, there was always a body of churchmen and their adherents who preferred dissent to conformity.

(c) Economic Developments, 1707-1750

Since agriculture in the first half of the eighteenth century is discussed in Section 8, our concern here is only with industrial developments during this period.

Undoubtedly, the first decades after the union brought only slow industrial expansion or prosperity, and there were several popular outbursts, for example, the Shawfield and Porteous riots - which reflected both dissatisfaction with the union as well as violent opposition towards government fiscal policy. Gradually, however, there were signs of an improvement in the economic situation especially in the linen industry which benefited from legislation such as that appointing the Board of Trustees for Manufactures (1727), the Bounty Act (1742) and the establishment of the British Linen Company in 1746. Likewise, trade with North America began to expand, particularly the importation of tobacco, although the zenith of this commercial enterprise was to be reached in the years after 1750.

By the mid-eighteenth century, the union of parliaments was firmly established. It had survived the Jacobite attempts at its overthrow and, if there was little affection for the Hanoverian dynasty, the highlands were the only part of Scotland where the Stewart cause had received any substantial support. While the church became increasingly preoccupied with the implications of the Patronage Act, not to mention various arcane controversies, trade and industry were slowly beginning to show some signs of benefiting from the treaty of union.

SAQs

1.	Why was disagreement over the succession a major factor in hastening the Treaty of Union?

2.	Account for the failure of the Jacobite rebellions in 1715 and 1745.

3.	To what extent was the union a success, from an economic standpoint, between 1707 and 1750?

4.	Why was lay patronage such a controversial issue in the first half of the eighteenth century?

FURTHER READING

R.H. Campbell (1985) *Scotland since* 1707, Chs. 1-4.

W.C. Dickinson and G. Donaldson (1961) A *Source Book of Scottish History*, Vol. III, pp. 469-495.

A Durie (1979) *The Scottish Linen Industry in the Eighteenth Century*.

W. Ferguson (1977) *Scotland's Relations with England*, Chs. 10-14.

H. Hamilton (1963) An *Economic History of Scotland in the* 18th *Century*.

B. Lenman (1980) *The Jacobite Risings in Britain* 1689-1746.

R. Mitchison (1970) A *History of Scotland*, Chs. 17-19.

P.W.J. Riley (1978) *The Union of England and Scotland*.

P.H. Scott (1992) *Andrew Fletcher and the Treaty of Union*.

C.A. Whatley (1994) *Bought and Sold for English Gold. Explaining the Union of* 1707.

THE LOWLANDS AND THE AGRICULTURAL REVOLUTION

OBJECTIVES

In this section we would like you to consider:

✿— land and agriculture in the Lowlands before the Agricultural Revolution,

✿— the role of landowners in agricultural "improvement" or modernisation,

✿— the links between land and industry,

✿— the social impact of these changes in the countryside.

READING

Much of the seventeenth century background is covered in Chapters 5 and 6 of Smout, while Chapter 12 and 13 describe the main developments during the eighteenth century. A more general picture is provided in Ferguson, Chapter 6 (especially pp. 166-174), so you might well want to read this first, before looking in detail at what Smout has to say.

Workhorses draw a binder at harvest time in Fife. G. M. Cowie.

SOME MAJOR THEMES

(i) The Lowlands before the Agricultural Revolution

As you will find in studying industrialisation (introduced in Section 11) historians have been reassessing earlier conclusions about the chronology of change during the seventeenth and eighteenth centuries. In agriculture as in industry modernisation probably began much earlier than previously supposed, though wholesale "improvement" - involving land enclosures, drainage, the introduction of improved crops and livestock, as well as new machinery, farm buildings and roads -

was still far from general in some backward parts of the Lowlands even at the end of the eighteenth century.

Lowland agriculture was essentially pastoral, though always with an arable base. In some areas distinct specialisation was apparent, for example, the relatively prosperous Fife and the Lothians, which were important cereal districts supplying expanding urban - and even export markets. Much of the West (including Ayrshire, Dumfries, and Galloway) was stock fattening country - and throughout the eighteenth century had important and developing connections with the cattle trade to markets South of the Border.

Despite this modest response to growing demand for farm products, traditional Lowland agriculture was generally regarded by observers as wasteful and inefficient. The great areas of waste moor and undrained marshland, as well as feudal systems of tenure and land use, reflected its essentially subsistence character. Yet - as Smout indicates - "pre-improvement" farming provided a living of sorts for three-quarters of the Lowland population (around two-thirds of a million in 1750), as well as feeding an expanding urban market. Admittedly the farming economy was poorly equipped to deal with harvest failure, when near starvation conditions often prevailed in places. Undoubtedly some of the accounts that survive of the various 'ill years' are harrowing enough, but how many contemporary reporters were comparing Scottish conditions at their **worst** with circumstances prevailing in the most advanced districts of England at the time.

Certainly the eighteenth century Agricultural Revolution in the Scottish Lowlands did not grow out of nothing and neither the agricultural economy or rural society were as static as has been imagined. Many of the elements we associate with the "improving" movement were present at the beginning of the century, such as money rents, stock breeding, the use of lime, improved crop rotations, and so on. Of course, the pace of change was slow and varied from district to district, with the Lothians in the van and upland districts everywhere in the rear. With the stimulus of demand from an expanding population landowners - even in the seventeenth century - had begun to modernise their estates, building new houses, enclosing and planting the land around, and even reclaiming land. The eighteenth century itself saw the gradual extension of agricultural improvement throughout the Lowlands.

(ii) Landowners and the Agricultural Revolution

Landowners - largely motivated by prospects of higher rents and increased profits - played a key role in agriculture and more general economic development throughout the eighteenth century. The early pioneers introduced English and Continental-style methods of the kind described on consolidated holdings let to tenant farmers. Enclosure and longer leases were essential prerequisites to further improvement in livestock and crops - well illustrated by the experiences of men like John Cockburn of Ormiston in East Lothian and Archibald Grant of Monymusk in Aberdeenshire. Other landowners (and Smout gives plenty examples) emulated the pioneers, and not only improved their estates and built planned villages, but also diversified into related industrial interests, like textiles or mining. Astute landowners therefore saw agricultural change as part and parcel of a much broader based economic and social transformation.

(iii) Land and Industry

This brings us to another significant point: the relationship between agriculture and industry, which was certainly much closer than might be imagined. There can be little doubt that agriculture played an important part in the whole process of industrialisation, not only in the provision of raw materials for processing trades like milling, brewing, distilling, leather, and textiles (both wool and linen), but also capital to finance other more obvious industrial activities (coal, iron, etc.) and transport - for the Transport Revolution of the eighteenth century owed as much to agriculture as to industry. Apart from urban demand for foodstuffs and raw materials, the countryside itself provided an expanding market for its own products, often in revitalised towns or new planned communities. Gatehouse-of-Fleet in Galloway was a prime example of a planned estate village with a range of appropriate industries including cotton spinning using water power, and ready access through its harbour for farm produce exported to the Firth of Clyde or across the Solway Firth to Whitehaven and Liverpool. As Smout shows, there were countless other communities where the links between agriculture and industry were actively fostered by landowners astute enough to see the advantages of a settled population and a mix of occupations. Enlightenment and efficiency walked hand in hand.

(iv) The Social Impact

Smout has a great deal to say on this (see Chapter 13), so it is enough here to identify the main points:

(a) peasant society, before the Agricultural Revolution was generally made up of the farmers or "gudemen", and a dependent class of cottars and farm servants, most of whom had some land in a small holding.

(b) the new farming class which emerged with "improvement" was as much entrepreneurial and capitalist as a tenant farming class, though in some areas of poorer land, or where farms were smaller, the old-style tenants survived.

(c) a landless labouring class was created, with its own stratifications, some paid partly in kind, others in money wages.

(d) the changes seem to have engendered little mass protest, although there were plenty minor disturbances (Smout instances the activities of the Levellers, who broke down enclosure dykes in the 1720s). Improvement may well have created new job opportunities despite depriving labourers of their holdings. And the planned estate villages also helped retain craftsmen in the countryside, besides bringing jobs for women and children in textile mills or other small-scale industries.

As with so many other aspects of Scottish history in the eighteenth century, there is still much we need to know in detail about what happened in different localities before we can make too many generalisations about the social impact of agricultural change throughout the Lowlands. Undoubtedly, though, agricultural improvement was part and parcel of more general economic growth - and in the Scottish context seems to have been of critical importance from the outset.

SAQs

1. How successful was Lowland agriculture before "improvement"?

2. What changes in farming practice were introduced during the Agricultural Revolution?

3. What was the role of landowners in agricultural improvement?

4. Was there a link between land and industry during the eighteenth century?

5. Why, according to Smout, did there seem to be so little conflict in Lowland society during the Agricultural Revolution?

FURTHER READING

T.M. Devine (1994) *The Transformation of Rural Scotland. Social Change and the Agrarian Economy, 1660-1815.*

H. Hamilton (1963), *An Economic History of Scotland in the Eighteenth Century.*

J.E. Handley (1963), *The Agricultural Revolution in Scotland.*

M.L. Parry and T.R. Slater (eds.) (1980), *The Making of the Scottish Countryside.*

N.T. Phillipson and R. Mitchison (eds.) (1970), *Scotland in the Age of Improvement.*

J.A. Symon (1959), *Scottish Farming: Past and Present.*

I. Whyte(1979),*Agriculture and Society in Seventeenth Century Scotland.*

THE SCOTTISH ENLIGHTENMENT

INTRODUCTION

During the eighteenth century and forward into the early nineteenth there was a remarkable surge in culture, though confined to the urban middle class and the aristocracy, embraced education, philosophy, art, architecture, and literature. There were also significant developments in science and notable contributions to the new 'social sciences', especially in economics. The Scottish experience was much in line with the European, though the Scots certainly made a forceful contribution to the advance of Reason.

OBJECTIVES

Your objectives in reading about this topic are as follows:

David Hume

✪— examine something of the origins of the Scottish Enlightenment,

✪— chart the main developments in each sphere,

✪— make some assessment of the impact of Enlightenment ideas on eighteenth century Scotland.

READING

Ferguson, Chapter 7, pp. 198-233 gives a useful account of education and culture in the eighteenth century; while Smout covers much the same ground - though with more detail on education (Chapter 18, pp. 421-450), and with a broader view of culture (Ch. 19, pp. 451-483).

SOME MAJOR THEMES

(i)   The Origins of the Scottish Enlightenment

According to Anand Chitnis Scotland provided a particularly "sympathetic environment" in which the new ideas of "Reason" became established. His view is that the roots of the movement lay deep in the nation's history - especially in the law, the educational system in schools and universities, and in the church - all institutions which had developed along Continental rather than English lines.

Scottish law was grounded in social law and social philosophy; and the legal profession was dominant in politics and economic affairs. In education - an extremely important influence on Enlightenment ideas - the arts were again distinctly philosophical. Medicine was concerned as much with research and teaching, as with caring and curing; while in science the concentration was on the physical and natural, with an emphasis on the application of ideas. The new "social sciences" - economics, history, politics, and sociology - sprang from the same philosophical tradition which prevailed in the arts. The church dominated the social affairs of the nation, yet at the same time (as Chitnis shows) theology was probably the original "social science", paving the way for the secular sciences of the eighteenth century. Many churchmen were distinguished men of letters.

(ii) Main Developments

Scotland in the eighteenth century saw significant developments in the sciences, social sciences, and culture generally. We only have space here to note the main features, but suggest you follow up the detail in Ferguson, Smout and the Further Reading.

(a) Science

Science made great strides and Scottish practitioners were essentially applied scientists, marrying research and teaching with practical application. Science had obvious links to technology and industry in the work of chemists and engineers. Outstanding were James Hutton (geology), David Gregory (mathematics), Joseph Black (chemistry, physics), and James Watt (engineering).

(b) Philosophy

The major figure is, of course, David Hume (1711-1776), author of A *Treatise of Human Nature* (1739-1740) and *Essays, Moral and Political* (1741-1742). Hume was greatly influenced by the European philosophy of the age, as were his contemporaries Francis Hutcheson, Thomas Reid, George Campbell, and Dugald Stewart, who together represented an important school of Scottish philosophy.

(c) Social Science

The leading social scientists had a sound grounding in the arts, philosophy, or theology, notably Adam Smith, Adam Ferguson, John Millar, and William Robertson. Smith's outstanding contribution, *The Wealth of Nations* (1776), established political economy as one of the leading social sciences.

(d) Culture

In literature, as we will find in Part II, notable contributions were made by the poets Allan Ramsay, James Thomson, Robert Fergusson, and Robert Burns, while Smollett and others worked in the novel genre. Literary styles changed greatly in the period, from the Classical, through transitional, to Romantic - the last seen at its best in the vernacular poems of Burns.

Art and architecture also reflected the styles of the age. Art was dominated by

Classicism - reflected in both portraiture and landscapes - produced, for example, by Allan Ramsay Jr., Henry Raeburn, David Allan, Alexander and Patrick Nasmyth, and Gavin Hamilton. The Scottish contribution to architecture was perhaps more significant - seen at best in the works of William Bruce, Colin Campbell, James Gibbs, Robert Mylne, and, above all, William and Robert Adam. In urban planning remarkable strides were made - from the grandeur of Edinburgh's New Town, to the modest estate villages built all over the Lowlands.

(iii) The Impact of the Enlightenment

Both Smout and Ferguson make their own assessment of the Scottish Enlightenment, but they agree that the advances in science and culture can hardly be seen in isolation from general social,and economic change. Some have argued that Enlightenment culture was essentially elitist, but while this might be true of art and architecture, it was hardly the case in the sciences, which contributed much to technology and industry. Scottish education - respected at all levels of society and long imbued with a democratic tradition - reinforced its position as a leading national institution, with schools and universities more committed to applied arts and sciences than their English counterparts. Finally, Enlightenment ideas of Reason and Order fitted in well with the new efficiency in agriculture and industry, and hence contributed in some measure to economic growth during the eighteenth century.

SAQs

1. Did the Scottish educational system encourage Enlightenment ideas or not?

2. Why did Scotland provide a "sympathetic environment" for Enlightenment thinkers?

3. Assess the contribution of either David Hume or Adam Smith to the Scottish Enlightenment.

4. What were the main cultural developments during the eighteenth century?

5. How much did the Enlightenment contribute to economic change?

FURTHER READING

R.D. Anderson (1995) *Education and the Scottish People 1750-1918.*

A.C. Chitnis (1976) *The Scottish Enlightenment: A Social History.*

D. Daiches, P. Jones and J. Jones (ed.) (1986) *A Hotbed of Genius: the Scottish Enlightenment.*

G.E. Davie (1981) *The Scottish Enlightenment.*

R.A. Houston (1994) *Social Change in the Age of Enlightenment. Edinburgh 1660-1760.*

B. Lenman (1981) *Integration, Enlightenment and Industrialisation 1746-1832.*

THE HIGHLANDS TO 1880

OBJECTIVES

More controversy and myth surrounds the history of the Highlands and Islands in the eighteenth and nineteenth centuries than perhaps any other topic in Scottish history, so let's be quite clear about objectives from the outset. By the time you have worked your way through this section you should understand:

A weaver's cottage on Islay.
The Trustees of the National Library of Scotland.

✪— the main historical developments after the Jacobite Risings,

✪— the socio-economic context of the Clearances,

✪— something of the nature of the Clearances themselves, particularly the various stages from the 1770s,

✪— the aftermath of the Clearances, especially the emergence of political action in the Crofters Movement and the Highland Land League.

READING

Smout, Chapter 14, pp. 311-337 takes us as far as 1830. Although Ferguson has no specific section on the Highlands, if you use the index carefully you can read what he says about the Clearances (pp. 276-277), society and economy (pp. 175-179), and subsequent nineteenth century developments like the Land League (pp. 325-326).

SOME MAJOR THEMES

(i)   The Highlands in the Eighteenth Century

Smout covers the ground adequately, so it is enough for us to identify some of the main points and controversies:

(a)   pre-eighteenth century Highland society had been increasingly exposed to

Lowland values over many centuries and the final blow against the old order was struck at Culloden and in the suppression which followed. The complicity of many Highland landowners was essentially motivated by self-advancement or profit, although in some of the "improving" lairds, like the Dukes of Argyll, the paternal instinct remained strong and found expression in assisted migration schemes or planned villages.

(b)   a remarkable range of economic developments were tried after 1750, designed to modernise the Highlands, including: in transport the building of roads, bridges, harbours, and two major canals, the Crinan and the Caledonian; the trade in cattle to the Lowlands; in textiles the development of the traditional woollen industry, in the main, but also linen and cotton, as in the Lowlands; in fishing, an industry revitalised from new harbours and planned villages like Helmsdale and Ullapool; in forestry the working of timber for shipbuilding, as in Speyside, or for charcoal used in iron smelting, as in Argyll; the development of the kelp industry, gathering and burning seaweed to produce potash for use in the chemical industry of the Lowlands and elsewhere.

But although these and other developments brought some employment, they did little to solve the fundamental problem of subsistence agriculture amongst a growing population.

(ii)   The Context of the Clearances

Try as we might, it's hard to escape from the fact that subsistence agriculture in the Highlands could hardly support its pre-eighteenth century population far less the growing numbers of later in the century. Much misunderstanding surrounds this basic point, for the earliest migrations were essentially seasonal, as folk came to Lowland towns seeking work, or to farms for harvest labour. Add to this the desire of landowners to "improve" their estates on Lowland lines and we have powerful incentives to encourage more permanent migration. The wickedness of the laird and tacksman (the laird's steward) is much vaunted, but a few did exhibit some humanity, others clawing paternalism, while most were apparently grasping capitalists.

Yet the encouragement to migrate further afield was a logical extension of existing custom, especially when the motive was preservation of a way of life, language, religion, and traditions - even on the other side of the Atlantic. Some Catholic clergy in the Western Isles, for example, favoured migration to Canada as a way of preserving religion and language in a cohesive community. Some of the early "clearances", or more properly migrations, were organised by the clergy, Catholic and Protestant - not as tools of the lairds - but as firm believers in the God-given virtue of their enterprise. We also tend to overlook the fact that the view of settlers in the United States and Canada (increasingly after the War of Independence) was often positive, for the search for land and a new way of life are perfectly understandable. This must certainly have motivated many in the later, and admittedly brutal, clearances, such as those on the Sutherland estates at the beginning of the nineteenth century.

(iii) The Clearances

As Smout makes clear, there were several stages in the clearances: from 1740 on a small scale, mainly at the initiative of the tacksmen, who probably recognised more clearly than most the increasing pressure on the land; after the 1760s the introduction of Lowland-style sheep farming accelerated clearance, with a rapid spread from the Southern into the Central and Western Highlands. The earliest large scale clearances took place in the 1770s and 1780s; much larger scale clearance during and after the Napoleonic Wars, notably

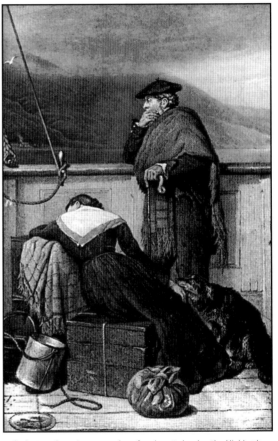

A nineteenth century engraving of emigrants leaving the Highlands.

in the 1820s. It was then that the harshness of wholesale clearance from the glens and straths was most acute - witness the Sutherland and Ross-shire experiences, for example. Smout has much useful analysis of this stage of events; later in the nineteenth century sporadic and occasionally numerically large instances, especially in the distress of the famine years in the 1840s.

In all of this there was much suffering and hardship, though at the same time life on poor, unproductive land must have been hard enough. Given a population explosion - partly as in Ireland the result of potato cultivation - the limit to numbers the land could support must have been reached. The motives of the landlords are often clear, but we know less about those of the people themselves. Certainly the desire for land and the preservation of a way of life was uppermost - even if the ultimate solution lay in emigration.

(iv) Aftermath

The Clearances left much bitterness, still part and parcel of Highland mythology after over two hundred years. Considering the scale of the upheaval it's surprising there was so little popular reaction or conflict, perhaps a reflection of the stranglehold of the tacksmen and clergy over much of the local population. But the aftermath saw considerable unrest, especially in food riots and demonstrations during the famine of the late 1840s, and in the stand against evictions which continued until late in the century.

The emergence of direct political action on the part of crofters was, as Ferguson indicates, as much influenced by the Irish experience as the extension of the franchise - especially in the formation of the Highland Land League. The passing of the Crofters Act in 1886 highlights both the success of political radicalism in the Highlands and the ultimate response of Gladstonian Liberalism to the need for change.

SAQs

1. How were the Highlands influenced by Lowland ideas during the eighteenth century?

2. How much did population pressure contribute to the Highland problem?

3. Were the Clearances an economic and social necessity?

4. Was there any protest against clearances and evictions and what form did it take?

5. Did the position of the crofters alter during the latter half of the nineteenth century, and if so, why?

FURTHER READING

J. Bumsted (1982) *The People's Clearance: Highland Emigration to North America*.

T. M. Devine (1988) *The Great Highland Famine. Hunger Emigration and the Scottish Highlands in the Nineteenth Century*.

T.M. Devine (1994) *Clanship to Crofter's War: The Social Transformation of the Scottish Highlands*.

M. Gray (1957) *The Highland Economy 1750-1850*.

J. Hunter (1976) *The Making of the Crofting Community*.

E. Richards (1982) A *History of the Highland Clearances*, Vol. 1: *Agrarian Transformation and the Evictions 1746-1886*.

E. Richards (1985) A *History of the Highland Clearances*, Vol. 2: *Emigration, Protest, Reasons*.

C.W.J. Withers (1988) *Gaelic Scotland; The Transformation of a Culture Region*.

A.J. Youngson (1973) *After the Forty-Five: The Economic Impact on the Scottish Highlands*.

THE INDUSTRIAL REVOLUTION

OBJECTIVES

Working through this section you should be able to understand:

✤— the concept of the Industrial Revolution and how the changes then affected Scotland 1780-1820;

✤— the main developments in the period preceding large-scale industrialisation before 1780;

✤— the key sectors of Scottish industrialisation - textiles, coal and iron;

✤— the immediate social effect of industrialisation.

READING

Ferguson, Chapter 6, especially pp. 180-197; Smout, Chapter 10, especially pp. 230-239. Optionally, Smout, pp. 355-365 and 371-392. There are optional case-studies of (i) Glasgow, (ii) the standard of living, and (iii) life in the textile mills. It could be that you will wish to read further in Smout, or perhaps investigate the effect of industrialisation in your own locality.

SOME MAJOR THEMES

(i)   The Concept

This is a complex subject to get to grips with in a single section, because industrialisation is part and parcel of the whole process of economic growth which involved not only an Industrial Revolution, but also new developments in agriculture, commerce and transport. The period for long described as the "Industrial Revolution" saw the introduction for the first time on a large scale of mass manufacture, applying new technology largely imported from south of the Border and in particular led to the growth of the "Factory System" in textiles. Scotland already had a well-established textile trade, particularly woollen and linen cloth production - but the new element was mechanisation using water power, and steam power, as prime movers. In both coal and iron there was parallel growth, partly stimulated by general home demand, and partly by the strategic needs of the Revolutionary and Napoleonic Wars, 1793-1815.

The Industrial Revolution - later in Scotland than in England - saw the "take-off" of these key sectors into what some economic historians have described as

The opening of the Glasgow and Garnkirk Railway, 1831. Glasgow Museums and Art Galleries.

'self-sustained growth', and helped lay the basis for further expansion after an initial spurt of activity before 1820. Not only this, demand was stimulated for the products of other sectors, notably agriculture, and processing industries like flour milling, drink, leather goods etc. None of this growth - essentially concentrated in the Lowlands and especially around Glasgow - would have been possible without significant inputs of capital, entrepreneurship, and labour. Capital came mainly from agriculture, and existing commercial and industrial enterprises, with banks playing a significant role in its mobilisation and application to new developments. Entrepreneurship was a quality Scots apparently had in abundance and some businessmen, landowners, and lawyers (among others) were quick to see the potential profits of dynamic enterprise.

Labour was more of a problem in the industrialisation process than you might think, though there was no shortage of skills in textiles and coal mining. More problematic was the attraction of labour to the new textile mills and iron works - many in remote locations. Problems of retaining labour, and of discipline, were often solved by resort to paternalistic planned villages, like New Lanark. Finally, and perhaps we should have started with this basic point, resources were geographically concentrated in the Lowlands, which made capitalist exploitation easier, given the development of transport facilities like the new turnpike roads, canals, improved harbours, and, ultimately, railways - a Transport Revolution coinciding with industrialisation.

(ii) Proto-Industrialisation

Historians have realised for some time now that the concept of an "Industrial Revolution" is a misnomer, because there is increasing evidence of longer-term development - in other words various stages of 'proto' industrialisation which in Scotland would find their origin earlier in the eighteenth century if not before. Agriculture certainly had a critical part to play, as had consumer industries like distilling, brewing, milling, salt, pottery, leather and textiles - all of which were becoming increasingly geared toward expanding urban and export markets long before the 1780s. Heat using industries - including lime burning and the nascent iron trade - stimulated further demand for coal, while urban building programmes led to expansion of stone quarrying and the timber trade. Finally, the problem of access to English and export markets overseas had been solved by the Treaty of Union, so an environment for potential growth existed as early as the 1700s.

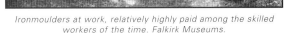

Ironmoulders at work, relatively highly paid among the skilled workers of the time. Falkirk Museums.

(iii) Key Sectors

a)   Textiles

There were few "dark satanic mills" before the 1820s, quite the contrary. For most of the early spinning mills using Arkwright's water frame were established in the countryside on rivers like the Clyde and Tay. New Lanark was the example par excellence of the planned industrial community, developed by the financier-entrepreneur David Dale from 1783, and managed by Robert Owen, the social reformer, after 1800. Yet much of the evidence would indicate that the larger mills were still atypical and that a fair proportion of output was still concentrated in smaller units even by the 1800s. Only after 1815 did cotton production really become concentrated in urban mills around Glasgow and Paisley, though linen and wool were still essentially rural or small-town enterprises. Alongside factory production there was a parallel development of the domestic sector - notably hand loom weaving. This soon became the first real casualty of mechanisation brought about by the introduction of the power loom.

(b)   Coal and Iron

Both industries were closely related geographically and in terms of technology, for the application of coke smelting (as opposed to the use of charcoal) stimulated coal mining. Steam engines - themselves coal-using -were applied to haulage and drainage in mines, and adapted for blasting air into furnaces. The first large coke smelting plant was established at Carron Ironworks (1760) near Falkirk, followed by later works at Wilsontown, Muirkirk, Shotts, and Clyde, near Glasgow. Coal mining was widespread and still smallscale throughout the Lowlands, though the opening of the Monkland and then the Forth and Clyde Canals greatly stimulated production in north Lanarkshire and Stirlingshire.

(iv) Social Impact

All of this was achieved at considerable social cost, though it has to be admitted (perhaps surprisingly) that the social climate was one of stability rather than conflict. The idea that people flocked to work in the new mills, mines and furnaces is certainly open to question; folk had to be persuaded and even cajoled into working as cotton spinners, colliers or furnace hands. Labour certainly came from the Highlands and from Ireland on a seasonal basis at first, later settling permanently in the Lowlands. But with the new skills and opportunities came the threat of cyclical unemployment, something that few had experienced in the subsistence life of the crofts or cott farms. As regards the standard of living of the working class it is difficult to make meaningful generalisations beyond the obvious fact that for some things got better, while for other groups the opposite was the case. You might like to think about the whole standard of living controversy in further detail following a reading of what Smout has to say.

Urban growth brought new challenges - the problem of the poor, bad housing, health and sanitation - most of which were already identifiable. But solutions, if only partial, were beginning to be found later in the 19th century, when things had got much worse. You can readily identify Glasgow's problems during the late eighteenth and early nineteenth centuries if you check up relevant references in your reading.

SAQs

1.   What main forces contributed to industrialisation in Scotland during the late eighteenth and early nineteenth centuries?

2.   Why did Scotland experience faster economic growth after 1780 than before?

3.   How did technology influence the growth of cotton spinning in the period 1780-1820?

4.   What was the relationship between the growth of the coal and iron industries in the Scottish Lowlands?

5.   What were the immediate social consequences of industrialisation in Scotland?

FURTHER READING

R.H. Campbell (1985) (2nd Ed.) *Scotland since 1707: the Rise of an Industrial Society.*

T. M. Devine and R. Mitchison (eds)(1988) *People and Society in Scotland. Vol.1, 1760-1830.*

P. Deane (1965) *The First Industrial Revolution.*

B. Lenman (1981) *Integration, Enlightenment and Industrialisation: Scotland 1746-1832.*

S.G.E. Lythe and J. Butt (1975) *An Economic History of Scotland 1100-1939.*

P. Mathias (1969) *The First Industrial Nation.*

GOVERNMENT AND POLITICS, 1789-1918

OBJECTIVES

Your aims in this rather long section should be to obtain a broad grasp of the following topics:

✪— the struggle for parliamentary reform, 1789-1832,

✪— Scotland and the political parties, 1832-1918.

READING

Ferguson, Chapters 8-11.

SOME MAJOR THEMES

(i)   The Struggle for Parliamentary Reform, 1789-1832

(Ferguson, Chs. 8-9.)

Before embarking on a study of the movements for parliamentary reform, it would be a good idea to check the defects in the Scottish electoral system, with within the counties and burghs (these are discussed earlier in Ferguson, pp. 134-137). While there was some tentative pressure on governments before 1789, it was undoubtedly the French Revolution which marked the start of serious demands for changes in the constitution. There are really three distinct phases between 1789 and 1832:

(a)   Radical Activity in the 1790's

The English Societies of the Friends of the People soon spread their activities into Scotland where they attracted the attention of various groups although the Friends of the People in Scotland was much less aristocratic in composition than their English counterparts. As soon as the war with France broke out, the government adopted a repressive policy towards reform movements. This took the form partly of a series of state trials of leading members of the Friends and their allies - the most celebrated, or notorious, was that of Thomas Muir of Huntershill by Lord Braxfield - and partly of reactionary legislation, e.g. The Seditious Meetings Act and the suspension of the Act against Wrongous Imprisonment (the Scottish equivalent of Habeas Corpus). Not surprisingly, there was a decline in radical activity for the remainder of the 1790's.

(b)   Radical Activity, 1815-1820

The post-war period with its dreadful economic recession was a time of considerable political agitation among radical groups on both sides of the border. Clearly, the efforts of the indefatigable Major Cartwright and his Hampden Clubs with their constitutional reform ideals produced some results in Scotland for instance the "Radical War" (1820). However, despite their demands for annual parliaments and universal suffrage, many of those involved in these years were more concerned about unemployment and food shortages than political change.

(c)   The Reform Act (Scotland), 1832

The campaign for parliamentary reform gained increasing momentum in the later 1820's with the Whigs and the radicals, who had now abandoned more violent solutions, mounting growing pressure on the Tory government, which eventually resigned in November, 1830. Regarding the details of the Act, you should pay particular attention to the increase in the number of Scottish constituencies, from 45 to 53, the introduction of the basic £10 householder qualification in the burghs, and the complex franchise system in the counties where, since there was no secret ballot, the landowning classes still dominated political affairs. You should also note that, although the Scottish electorate jumped dramatically from around 5,000 to over 60,000, the working classes, in most areas, were still without the vote and that Scotland was still under- represented at Westminster.

(ii)   Scotland and the Political Parties, 1832-1918

(Ferguson, Chs. 10-11.)

This is best divided as follows:

(a)   1832-1886

The outstanding political phenomenon of this period is that the Whigs, or Liberals, as they soon came to be called, had a unique preponderance of electoral support in Scotland. Although it was their rivals, the Conservatives, who passed the Second Reform Act in 1867, extending the vote to rate-paying householders and £10 lodgers in the burghs, widening the county franchise and giving Scotland seven more seats in Parliament, it was the Whigs/Liberals who were responsible for the important Burgh Reform Act (1833) and the very significant Third Reform Act of 1884-1885. This latter statute completed parliamentary reform in the 19th century by giving male suffrage to all householders in the counties as well as the burghs, adding twelve more members to Scotland's complement at Westminster and by making an extensive reallocation of parliamentary seats based on the distribution of population.

The main radical challenge to both Whigs and Tories in the 1830's and 1840's was Chartism. Although largely a movement which acted as a barometer for social and economic conditions in Britain, it did have as its programme a number of demands (the "Six Points"), all of which sought political reform of one kind or another. The Chartists had a considerable following in Scotland and, while the details of their rise and fall need not be traced in any depth, it is worth observing some of the aspects of the movement, e.g. the emphasis on temperance, pacifism and the abolition of capital punishment which were particularly stressed by Scottish Chartists. The fact that Scottish Chartism was not bedevilled so much by the "lunatic fringe" as elsewhere in Britain is also worth noting.

(b) 1886-1918

This period saw the end of the liberal hegemony in Scotland. This was a process which began in 1886 with the divisions within the party over Gladstone's Irish Home Rule policy and culminated in the crisis over Asquith's leadership in 1916.

Obviously the rise of the Labour Party in Scotland in these years is a major political development, and you should familiarise yourself with the details of its early origins, especially the role played by its key figure, Keir Hardie. The activities of its militant left wing in the West of Scotland during 1914-1918 war deserve some attention although it should be remembered that Maxton and his colleagues were largely discounted by the official parliamentary Labour party.

The Irish Home Rule issue, apart from its impact on the Liberal party, also stimulated Scottish nationalism. You should note the various Liberal "sops" to placate this movement, e.g. the appointment of a Secretary of State for Scotland, the establishment of a Scottish Grand Committee at Westminster and even a Scottish Home Rule bill before the war broke out in 1914.

Aside from the very important act establishing popularly-elected county councils in 1889, the main political reform, the Representation of the People Act, comes at the very end of our period. This was a momentous measure for Britain generally, giving all males over twenty-one and all women over thirty the vote, but, as far as Scotland was concerned, its most notable feature was the widespread redistribution of burgh and county constituencies.

By 1918, as a result of the four major reform acts (1832, 1867, 1884-1885, and 1918), political reform was no longer a key issue in Britain. Similarly, as a consequence of various other statutes, e.g. the Burgh Reform Act (1833) and the County Councils Act (1889), local government in Scotland had been completely transformed. From a party standpoint, the fortunes of the Liberals in Scotland were clearly in decline as the divisions over Ireland and party leadership provided obvious opportunities for their rivals both to the right and left of the political spectrum.

Masthead of 'Forward', the socialist newspaper edited by Tom Johnston.

SAQs

1.   Describe and account for the growing interest in parliamentary reform between 1789 and 1832.

2.   Which of the three parliamentary reform acts of the 19th century was, in your opinion, the most important?

3.   Estimate the significance of the Irish Home Rule question in Scottish politics between 1886 and 1918.

4.   Trace and account for the rise of the Labour Party in Scotland.

FURTHER READING

I. Donnachie, C. Harvie and I. Wood (eds.) (1989) *Forward! Labour Politics in Scotland 1888-1988.*

M. Fry (1987) *Patronage and Principle. A Political History of Modern Scotland.*

I.G.C. Hutchison (1986) A *Political History of Scotland 1832-1924.*

I. McLean (1985) *The Legend of Red Clydeside.*

G.S. Pryde (1962) *Scotland from 1603 to the Present Day*, Chs. XI (pp. 120-126), XVII-XIX.

A. Wilson (1970) *The Chartist Movement in Scotland.*

VICTORIAN SCOTLAND: WORKSHOP OF THE EMPIRE?

INTRODUCTION

The nineteenth century saw the triumph of Scottish industry, particularly on Clydeside, where the traditional industries of coal and iron (ultimately steel) provided the basis for diversification into related engineering, shipbuilding, and railways. Textiles, a key sector in earlier industrialisation, remained important, though like chemicals gradually lost out to English and foreign competition.

OBJECTIVES

Your objectives in this section are to look at:

✸— the key industrial developments of the period 1830-1914,

✸— labour and trade union organisation during the same period.

You will have to relate your reading for this section to that for the following one, as some of the social issues of the Victorian and Edwardian eras are introduced there.

READING

Ferguson provides general coverage of the period in Chapters 10 and 11, and the Further Reading indicated here will help if you want to follow up specific topics.

SOME MAJOR THEMES

(i) Economy and Industry

The basis of an apparently sound economy was provided by the key sectors of earlier industrialisation, though the emphasis shifted from textiles to coal and iron, mainly but not exclusively in the West of Scotland. The iron industry in particular grew rapidly after 1840 - stimulated by railway demand and by exports. Steel making was at first slow to develop, partly for technical reasons, and partly because of the high profits in the pig iron trade. The rise of malleable iron manufacture was closely tied to shipyard demand, and by the 1860s and 1870s shipbuilding absorbed 70 per cent of production. In the West coal mining was stimulated by demand from the local iron and steel industry, whereas in the East, especially after 1875, the emphasis was on exports, mainly to Eastern Europe and the Baltic.

It is easy to see shipbuilding as being critical to Scottish economic growth in the Victorian period, such was its pre-eminent position on Clydeside after the change to iron and the development of more efficient marine engines. Engineering itself was of major importance, particularly locomotive manufacture and marine engineering, both of which had direct and obvious links to iron and steel. Such was the diversity of export engineering products originating from Clydeside before the First World War that the area could justifiably claim the title of 'Workshop of the Empire'.

Given the general prosperity of the heavies and other traditional trades like textiles, it is perhaps not surprising that newer industries were less important than they might have been. But efforts in this direction - shale oil, chemicals, and rubber (established with American capital) were relatively small-scale, as were light engineering and, later, vehicle manufacture. Scottish businessmen also eschewed consumer durables, preferring to concentrate on established heavy goods. But even in a key industry like shipbuilding - as Ferguson shows (pp. 330-331) - the Clyde soon began to fall behind its competitors.

A key question which emerges from any study of the economy before 1914 is whether or not there was a failure of entrepreneurship and innovation in late Victorian and Edwardian Scotland? Did business and industry prefer to concentrate on familiar products for established markets - or on highly profitable overseas investment - rather than devote energy and capital to fresh enterprise? For modernisation was slow, and even in the heavy industries the cold wind of foreign competition was being felt in Scottish industry long before the Great War.

(ii) Labour and the Trade Unions

Weavers in a Dundee jute works c1908.
Dundee University Library.

This is clearly a major topic which relates as much to political development as to the economy before 1914. Whether or not industrialisation had created a new working class by the 1830s (as E.P. Thompson suggested in his *Making of the English Working Class*), it certainly generated grievances about wages, working conditions, and political representation which were articulated first by the skilled workers. In the early nineteenth century a whole host of Radical popular movements seeking reform united sections of both working and middle classes throughout Britain - so the early development of trade unions need to be seen in a wider context.

During the 1830s and 40s trade unionism and Chartism were closely associated, though neither was particularly effective in challenging the ascendant capitalism of industrial Scotland. There were several major efforts by skilled operatives during the 30s - weavers, cotton spinners, carpenters, and masons - which coincided, as in the 40s, with peaks of Chartist agitation.

There was a revival of activity in the 1850s spearheaded by the United Coal and Iron Miners' Association of Scotland, and followed by others in the collieries, building trades and engineering. The Amalgamated Society of Engineers was the first English-style "New Model" union to organise in Scotland; in other trades local unions dominated. In mining, for example, despite Keir Hardie's efforts, the Scottish Miners' Federation (1894) was still only a loose-knit amalgamation of county unions. But it grew steadily and had 87,000 members by 1913, and Scottish miners played an active part in several major strikes, notably in 1894 and 1912.

Although mining unions were most militant, others showed comparable growth, especially among the lower paid (like the farm workers). By the 1880s trade unions in Scotland - as elsewhere - concerned themselves increasingly with the political representation of labour as well as the fight for improved wages, shorter hours and better conditions. Given the maldistribution of wealth and power in Victorian Scotland the unions had much to fight for.

SAQs

1.   Why was Scottish industry so apparently successful in the latter half of the nineteenth century?

2.   Can you suggest why shipbuilding occupied such a key place in the economy of the West of Scotland before 1914?

3.   Were Scottish trade unions more motivated by self interest than political action?

FURTHER READING

A.B. Campbell (1979) *The Lanarkshire Miners: A Social History of their Trade Unions 1775-1974.*

R.H. Campbell (1980) *The Rise and Fall of Scottish Industry 1707-1939.*

R.H. Campbell (1985) *Scotland since 1707.*

S. and O. Checkland (1984) *Industry and Ethos. Scotland 1832-1914.*

W. H. Fraser and R. J. Morris (eds)(1990) *People and Society in Scotland Vol.II, 1830-1914.*

R.Q. Gray (1976) *The Labour Aristocracy in Victorian Edinburgh.*

B. Lenman (1977) *An Economic History of Modern Scotland 1660-1976* (Ch. 6).

P.L. Payne (1992) *Growth and Contraction. Scottish Industry c. 1860-1990.*

A.Slaven (1975) *The Development of the West of Scotland 1750-1960.*

PEOPLE, TOWNS AND CITIES

OBJECTIVES

Population growth and migration from countryside to town as well as overseas have been major features of Scottish social history since the eighteenth century. In this section we want to examine:

✿— population growth after the middle of the eighteenth century and the main causes,

✿— the rise of towns and cities, notably the major centres of Edinburgh and Glasgow,

✿— social changes and conditions.

Clearly these are wide-ranging themes, so we can only really expect to pinpoint the main issues here. You can follow up the details in your reading of Smout and Ferguson.

READING

Smout, Chapter 11 (pp. 240-260) gives an excellent account of population growth, while his sections on the major cities provide case-studies of the differing experiences of Edinburgh and Glasgow. Ferguson, Chapter 10 describes developments during the nineteenth century, and is especially good on the social consequences of urban growth and industrialisation.

SOME MAJOR THEMES

(i)   Population Growth

Smout gives a detailed analysis of developments before 1830, so we need only provide a summary here. Let's start with some figures:

Population (millions)

c 1755	1.2	1841	2.6	1901	4.4
c 1795	1.5	1851	2.9		
c 1801	1.6	1861	3.0		
1811	1.8	1871	3.3		
1821	2.1	1881	3.7		
1831	2.3	1891	4.0		

Now we'll look at the main developments in the eighteenth and nineteenth centuries.

(a) The Eighteenth Century

As Smout makes clear, lack of accurate data is a major problem, but we do know that population growth was very slow before 1740, perhaps only restoring the level of the 1690s, preceding the "ill years" of harvest failure and famine during that decade. There was marked and sustained growth from the late 1740s, maintained except for a slight dip in the early 60s until the late 80s. After that the rate of growth, though still positive, appears to fall slightly in the last decade of the century.

The obvious problems we can identify in trying to explain eighteenth century growth are:

(1) can population expansion be attributed to economic growth?

(2) to changes in social organisation?

(3) to changes in the impact of disease or physical environment?

The evidence available indicates the importance of falling death rates, brought about by a combination of favourable factors:

(a) there was no widespread famine of the kind that occurred in the seventeenth century; the potato provided an important new food crop; and better transport ensured more efficient distribution of available food.

(b) the poor relief system was improved, with increasing government intervention.

(c) medical and environmental improvements contributed to the falling death rate, especially through the provision of infirmaries, dispensaries, and vaccination.

As well as the falling death rate, you should note that fertility probably increased thanks to modest improvements in the standard of living, especially in the second half of the century.

(b) The Nineteenth Century

Much more accurate data is available from the first census of 1801. In general, population growth was faster before 1851, but both the 70s and the 90s achieved rates comparable with those of the first half of the century.

Migration played an important role in Scottish demography during the nineteenth century. Emigration both to other parts of the UK and abroad was significant, not only those forced to leave by the Highland Clearances, but also increasing numbers voluntarily seeking new lives and opportunities in North America, Australia, New Zealand, and elsewhere. But immigration was also important, especially from Ireland, England, and the Continent (e.g., the Italians and Lithuanians).

The Highlands experienced a persistent decline in population from midcentury. Indeed, most rural areas had reached their peak by 1851, although some country towns continued to grow. Improved transport - notably the railways - probably encouraged movement to the towns. So urbanisation was a significant feature of the period, and it is to it we now turn.

(ii) Urbanisation

Towns grew rapidly with industrialisation, but urban growth had already begun before the end of the eighteenth century. There was a notable change in the rank order of the larger towns and cities, for industrial centres, like Glasgow, Dundee, and Paisley, expanded rapidly in the early nineteenth century. This is not to deny the growth of towns and villages everywhere - a clear function of economic growth - from the classical Edinburgh New Town to countless humbler planned estate or industrial villages.

Glasgow (see Smout, pp. 355-365) is an excellent case study in urban industrial growth, with all of its associated social problems. You can see from the table here how rapid the city's growth was: the population trebled between 1755 and 1801 and trebled again in the three decades to 1831. Later expansion was equally dramatic (with a massive influx from Ireland in the 1840s) so that Glasgow ultimately became the Second City of the Empire and one of the great Victorian cities of the world.

The Growth of Glasgow (thousands)

c1755	23	1841	275
1801	77	1851	345
1811	101	1861	420
1821	147	1871	522
1831	202	1901	762

Edinburgh's earlier experience had created the Georgian New Town, away from the squalor of the Old Town's ancient tenements. But to this was added - mainly during the late nineteenth century building boom - the ordered tenement suburbs that make the city as much Victorian as Georgian. Dundee was a microcosm of the Glasgow experience with its juxtaposition of jute mills and overcrowded tenements, a telling indictment of industrial capitalism at its worst and a manifestation of the social problems urban growth seems to have brought in its wake.

(iii) Social Problems

Again these are tackled in some detail by both Smout and Ferguson, so we need only note the main points you might want to look out for:

(a) the urban poor: urbanisation greatly increased the problem of poverty (the Irish were often blamed). The reformed Scottish Poor Law (1845) may have tightened up on administration, but it did little to humanise a system - which sought economy more than providing genuine aid to the poor.

(b)   housing became one of Scotland's major social problems during the nineteenth century, for overcrowding and slum conditions were all too common in Scottish towns and cities. Modest improvements were made later in the century - in Glasgow and Edinburgh, for example - but they did little to solve the problem.

(c)   disease was an inevitable outcome of overcrowding and poor conditions, particularly waterborne diseases and those of malnutrition. Only when epidemics like the cholera outbreaks threatened the middle and upper classes was much action taken. But diseases like smallpox and tuberculosis remained major scourges throughout the period.

(d)   water supply and drainage: some improvements were affected in the Victorian period -Glasgow's Loch Katrine water supply being a pioneer - though many smaller towns also made provision for public water supply and drainage.

In general, civic improvement in the cities and larger towns was a product of the later Victorian era - partly a response to the poor conditions themselves, and partly to the extension of municipal government.

SAQs

1.   Was eighteenth century population growth a function of economic growth rather than medical and environmental improvements?

2.   Why did Glasgow grow so rapidly during the nineteenth century (refer to Smout and Ferguson)?

3.   How important was migration in shaping of Scotland's population during the period 1750-1900?

4.   What were the major social problems of Scottish towns during the nineteenth century?

FURTHER READING

I. Adams (1978) *The Making of Urban Scotland*.

R.H. Campbell (1985) *Scotland since 1707*, Ch. XI on Social Reform.

M.W. Flinn (1977) *Scottish Population History from the 17th Century to the 1930s*.

M. Gray (1990) *Scots on the Move. Scots Migrants 1750-1914*.

S.G.E. Lythe and J. Butt (1975), An *Economic History of Scotland* 1100-1939, Ch. VII on Population and Economic Growth.

T.C. Smout (1986), A Century of the Scottish People.

THE INTER-WAR YEARS

OBJECTIVES

Working through this section should enable you to understand:

✿— the background to Scotland's economic problems in the 20s and 30s,

✿— the political response to the socio-economic difficulties of the Depression years in Scotland.

READING

Ferguson, Ch. 12, pp. 359-382. More specific background on the economy than Ferguson contains is provided here, while further reading will supplement both economic and political aspects if necessary.

INTRODUCTION

It is certainly a mistake to regard World War I as some great discontinuity in Scotland's socio-economic development during the early twentieth century, for despite the disruption the war simply emphasised forces long at work and highlighted underlying problems in the economy and social fabric. Politically there was a sharpening up of traditional Scottish radicalism, in opposition to the war, in labour and trade union organisation, in the politics of the left, especially on "Red" Clydeside where industrial militancy was most notable and found early expression in the famous Rent Strike, the Clyde Workers' Committee activities, of the war years and the Forty Hours Strike (1919).

(i) The Economy

An understanding of Scotland's economic problems during the inter-war years is critical to any analysis of social and political developments in the period. Ferguson (pp. 361-363) discusses the economy briefly and emphasises that Scotland's problems presented a microcosm of the UK experience. The problems of industrial structure were certainly deepseated, with Scotland's over-reliance on the old industries like coal, iron and steel, shipbuilding, heavy engineering, and textiles dating back to the early nineteenth century. Old fashioned technology and perhaps even more traditional managements and patterns of industrial relations held little hope for modernisation. At the same time, the needs of war strategy simply compounded the problems of an economy over-dependent on outdated heavy industry. As elsewhere in Britain - Tyneside, South Wales, or Merseyside, for example, the loss of export markets during and after the First World War has been consistently emphasised as a central **short-term** factor contributing to economic malaise - yet **longer-term** forces seem altogether more significant. Scotland, and Clydeside in particular, had probably lost her status as "Workshop of the Empire" long before 1914 - partly a reflection of competition from foreign rivals, notably Germany and the United States, partly the result of industrial development in the colonies.

If things seemed gloomy after the collapse of a short post-war boom between 1919-1921, they got much worse as Scotland slid into a depression, characterised by alarming levels of unemployment and a widening gap with the UK experience.

Percentage Unemployed and Indices of Insured Labour Force and Numbers in employment, Scotland and Great Britain, Selected Years, 1923-1939

(1923 = 100)   Source: Ministry of Labour Gazettes

	(1) Unemployment (%)		(2) Insured Labour Force		(3) Numbers in Employment	
	Scotland	Gt. Britain	Scotland	Gt. Britain	Scotland	Gt. Britain
Britain						
1923	14.3	11.6	100	100	100	100
1927	10.6	9.6	101	106	108	109
1929	12.1	10.3	102	109	105	110
1932	27.7	21.9	107	115	91	101
1934	23.1	16.6	108	116	98	110
1936	18.7	13.0	110	120	106	118
1938	16.3	12.6	114	124	111	122
1939	13.5	10.3	115	128	116	128

As the data here show, the actual number in employment only reached its 1929 level as late as 1935, with any real recovery delayed until 1936, rather than 1934 for the UK in general. Differences in industrial structure were also reflected in lower productivity and persistently lower earnings, so the social consequences of the depression were more deeply felt in Scotland than elsewhere, with the possible exceptions of South Wales and Tyneside, which shared similar problems. More positively, the 'thirties saw a modest growth of "new" industries, which by 1935 represented about 11 per cent of net output. Even this development left over 30 per cent of the labour force in Scotland's traditional trades of coal-mining, iron and steel, shipbuilding, heavy engineering, and textiles. The upturn when it came was based largely on improved exports and rearmament, though even in 1939 unemployment - at 13% - exceeded the 1929 level.

(ii) Socio-Political Context

Against this background Scotland in the inter-war years presented pockets of deep poverty, severe over-crowding, disease and poverty. Infant mortality rates were among the worst of any industrial country, and Scotland was one of the worst housed area in the UK. These two features alone could hardly merit self-congratulation on the part of any government, whether or not it understood the causes. But governments of the period - Tory or Labour - could hardly be blamed for their failure to understand the causes of industrial collapse and unemployment, when the underlying economic mechanisms were just beginning to be identified by theoreticians like J.M. Keynes.

No-one could deny the severity of social distress caused by the Depression, yet thinking about the period is coloured by misery and despair, while more optimistic developments are often overlooked. Some good emerged from the inter-war years in Scotland, especially the political will for improvement through schemes designed to aid the Distressed Areas and assist agriculture. Although the problem of unemployment inevitably dominated the thinking of politicians local and national, modest efforts were also made in such fields as slum clearance, housing, health, and education. Given the scale of the problems in places like Glasgow and Dundee - and conditions were actually worse in some of the distressed colliery districts - the attempt at improvement was too little too late (a catch-phrase for the period), but at least the framework was laid for more positive developments in the future.

The Labour Party became a major political force in Scotland after its partial breakthrough in 1922, though success in local rather than national politics was delayed until the 'thirties. In general Scotland's contribution to radical politics in Britain during the inter-war period must be measured not by sub-revolutionary confrontations with authority such as that in 1919, but more by the impact of a few key figures (and even they were thin on the ground) like J. Ramsay MacDonald, John Maclean, John Wheatley, James Maxton, and Tom Johnston. Despite the impact of the "Clydesiders" some would maintain that 'Red' Clydeside is another of the great

'The origin of 'Red Clydeside' ~ a 'Bailie' cartoon from the 1923 Parliamentary election, showing James Maxton, George Buchanan, John Wheatley and Campbell Stephen

myths of Scottish history. For although Labour did well before the debacle of 1931 industrial Scotland presented an image of radicalism which hardly reflected reality, or its parliamentary representation. Certainly the two short-lived Labour governments can no more be accused of failure to get to grips with Scotland's problems than the Tory-Unionist or National governments - for politicians of all parties, and in so many other countries, were trapped both by the failure of industrial capitalism and by their own essentially conservative outlook.

SAQs

1.   Was 'Red' Clydeside revolutionary? Discuss with reference to ideology, personalities and events before 1920.

2.   Why did Labour make such a breakthrough in Scotland at the 1922 General Election?

3.   Assess the economic and social impact of the Slump in Scotland.

4.   What efforts were made to regenerate the Scottish economy in the 1930s?

FURTHER READING

B.W.E. Alford (1972) *Depression and Recovery? British Economic Growth, 1918-1939.*

D.H. Aldcroft (1970) *The Inter-War Economy: Britain 1919-1939.*

S. Glynn and J. Oxborrow (1976) *Interwar Britain: A Social and Economic History.*

J. Stevenson and C. Cook (1977) *The Slump: Society and Politics During the Depression.*

C.T. Harvie (1981), *No Gods and Precious Few Heroes: Scotland 1914-1980.*

SCOTLAND SINCE 1945

OBJECTIVES

The proximity of the post-1945 era means inevitably that any analysis of events is coloured by our own views and experience - and historians, who ought to be objective, are just as guilty of subjectivity as the rest of us. Yet even subjective judgements are better made with some understanding of the recent past, so once you have read this section and the appropriate chapter in Ferguson you should know something about:

✿— the main economic and social developments in Scotland since 1945,

✿— the political background, both in Scotland and the UK.

These are clearly immensely complicated issues in themselves, but at the same time we need to take account of the many interrelationships between political, economic and social change if we are to understand the historical process since the Second World War. Additionally it is impossible to separate the Scottish from the British experience as a whole, seen for example, in the discovery and exploitation of North Sea oil, or the great public debates about Europe or Scottish devolution.

READING

Ferguson, Ch. 13, pp. 383-421. The 1978 edition has a Postscript that takes events to 1977; but see the suggested Further Reading for alternative analyses.

SOME MAJOR THEMES

(i) Economic and Social Developments

(a) The Economy

If the economy and its problems hold the key to an understanding of Scotland in the 'twenties and 'thirties, this is perhaps even more relevant in the post-war period. Just as World War I had confirmed the dominance of Scotland's heavy industries, so the strategic needs of the Second World War brought about a reassertion of coal, iron, steel, engineering and shipbuilding production - vital to the war effort. The attempt to diversify into newer industries, started in the late 1930s, was temporarily suspended, so that the Scottish economy emerged from the war with much the same narrow base as before.

After 1945 there were many difficulties: modernisation of older industry was limited by lack of investment, and new industry slow to develop. But in the longer term, and with government assistance, much was achieved, especially in the New Towns and on the industrial estates. Post-war recovery therefore brought much needed diversification to the Scottish economy in industries like vehicle manufacture, petro-chemicals, nuclear power, electronics, electrical and other light engineering. But despite the growth of new industries of the kind that typified the regional economies of the English Midlands or the South East, much of the prosperity of the 1950s and 60s still arose from heavy industry, revitalised by post-war recovery, for example, in the steel industry. The run-down of older plant in coal mining, textiles, and shipbuilding among others continued - creating profound difficulties for the communities concerned.

The continuing challenge of foreign competition after the 1960s gradually eroded much that had been achieved by modernisation, despite large-scale investment during the 'seventies in growth industries like electronics and oil-related activities. Certainly, the discovery and exploitation of North Sea oil and gas were the most dramatic developments of the post-war era, though it is difficult to assess the long-term direct impact of oil and gas recovery on the Scottish economy, given central government policy of absorbing all revenue. Add to this the uncertainty created by the energy crisis and an associated recession in the later 1970s, and the historian reviewing the situation might be forced to conclude that despite some economic achievements of the period, many deepseated problems remained unresolved. Paramount were those related to recession and unemployment, though some industries and the areas in which they were located prospered. As in so much besides, Scotland's fortunes were bound up with those of the UK, so it is almost impossible to escape the conclusion that common solutions to common problems were required.

(b)   Social Conditions

The social condition of post-war Scotland, like its economy, presented many paradoxes. For amidst the fragile prosperity of the new consumer society there remained pockets of deep poverty and social depression, mainly found in the cities and older industrial districts. Inevitably, with the coming of the Welfare State, the poverty line moved upward, so that the new poor of the post-war years could at least count on some hard won state benefits previously denied this during the earlier Depression era.

Apart from unemployment and endless attempts to create new and permanent jobs to replace those lost by closures, housing was probably Scotland's major problem before the 1960s - as it had been in the 20s and 30s. Major progress of slum clearance and house-building by local authorities and the Scottish Special

Housing Association did much to improve matters; while there was a parallel development of the New Towns and overspill to growth areas around older centres elsewhere. The character of older communities, especially in Glasgow, was thus greatly altered - to the extent that only in the 1970s was urban renewal tackled as a serious alternative to the creation of new communities. In the longer term the falling birth rate after the 1960s did something to alleviate the housing problem, though in much remained to be done.

Scottish society experienced significant changes between after 1945, partly a reflection of improved standards of living and partly through minor modifications in class structure brought about by wider educational opportunity. Paradoxically Scotland became an increasingly polarised society, with a widening gap developing between the old working class and the new middle class - especially what Stephen Maxwell has called "the state-sector middle class", who came to constitute the new elite. As before, it was the skilled working class - often with middle class values and aspirations - that dominated trades unions, and the Left in local and national politics. The Scottish Establishment, mainly but not exclusively Edinburgh based continued to present a remarkably old-fashioned Unionist image, as did the landed class, where it survived alive and well in the counties.

(ii)   Political Developments

As Ferguson indicates, Scottish politics since 1945 have reflected both the acute differences between Scotland and other parts of the UK - and at the same time the essentially radical nature of urban industrial Scotland. Geographical voting patterns highlight the traditional Conservative-Unionist dominance of the counties, though Liberalism always retained a foothold in rural areas with either a radical agricultural tradition, or with working class towns, like those in the Borders. Elsewhere Labour dominated, both in local and national politics.

The major phenomenon in Scottish politics during the 1960s was the emergence of the Scottish National Party, which made remarkable headway after years of largely unrewarded effort following its establishment in the 1930s. Even if it was a party whose strength lay in the protesting voter, the SNP nevertheless made a remarkable contribution to national politics in the 1970s, when its exertions on behalf of independence provoked Westminster recognition of demands for devolution of political power to a Scottish Assembly. Labour was only partly converted to the devolution objective, while the Tories were even more ambivalent. Only the Liberals could claim to be whole-heartedly in favour of devolution - within a federal structure. Although the final devolution proposals were less than satisfactory - including a 40 per cent ruling incorporated in the enabling legislation after pressure from Westminster (mainly English) MPs - the Referendum went ahead on 1 March 1979. In the run-up to the ultimate debacle confusion reigned: neither "Yes" nor "No"

campaigns made clear the obvious historical fact that a Scottish administrative state had long existed and that what was sought was some measure of democratic control over it. As events had it devolution failed -as much through traditional Westminster manipulation as lack of enthusiasm on the part of the Scottish voter.

Another major public debate had earlier focussed on Britain's membership of the then European Economic Community, and here again Scotland had proved to be almost equally divided in its opinion. Following a debate which cut clean across party lines - although the "Anti" side was dominated by Labour and the SNP - the pro-Europeans won by 58 to 41 per cent, on a low poll. The pro-European camp had prepared a carefully orchestrated campaign designed to persuade the electorate that withdrawal from the Common Market would spell disaster and may well have secured a majority in Scotland because economic concerns were uppermost in voters' minds. Certainly, Scottish politics were still dominated by the economy in 1990s - when constructive and farseeing solutions to the country's economic problems were as urgently needed as they had been in the dark days of the Slump sixty years earlier.

SAQs

1.　What attempts were made at economic diversification in post-war Scotland - and were they successful?

2.　What impact did the energy crisis of the 70s have on the Scottish economy?

3.　What major social changes occurred after 1945?

4.　What were the main developments in education after 1945? (See Ferguson, pp. 404-408.)

5.　Why did the SNP make a political breakthrough in the 1970s and what did its policies achieve?

FURTHER READING

G. Brown (ed.) (1975) *The Red Paper on Scotland.*

C.T. Harvie (1977) *Scotland and Nationalism: Scottish Society and Politics 1707-1977.*

C.T. Harvie (1981) *No Gods and Precious Few Heroes: Scotland 1914-1980.*

T.L. Johnston, N.K. Buxton and D. Mair (1971) *Structure and Growth of the Scottish Economy.*

J.G. Kellas (1978) *The Scottish Political System* (2nd ed.).

J.G. Kellas (1980) *Modern Scotland* (2nd ed.).

G. McCrone (1969) *Regional Policy in Britain.*

PART 2:
LITERATURE

A Merry Meeting by Walter Geekie

INTRODUCTION

Part II of this volume is designed to help the reader direct his or her own study of any or all of the major periods and authors in the Scottish literary tradition.

Further Reading lists are provided for each chapter. More generally, we recommend *The History of Scottish Literature*, Aberdeen University Press (1987), 4 vols.

In addition, Roderick Watson, *The Literature of Scotland*, Macmillan (1984), is an excellent short introduction to the subject and so we refer to in by Chapter throughout, as we do in some cases to Kurt Wittig's *The Scottish Tradition in Literature*, The Mercat Press, 1978. Finally, reference is often made to Edwin Muir's *Scott and Scotland*, originally published in 1936 and reissued by Polygon Books in a 1982 edition.

Sadly, many important texts and critical studies are out of print. However, most public libraries make some attempt to cover our subject. We have indicated at the start of each section texts which seem to us essential and which should be readily available, even if not in print.

To help you test your own understanding of our chosen topics, we have designed self assessment questions at the end of each section, which might be used as topics for essays or simply as points for further discussion and thought.

For a small country, Scotland has produced a remarkable body of literature, which furthermore exists in three languages, Scots, Gaelic and English. Some leading authors - Burns, Scott, Byron, Carlyle, Stevenson, and Conan Doyle in particular - have been famous and influential all over the world, but other work of high merit has suffered neglect even in Scotland, and Scots, as Muir exemplifies, are often self-doubting when they speak of their literature. We believe that the time has come to be less bashful. Just as Henryson and Dunbar matched - indeed, outmatched - their contemporaries south of the Border; so MacDiarmid must be recognised as one of the greatest of Modernist poets, writing anywhere, Grassic Gibbon as arguably the best 'proletarian' novelist publishing in Britain in his period, and, to come up to date, McIlvanney's *Docherty* Gray's *Lanark* and Kelman's A *Disaffection*, as novels of the highest quality by international standards.

The vigour of Scottish writing, and of debate over Scottish Literature is well represented in such literary magazines as *Cencrastus*, *Chapman* and *Edinburgh Review*. Important articles on authors discussed here have appeared and will continue to appear in such journals, and you could follow up your interest by subscribing to one or more of them. Scholarly articles can be found in *Scottish Literary Journal* and *Studies in Scottish Literature*.

SOME ASPECTS OF EARLY SCOTTISH LITERATURE

OBJECTIVES

This section provides a general introduction to:

✪— Scottish culture to the mid-fourteenth century

✪— the emergence of the Lowland vernacular: themes medieval and Scottish.

READING

The poets considered here and throughout Part II are well represented in R. Watson (ed.) (1995), *The Poetry of Scotland: Gaelic, Scots and English.*

Watson, Ch 1 and 2

Wittig, Ch 1 and 4

SOME MAJOR THEMES

(i)   Scottish Culture to the Mid-Fourteenth Century

In the mid-fourteenth there existed in Scotland both Latin and Gaelic cultural traditions. Latin remained the international language of educated Christendom. Scotland provided her share of scholars, for example John Duns Scotus (1265?-1308?), who provided the main opposition to St Thomas Aquinas in the great theological debates of the time. The international basis of this Church-centred Latin culture is reflected in the fact that many of its contributors, like Duns Scotus himself, spent much of their time outwith their native country, in monasteries and universities throughout Europe. Even with Renaissance and Reformation this internationalism lingered. The most powerful Scottish intellect in sympathy with the Reformers, George Buchanan (1506-1582),nonetheless taught at Paris and wrote in Latin. Moreover, with the Reformers triumphant in Scotland, many clerics adhering to the old religion chose exile on the Continent. From the various Scots Colleges which they established, they continued in the Latin tradition. On a more secular level, the neo-classicism which was a feature of the Renaissance encouraged the continuation of Latin poetry. Well into the seventeenth century, Scotland was responding to that encouragement with verse of a very high quality. (See section 4 on the 'Aberdeen Doctors').

Apart from the classical cultures of the Mediterranean, Gaelic is perhaps the oldest European poetic tradition. For centuries the Gaels of Scotland and of Ireland shared this tradition in sharing the language that expressed it and, to a large extent, the loyalties of which that language was a symbol. With the Anglo-Saxon plantation of Ulster in the seventeenth century, this Gaelic connection was dislocated. The poetic traditions of Gaeldom continued however, and thus isolated the achievements of the Scottish Gael became increasingly distinctive. You will find a special section devoted to Gaelic literature later.

By the mid-fourteenth century, the language of the northern English had for several hundred years displaced the Celtic tongues in the lowlands of south and east Scotland. However, the political boundary between the two countries was also long established, as was the hostility between them, and with a dialect from Southern England emerging as the standard for that nation, the language of lowland Scotland likewise developed in its own distinctive direction. Thus linguistic and national distinctions combined to voice the existence of a non-Latin, non-Gaelic and decidedly Scottish literature.

Encounter between Bruce and De Bohun

(ii)   The Emergence of the Lowland Vernacular - Themes Medieval and Scottish

Throughout Europe, the Middle Ages saw the emergence of literatures written in the vernacular - Italian, French, English etc - as opposed to Latin. Literature in Scots, as distinct from Gaelic, began relatively late and like the other vernaculars showed the influence of earlier traditions - notably the Classic and the Celtic - and of the innovations being wrought by the vernacular writers themselves. However, the Scottish poets brought their own personal and national temperaments to bear, thereby creating a tradition distinctively their own. Finally, in reading these early Scottish poets you should be conscious that they write from the basis of a medieval vision of existence which differed radically from that of the world by which it was replaced.

(a) The Epic

The long narrative poem dealing with a heroic subject is one of the oldest literary forms. In the feudal world of medieval Europe, the tone of such poetry normally reflected the values held - at least in theory - by the courtly audiences for which it was written. What are celebrated are chivalric ideals, and the poet rarely allows reality to inconvenience him. The first major poem in Scots was in the epic tradition, but *The Bruce* by its very title indicates the distinctively Scottish experience

William Wallace by the 11th Earl of Buchan after unknown.
Scottish National Portrait Gallery

of the War of Independence. The poem was written by John Barbour, the Archdeacon of Aberdeen, in the 1380's, within living memory of Bannockburn. Such proximity to the great national struggle gives the poem a new realism. Moreover, the nature of that struggle, the defiance - ultimately by an entire people - of the might of English feudal assertion, makes *The Bruce* as much a statement of national integrity as it is a heroic romance. 'Freedom', that is 'freeliking' or free will is what is at stake, and there is no doubt that since free will is the gift of God, the Scots are justified in defending it from English usurpation. Wittig is right to point out that this gives the poem 'a remarkable quality that can perhaps best be described as 'poise': he (Barbour) need not hotly assert his patriotism, but can afford to be

objective in judging his enemies'. Further, as he continues, it is 'essential to grasp the fact that the conviction on which Barbour's poise was based had itself a religious basis'. This quality is likewise to be seen in *The Wallace*, the other great epic of the period, written by Blind Hary the Minstrel about one hundred years after Barbour's work. Hary's poem reaches its climax, not in the awesome brutality of Wallace's death, which is treated with great tact, but in the spiritual vindication of his career, and the condemnation of that of Edward I, by the Bishop of Westminster, a conclusion which all good Englishmen recognise as just. Wittig goes on to see in Barbour's religiosity a foretaste of the attitudes of the Scottish Reformers. It is an opinion that comes up regularly in his treatment of pre-Reformation Scottish poetry, and it should be considered with the utmost caution. In the case of Barbour for example, the very universality indicated above might more accurately be seen as a particularly medieval attitude which the nationalisms and factionalisms of the Reformation era would actually undermine.

(b)   Beast Allegory

An interesting, early Scottish example of beast allegory is *The Buke of the Howlat* written by Sir Richard Holland (1420-85), an adherent of the House of Douglas. The heavy alliteration which dictates the poem's rhythm is a reminder of Middle English heroic poetry, undercut on this occasion by the nature of the subject matter. The owl, or 'howlat' appeals to the Pope and to the Emperor of birds concerning his dowdy appearance, that they might intercede with Nature on his behalf. As a result he obtains a brilliant plumage, only to lose it again through his consequent pride. The mood of the poem is essentially comic. At the same time however, it suggests parallels that satirize contemporary events. Soon after the poem was written, the immense power of the House of Douglas was ruthlessly destroyed by James II. The lesson on the dangers of pride could thus be read as a warning to the Douglas dynasty. However, Holland was part of that House and the poem ends with a long eulogy on its achievements. Nor can the warning be aimed squarely at the king, for the essence of the eulogy is the glories wrought through Douglas' loyalty to the Crown. Perhaps this problem is part of the reason why critics tend to pass over the poem. Scottish independence was largely achieved through the cooperation of Bruce and his mightiest subject, James Douglas. The growing tension between the descendants of these two powers in Holland's generation appeared extremely ominous, being the disintegration of the foundation on which the nation's independence and security was based. This tendency of events was paralleled on a wider scale by schisms within the Church which threatened the unity of Christendom, and these too are alluded to in Holland's poem. *The Buke of the Howlat* considers the nature of harmony and the causes of disharmony. Ultimately, the source of the latter is pride, and the lesson of the poem is for all those to whom it is applicable.

(c)   Courtly Love

The Courtly Love tradition in medieval poetry had its origins in Provence in Southern France, its most famous expression being *Le Roman de la Rose*. The central theme is the courtier's love for his lady, who is invariably married to someone else. The Scottish poem belonging most fully to this category is the *Kingis Quair* of James I of Scotland. James was captured by the English on his way to France in 1406, and grew up in captivity in London until he was ransomed by his subjects in 1424. In these years he was no doubt influenced by the French courtly tradition and its English imitations, and his poem, written at the end of his captivity, employs many of its conventions, while his language is, understandably, somewhat anglicised. However, James' poem is distinctive in being at once more realistically personal and more universal than is normal in such poetry. To begin with, the romantic content of the poem is centred, not on the idealised and adulterous affair traditional to the courtly love genre, but on an actual woman, Joan Beaufort, whom the poet courted and married. Secondly, a very different influence is the writing of Boethius, the great Roman thinker who found solace against the evil fortune which had reduced him from honour to poverty and exile in the meditations which he recorded in his *Consolation of Philosophy*. The legitimate and constant nature of the poet's love allows him to reconcile his personal predicament in accordance with the Boethian philosophy. Unable to sleep, the poet reads how Boethius found peace and overcame the vagaries of Fortune through philosophy. He recognises a similarity in the ill-fortune of his own exile and imprisonment, and resolves to write an account of his predicament. He tells how the misery of his condition is brought home to him when, from his prison window, he sees and falls in love with the seemingly unattainable Joan Beaufort. He later falls into a dream in which he is gradually brought to learn that, beyond what seems to be the indifferent working of Fortune, there exists the unwavering hand of God. Through the constancy of his affection, he ultimately wins his freedom and his love. Constancy is the key. Through it we reflect our allegiance to God who is permanence, and Fortune is transcended.

> Tak him before in all thy governance,
> That in his hand the stere has of you all;
> And pray unto his hye purueyance
> Thy lufe to gye, and on him traist and call,
> That corner-stone and ground is of the wall,
> That failis nought; and trust, withoutin drede,
> Unto thy purpose sone he sall the lede.

(d) The Moral Tale

The blending of moral lesson and entertainment is another feature of medieval poetry. Without doubt the finest Scottish example of this type of literature is Henryson's *Moral Fables*, which we will look at in the following section. In the anonymous *Thre Prestis of Peblis*, three priests, at ease before the fire of a Peebles inn decide that to pass the time each will in turn entertain the others with a story. Precedence is given to the wisdom of experience. Thus the first tale is told by Master John, for he has seen, among other places, Portugal, the five kingdoms of Spain, Flanders, Venice and Rome. He is followed by Master Archibald, for he has at least been to Rome, while William, who has been nowhere and done nothing comes last.

All three offer sound advice on various aspects of human existence. But of course the spirituality of that advice increases in direct proportion to the lack of worldly wisdom, culminating in William's final tale. The interplay of the material and the spiritual is a feature of pre-Reformation poetry however, and there is no contradiction in the fact that the tales are told before a blazing fire, to the accompaniment of roast capon and home-brewed ale.

(e) Popular Poetry

Other poems could have been mentioned, and there are references in some existing pieces to many more that have been lost. One other type that we should note, is a continuing body of anonymous poetry dealing with popular subjects - fairs and holidays, brawls and wooings - which began at this period and was maintained by the common people through the centuries. (Eg *The Wife of Auchtermuchty, Kind Kittock, Rauf Colyear* and the *Colkelbie Sow*.) In the medieval period itself, such pieces were known to the most sophisticated, side by side with the most elaborate Courtly Love convention. Indeed, some have credited William Dunbar with *Kind Kittock*, while two other examples of these 'folk' poems, *Christis Kirk of the Green*, and *Peblis for the Play*, have been attributed to James I and James V. The people maintained such poems, so that three hundred years later their influence is plainly seen in the poetry of Fergusson and Burns.

SAQ

What would you say were the essentially national ingredients that the advent of Scots brought to European literature and what were the main European influences upon medieval Scottish literature?

FURTHER READING

There is a shortage of material on the writers discussed in this section. In any case, maybe at this stage you are better to spend the time on the poetry itself. If you wish to forge ahead in coming to terms with the period, the reading for the following two sections should be helpful.

ROBERT HENRYSON (C1420-1490)

OBJECTIVES

Of all the medieval Scottish poets Henryson is perhaps the most accessible, both linguistically and in terms of subject matter. His work certainly provides the fullest insight into the thoughts and attitudes of the time. We will try to indicate this under the following headings:

✺— human dilemmas and Christian solutions - from *Orpheus* to 'The Annunciation'

✺— the *Testament of Cresseid*, a synthesis?

✺— the *Moral Fables*

READING

Henryson (1974), *Poems*, ed Charles Elliott, Oxford

Watson, Ch 2

Wittig, Ch II

SOME MAJOR THEMES

(i) Human Dilemmas and Christian Solutions

(a) Orpheus and Eurydice

Orpheus and Eurydice contains Henryson's bleakest depiction of the human condition. The laws with which humanity must comply, the rigid allegorical parallels that the concluding 'moralitas' asserts, take no account of human frailty. The tragedy of such a position is expressed in the disjunction between the inflexible ideals of the 'moralitas' and the reality of life as displayed by the events of the 'taill' itself. The demands of the ideal are indicated in the poem's opening statement:

> *It is contrar the lawis of nature*
> *A gentill man to be degenerate.*

Orpheus, as a human offspring of the gods, cannot meet such demands. His mother is the Muse Caliope, through whom he has inherited the ability to create the 'sweit licour of all musike perfyte'. His father is Phebus, the god of reason, and this too he inherits. The essence of these gifts is that through the application of reason, he should be able to create a harmony in human affairs at one with the ideal. His role as musician is an expression of this, for music, personified in his mother, is called the 'fyndar of all ermonye'. Orpheus' marriage to Eurydice, is the union of reason to the legitimate power of human desire. Ideally, the two forces should complement each other. As the 'moralitas' puts it:

> *Bot Orpheus has wone Erudices*
> *Quhen our desyre with resoune makis pes.*

In reality however, both reason and music are silenced by the predominance of Eurydice, as expressive of desire, who thus isolated, embraces sensuality - the serpent sting that takes her to Hell.

Such are the clear equations by which Henryson, in his 'moralitas' translates the 'taill' of Orpheus and Eurydice. The moral values to which the allegory converts the affairs of men with unyielding precision, stands in stark contrast to the confused reality in which these affairs are enacted. The pre-requisite to salvation is a god-like perfection, and no mitigation of this condition is allowed for what can be achieved by a flawed creature in a flawed world.

As he searches the universe for Eurydice, music, and therefore reason is rekindled in Orpheus. But only in that he is among the spheres, in the presence of the gods. When, having followed her to Hell, he is

Orpheus and Eurydice

faced with the possibility of regaining his queen, reason is again confounded, and the backward glance by which the lovers are thwarted is all but inevitable.

The 'moralitas' follows remorselessly. But our sympathy remains with Eurydice, and with Orpheus as he mourns his loss and laments the dilemma of fallen humanity:

> *Quhat art thow luf? How sall I the diffyne?*
> *Bitter and sweit, cruell and merciable, ...*
> *Quha servis the, thocht he be never so trew,*
> *Perchance sum tyme he sall have caus to rewe.*

(b) The Religious Poems

Most critics recognise a great deal of human sympathy in Henryson's poetry. However, there is considerable divergence as to the precise tone of that sympathy. Some see the shadow of the cruel dilemma expressed in *Orpheus and Eurydice* throughout the poetry, and therefore attribute Henryson with an essentially pessimistic, or at times rebellious view of existence. Matthew P McDiarmid is one such critic. Others point to the medieval Christianity which was the central feature of the poet's world, as the basis of an ultimately optimistic vision. Either way, it is necessary to recognise this centrality if we are to avoid imposing on the poetry the attitudes of a later age.

The moral universe in which *Orpheus and Eurydice* is placed is non-Christian. Christianity proposes a solution to the dilemma it presents, and Henryson is keenly aware of this in his religious poems. Like *Orpheus*, 'The Bludy Serk' is divided between 'taill' and 'moralitas'. Like Eurydice, the princess of the poem, who in terms of the 'moralitas' becomes 'manis saule', is captured by the 'gyane' Lucifer. As the Christian features of the poem emerge however, a new factor comes into play: 'Chryst that deit on tre' is the knight who redeems man's soul, and Lucifer is cast down, not with his captives, but 'allane withoutin feir'. When the last line of the poem asks the reader to 'Think on the bludy serk' it is as the symbol of the means by which the world of *Orpheus and Eurydice* is renewed.

A favourite expression of this renewal was the Annunciation scene, and Henryson's poem is as exquisite as the painting by his contemporary, Botticelli, that hangs in Glasgow. While the language of the first third of the poem mirrors the mood of Mary's confinement, the rest of the poem is, by contrast, a celebration of the great outflow of grace from 'luffis ryver' that is to follow, whereby past, present, and future are redeemed.

(ii) The Testament of Cresseid, a Synthesis?

In Chaucer's *Troilus and Criseyde*, Criseyde deserts Troilus for the Greek Diomede. Thereafter Chaucer's concern is Troilus and he takes no further interest in his heroine. Henryson's *Testament* takes up her story. Diomede tires of her and she in turn is deserted, to live as best she can by her charms in the 'court commoun'. Ultimately rejected by all, she returns to her father's house, where an outburst against the cruelty of the gods for her misfortune, results in her being brought before them in a dream-vision to be judged. When she wakes, she finds herself striken by leprosy, in accordance with their verdict. The venereal implications held by that disease in the Middle Ages, unites the punishment of her blasphemy with the results of her recent mode of existence. At first, she remains resentful of the gods, but gradually she accepts the fact that:

> All welth in eird away as wind it weiris ...
> Fortoun is fikkill quhen scho beginnis and steiris.

and learns to 'leve efter the law of lipper leid'. As in *Orpheus and Eurydice*, the world of the poem is pagan. Having thus reconciled herself to her fate, Cresseid parallels the widowed Orpheus and there seems little more to be said. However, we have employed the term 'synthesis' because several critics, including Professor MacQueen, see in the remainder of the poem a resolution of Cresseid's fate, ultimately Christian, though conveyed imaginatively, not dogmatically.

As Cresseid begs with the other lepers, she is passed by Troilus returning from battle. They do not recognize each other, but he is reminded of her and 'For knichtlie pietie and memoriall of fair Cresseid' he throws her a purse of gold. On being told by the other lepers who has done her this charity, Cresseid perceives a constant value beyond the realm of 'fikkill' fortune which fundamentally transforms her vision of existence. Resignation becomes repentance as she discovers and acknowledges the existence of 'trueth'. By Christian implication she is at once quit of her sin through the sorrow it evokes, and taken beyond the jurisdiction of the powers that had condemned her. It should be noted that not everyone agrees with this positive conclusion. Matthew P McDiarmid for example, sees the poem as tragic to the end, though this perhaps discounts the poet's medieval context. But, in drawing your own conclusions you will get to the heart of an excellent poem.

(iii) The Moral Fables

The world of the *Fables* is the redeemed world of the Christian era. Nonetheless, as Henryson informs us in the Prologue, it is still the case that:

> ... mony men in operatioun
> Ar like to beistis in conditioun

At their most serious, the *Fables* seek to combat this situation. Here, as everywhere in medieval poetry:

> ... dois spring ane morall sweit sentence
> Oute of the subtell dyte of poetry,
> To gude purpois quha culd it weill apply.

However, it is simultaneously Henryson's intention:

Amangis ernist to ming ane merie sport
To light the spreit and gar the tyme be schort.

The balance of earnestness in relation to merriness varies from fable to fable. In this redeemed world however, they always mingle, 'taill' and 'moralitas' are no longer distinct but part of the inseparable whole of human experience. We cannot deal with the thirteen poems of the *Moral Fables* individually, but a discernible group concerns the folly of individuals - all featuring Lawrence the Fox, Chanticleer, and the Town and Country Mice - in which comedy is most prominent. A second group concerns more serious social criticism. Those featuring the lion allude to monarchy with reference to contemporary conditions. Thus, in the *Parliament of fourfuttit Beistis* the lion's pride is deflated by the reaction of the mare, representative of the religious, while the *Taill of the Lyoun and the Mous* reflects the torturous relationship between James III and his nobility. Criticism turns to condemnation when Henryson speaks of the oppression of the weak by the strong, with the connivance of the law, as in the *Taill of the Sheip and the Doig*, or the *Taill of the Wolf and the Lamb*. Finally, there are those fables in which the lesson is essentially theological and philosophic: *The Cok and the Jasp*, *The Paddok and the Mous*, and *The Preiching of the Swallow*. In every case, the emphasis rests on the medieval assumption that life is at heart an inter-relationship of the 'taill' and the 'moralitas', temporal and eternal. Moreover, while Henryson most fully expresses this vision of life, it likewise lies behind all the poetry of the period.

SAQs

1.   The Annunciation was a favourite topic for artists, as a succinct expression of divine intervention in human affairs. Consider Henryson's treatment of the subject.

2.   How does the position of the narrator in the *Testament* relate to the events of his story?

3.   How successful is Henryson's characterisation of the animals in *the Moral Fables*?

FURTHER READING

M.P. McDiarmid (1981) *Robert Henryson*.

J. MacQueen (1967) *Robert Henryson: A Study of the Major Narrative Poems*.

Scottish Literature in the Sixteenth Century

OBJECTIVES

Nowadays, we look upon the late medieval period as something of a golden age in Scottish poetry. Dunbar, in the poem that is known as the 'Lament for the Makaris' names twenty one Scottish poets, many of whom have come down to us as nothing more than names. Nevertheless, a sufficient amount of work has survived from the period to bear witness to a mature and flourishing culture. The title of this section begs questions. The poetic careers of Dunbar and Douglas did not extend beyond the fateful year of Flodden (1513), and taking that date as the end of an age, either or both could be considered with Henryson in the fifteenth century. Watson treats Dunbar in this way. Conversely, as the dates of MacQueen's anthology suggests, Henryson can be seen with Dunbar, Douglas and Lindsay, as part of an era that ended with the Reformation. Again, it could be argued that the poetic continuity is only broken absolutely with the Union of Crowns in 1603. In any case, we will now look at the major poets of the period after Henryson.

✪— William Dunbar

✪— Gavin Douglas

✪— Sir David Lindsay

✪— Scottish poetry 1560-1603

READING

J. and W. MacQueen, eds. (1972) A *Choice of Scottish Verse* 1470-1570.

R.D.S. Jack, ed. (1978), A *Choice of Scottish Verse* 1560-1660.

Watson, Chs 2 and 3

Wittig, Chs II, III and IV

SOME MAJOR THEMES

(i)   William Dunbar (c1460-c1513)

What ultimately impresses us about Henryson is the combination of spiritual wisdom and human sympathy. By contrast Dunbar, the townsman and the courtier, conveys in his poetry before all else the great variety of sights and sounds and smells which made up urban life in sixteenth century Scotland, together with the responses, fluctuating between attraction and revulsion, that they provoked. This variety of subject matter is matched in Dunbar's poetry by an immensely rich hierarchy of linguistic expression, for he is a complete master of language and style operating within a highly sophisticated cultural tradition. At one extreme is the 'High Style' of such poems as 'The Thrissill and the Rois' or 'The Golden Targe', written as much as anything else, one feels, out of the poet's sheer delight in his own stylistic mastery:

> The cristall air, the sapher firmament,
> The ruby skyes of the orient
> Kest beriall bemes on emerant bewis grene ...
> (from 'The Golden Targe')

In such poetry Dunbar employs a great many 'aureate' terms of Latin or French derivation. At the other end of the spectrum, as in the 'Flyting' poems (linguistic battles of abuse between two poets) he taps the full strength of Scots with equal assurance:

> ... Muttoun dryver, girnall ryver, yadswyver, fowll fell the;
> Herretyk, lunatyk, purspyk, carlingis pet,
> Rottin crok, dirtin dok, cry cok, or I sall quell the.
> (from 'The Flyting of Dunbar and Kennedie')

Certainly such stylistic 'extremes' present difficulties for the modern reader, but both types of poem repay the effort, and such an effort is necessary for those who wish to come to anything like a full understanding of Dunbar and the tradition in which he worked. However, there is a central body of poetry in a 'middle' style - the regularly anthologised pieces such as 'Meditation in Winter', 'To the Merchants of Edinburgh', 'To a Lady' etc, as well as many Moralities and poems to the King - in which language and intention are more accessible.

Dunbar's linguistic variety is matched by the extremes of his personal response to existence. His attitude to life wavers between a consciousness that:

> Heir nocht abydis, heir standis nothing stabill;
> This fals warld ay flittis to and fro;
> (Vanitas Vanitatum et omnia Vanitas)

and the more positive response;

> Be mery man, and tak nocht fer in mynd
> The wavering of this wrechit vale of sorow;
> (Without Glaidnes avalis no Tresure)

Dunbar's sheer professionalism as a 'Makar' makes it notoriously difficult to distinguish the man beyond the poem. However, in the combination of these two responses we perhaps get some idea of a vision which, whether merry or morose, sees something essentially absurd about the life of which the poet is himself a part.

His longest poem, 'The Tretis of the twa mariit Wemen and the Wedo' finds the poet in a beautiful garden on Midsummer's Eve, where, through a hedge he hears the conversation of three ladies. It is the traditional setting for a courtly romance. However, the audience has been lulled only to be assailed by a cynical and scurrilous interpretation of the realities of life and love. The attitudes of the women are the responses of experience to the reality of what society, in the persons of their lovers and husbands, demands of them. A similar feel for the absurd is found in many of Dunbar's poems. In 'The Telyour and the Sowtar's War' (Nixt that a turnament wes tryid) the tailor and the souter ape the chivalric conventions of the nobility. Wittig sees in this Dunbar's denigration of the commons. This is no doubt a factor, but surely the chivalric pose of the nobility itself is simultaneously ridiculed. Certainly, in the many poems of court life, for example 'Of a Dance in the Quenis Chalmer' the portrayal of the courtier is little more elevated than that of the tradesmen. Again, this court dance both echoes, and is echoed in 'The Dance of the sevin deidly Synnis'.

The degree to which such parallels are serious or jocular depends on Dunbar's mood. Probably, there is always a bit of both. What is certain is that in the world he portrays, values are often distorted if not inverted.

No doubt the source of this attitude is to a considerable degree personal. The many poems to the King in which Dunbar seeks some reward - money, a church appointment, but essentially the recognition of his worth - show how he felt himself undervalued by a society thats values are, by implication, false. However, this does not negate entirely a note of genuine moral outrage. In the first half of 'Remonstrance to the King' for instance, Dunbar gives a list of valuable and honoured members of society, while in the second half he names those who, though equally honoured, are wholly parasitic. As MacQueen has pointed out (Scottish Verse 1470-1570, Introduction) the two groups are in fact the same, described firstly at their own estimation, and secondly in relation to their true worth. Such criticism is perennial, but, as MacQueen indicates, the unique distortion of the period was the intrusion of the Crown in the making of important appointments within the church, in favour of its own relations and favourites. One such favourite was the charlatan Damian, whose attempt to fly from Stirling Castle forms the basis of 'The fenyeit freir of Tungland'. To the medieval man such usurpation of spiritual authority, of the source from which guidance and correction was traditionally sought, must have been fairly awesome, and Dunbar is such a man declaring his outrage.

Dunbar's poetry is intensely involved in the material concerns of day to day life. But as with the other poets of the period, one often gets the feeling that at heart, these concerns exist for the poet in their relationship to, (or contrast with) eternal verities.

Whatever the subject of Dunbar's poetry, this spiritual framework lies somewhere in the background, for him, the ultimate reality. It finds its most overt expression in such superb liturgical pieces as 'Of the Nativitie of Christ' (Rorate celi desuper) or 'On the Resurrection of Christ', (Done is a battell on the dragon blak). Wittig's opinion that the Nativity poem is 'mechanical' and 'theatrical' betrays a failure of sympathy for the medieval spiritual order on his part, rather than a flaw in the poem. 'Of the Nativitie of Christ' is not simply a parallel to a modern Christmas carol, expressing joy at the birth of Christ. It does that of course, but it also recognises the meaning of the birth, whereby all things in heaven and on earth are reconciled and harmonized:

> *Syng hevin imperiall, most of hicht,*
> *regions of air mak armony;*
> *allfishe in flud and foull of flicht*
> *be myrthfull and mak melody:*
> *all **Gloria in excelsis** cry,*
> *hevin, erd, se, man, bird, and best,*
> *he that is crownit abone the sky*
> *pro nobis Puer natus est.*

Only by referring directly to the Christian liturgy can Dunbar express such harmony. Beyond that, where Henryson could apply its solutions imaginatively in order to reconcile the contradictions of life, Dunbar can only acknowledge the contradictions. As a courtman, Dunbar was perhaps himself too close to those contradictions, recognising in fact that he was a part of them. And perhaps the Scottish capital a generation after Henryson's death presented more profound anomalies to the medieval vision of existence.

(ii) Gavin Douglas (c1475-1522)

Apart from being attributed authorship of *King Hart*, an interesting morality poem of doubtful origin, Douglas is remembered for the long allegorical poem *The Palice of Honour*, and for his *Eneados*, which Wittig rightly calls 'one of the great Renaissance translations'. He completed this enormous achievement in 1513, the year of Flodden, and thereafter, as Provost of St Giles, and later Bishop of Dunkeld, abandoned poetry for more serious matters. *The Palice of Honour* is a dream allegory, in a medieval mode which, as Priscilla Bawcutt puts it, was at heart 'a vehicle for psychological investigation and the discussion of ideas'. Here as elsewhere, the question is how man, faced with the vagaries of human experience, might gain access to the Palice which is the presence of God (the description of the Palice is based upon the Revelations of St John). The dreaming poet witnesses a procession of the goddesses who represent the various means - Wisdom, Chastity, Love - through which access to the Palice is sought. Ultimately, he gains a brief glimpse of it with the help of the Muse Calliope, and learns that moral virtue is the eternal value through which eternal honour is achieved. It is interesting that it is through the efforts of the Muses that the poet is saved. The court of the Muses is described thus:

> Yone is the Court of plesand steidfastnes,
> Yone is the Court of constant merines,
> Yone is the Court of loyous discipline.

The role of the Muses, and therefore of poetry, implied in this description, is that of reconciling contradictions, ultimately with regard to the relationship between the temporal and the eternal. This view is familiar in medieval poetry (Henryson, in his prologue to the *Moral Fables*, alludes to the Parable of the Sower, and sees himself as tending the growth of the 'good seed'). For Douglas however, the *Palice of Honour* seems at least as much a vehicle to express his erudition and poetical virtuosity, and there is a distinctly Renaissance energy about this aspect of the poem.

Calliope

Perhaps his most original and accessible work is in his Prologues to the *Eneados*, particularly the 'Seasons' Prologues, with their close observation of the workings of nature. The success of Douglas' translation of Virgil's *Aeneid* lies in the happy combination of the medieval and the Renaissance. In his learned approach, his respect for his original, in his immense and successful efforts in expanding the scope of the Scots language to contain even the great Virgil, he shows the spirit of the new learning. In doing so without the pedantry and dryness which overtook later classicism, and responding instead to all that is enduringly human in the ancient poet, he brings to bear the heritage of medieval Scottish poetry. C.S.Lewis notes that:

Time after time Douglas is nearer to the original than any version could be which kept within the limits of later classicism. And that is almost another way of saying that the real Virgil is very much less 'classical' than we had supposed. To read Latin again with Douglas's version fresh in our minds is like seeing a favourite picture after it has been cleaned. Half the 'richness' and 'sobriety' we have been taught to admire turns out to have been only dirt; ... Douglas gives us new eyes - unless, of course, we approach him with the assumption that wherever medieval

Virgilianism differed from humanistic, the medieval must have been simply wrong.

This discovery is echoed by all those who encounter Douglas' *Eneados*. On this basis, ultimately, we could discount Wittig's suggestion that Douglas - and virtually everyone else in pre-Reformation Scottish literature - is 'very close to Calvin'. On a more obvious level, where Wittig cites references at one with Calvinist theory, it should be pointed out that they are no less at one with medieval religious theory. Wittig presumably considers features not at one with Calvinist theory - for example the fact that 'Douglas retains the Catholic system of thought' - to be the dismissable lapses of 'the bishop to be' into 'religious orthodoxy'. But whatever we may think of that 'system of thought' we must accept the fact that it is the base on which the poetry of the Makars stands. It is Catholic in the sense that it is universal, in the sense that the universe is assumed to be redeemed, and in the sense that a central role of the Muse is to reconcile the contradictions raised by human imperfection. Hence, Douglas' Eneados is everywhere pointing a Christian moral. This approach is also the source of the features to which Lewis and others respond, for it is one which alights on that which is of enduring human applicability. Calvinism was of course an immensely important influence upon later Scottish culture - in determining, for example, the directions in which the men of the eighteenth century Enlightenment would excel. But these are not in any fundamental way the directions of the pre-Reformation poets, and the relationship which Wittig suggests is more likely to create barriers between ourselves and their period, than to provide insights.

However, the world in which the Makars wrote was soon to be changed in many ways. In his *Eneados*, Douglas demonstrated that there was no limit to what could be expressed in the Scots language. Less than a century later, that language was coming to be regarded as a socially inferior dialect.

(iii) Sir David Lindsay (1486-1555)

In 'The Dreme of Schir David Lyndsay' Jhone the Commoun Weill declares:

... thare sall na Scot have comfortyng
Of me, tyll that I see the countre gydit
Be wysedome of ane gude auld prudent kyng.

The central theme of Lindsay's work is the ruin that comes to the country and the common people when such guidance is absent, through the abuses practised by the 'three estates' of Church, lords and merchants, but particularly those of the churchmen. The fact that Lindsay was writing in the decades immediately preceding the Reformation Settlement of 1560 has given this aspect of his work a special prominence. But there is little that is new in such criticism which is, for example, an important aspect of Henryson's *Fables*. What is, crucially, new, is Lindsay's response to such abuses. Henryson shamed evil by contrasting it with universally accepted religious truth. Lindsay seeks the correction of the Church's ills at the throne of the secular authority. The confusion over the relationship between Church and State noted in relation to Dunbar has taken a step towards resolution in favour of the latter. One result of this is that poetry moves away from the kind of kinship with theology and philosophy we find in Henryson, towards a closer relationship with politics as in much of Lindsay's work. At worst, the somewhat polemical results of this shift, through being intensely related to the details of the period, court obsolescence, as in 'The Tragedie of the Cardinall' and long sections of 'Ane Dialogue betwix Experience and ane Courteour'. Perhaps Lindsay's best poetry is found where he is least influenced by this spirit, as in *Squyer Meldrum*. But the same spirit, applied in drama, resulted in what is far and away Lindsay's masterpiece, *Ane Satyre of the Thrie Estaitis*, which will be considered in a later section.

(iv) Scottish Poetry 1560-1603

> In this new yeir I see but weir,
> Nae cause to sing.

So goes the refrain of Sir Richard Maitland's poem 'On the New Yeir 1560', while in his 'Satire on the Age' he mourns the fact that 'All merriness is worn away'. In the face of such conditions, some poets tended to withdraw within the confines of the court, where, however, a good deal of singing did continue - literally, since the love poetry that dominated the period was normally written to be sung. The outstanding figure of the mid-century was Alexander Scott (c1515-1538) author of many beautiful love poems and of the memorable plea for moderation 'Ane New Yeir Gift to the Quene Mary'. Later, the leading poet at the court of James VI was Alexander Montgomerie (c1545-1597). Centrally, Montgomerie too is a love poet, though he could also take part in 'Polwart and Montgomerie Flyting', and, on the other hand write the long philosophical and theological allegory *The Cherrie and the Slae*. The period produced many poems of high accomplishment by other named authors (as well as many anonymous pieces) and several of them are quoted and referred to by Muir, as evidence of what he considers a level of civilisation which was soon to be undermined.

SAQs

1.   How far, if at all, do you think that Dunbar's 'spiritual framework' manifests itself in the many poems that are not overtly religious?

2.   Which do you consider to be the most accomplished of Douglas' nature prologues? Give reasons for your selection, and examples to support it.

3.   Compare and contrast Lindsay's *Dreme* and Henryson's *Parliament of Beasts* with regard to the social changes implicit in the differences between them.

4.   Summarise the achievement *particular* to Scottish poetry after 1560.

FURTHER READING

(a)   Texts

G. Douglas (1964) *Selections*, ed. D.F.C. Coldwell

W. Dunbar (1958) *Poems*, ed. J.Kinsley

Sir D. Lindsay (1989) *Ane Satyre of the Thrie Estaitis*, ed. R. Lyall

Sir D. Lindsay (1959) *The Historie of Squyer Meldrum*, ed. J. Kinsley

(b)   Secondary Material

P. Bawcutt (1976) *Gavin Douglas*.

P. Bawcutt (1992) *Dunbar: The Makar*.

T. Scott (1966) *Dunbar: A Critical Exposition of the Poems*.

J. Speirs (1962) *The Scots Literary Tradition: An Essay in Criticism* (2nd ed.).

SCOTTISH LITERATURE FROM REFORMATION TO ENLIGHTENMENT

OBJECTIVES

Here we are faced with an extended period, marked by an exceptional rate of change. The following headings seem helpful:

❂— the cultural effects of the Union of Crowns - Scottish literature in the seventeenth century

❂— the Ballads

❂— from Covenants to Enlightenment

❂— the eighteenth century cultural revival

READING

R.D.S. Jack ed. (1978), A *Choice of Scottish Verse* 1560-1660.

Faber Oxford and Penguin Books of Ballads

Editions of Ramsay and Fergusson poems are available in most libraries; selections in Oxford and Penguin Books of Scottish Verse.

Watson, Chs 3, 4 and 5

Wittig, Chs V and VI

SOME MAJOR THEMES

(i)   The Cultural Effects of the Union of Crowns - Scottish Literature in the Seventeenth Century

Before the Reformation, Scottish literature expressed, in language and in content, the interplay of the entire spectrum of society. In the decades following the Reformation settlement of 1560, parliament sought to suppress such vehicles of popular culture as minstrelsy, pageants and plays with a regularity which indicates both the determination of the Reformers and the persistence of the revellers. In these circumstances, literary activity which had always centred on the court became increasingly confined within the court, and this is reflected in a narrowing, in terms of language and of content, in the poetry of the period. This process was gradual, being less evident in the reign of Queen Mary than in the work of the 'Castalian Band', as a group of poets who surrounded James VI was termed. This is not to downgrade such poetry, just to point out that in language and in content it becomes more exclusively courtly. Muir, (p.60) calls the marriage of experience and reflection that still marks such work 'as good a criteria of civilisation as one could find'. In the decades after 1560 the court provided a haven for the literary tradition, even if it had become, to some extent, a walled garden.

In 1603, the court moved from Edinburgh to London. The cultural effect was profound. Firstly, a London court, as centre of a United Kingdom, confirmed the primacy of England and of English, which the political tendencies of the reformers and the language of their Bibles had already inaugurated. Secondly, with the removal of the court from Scotland, the cultural tradition was deprived of its base - and as that base had latterly become a sanctuary, its demise left the tradition isolated in an atmosphere more hostile than ever. The 17th century was a sparse period in Scottish literature. Yet it is important in considering the great changes which distinguish the poetry of the 18th century from that produced before 1603.

The most notable figure in the seventeenth century is William Drummond of Hawthornden (1585-1649). Like much contemporary European poetry, his work centres on the neo-Platonic idea which sees human love as an expression of divine love. Individual poems often convey this, and his two major collections, the sonnets and madrigals brought out as Poems in 1616, and the spiritual pieces contained in *Flowers of Sion*, 1623, express en masse the twin aspects of the same idea. Linguistically, the important point is that Drummond writes in English, reflecting how much and how quickly Scots as a literary medium had been undermined. Perhaps what is further indicated is a sort of

William Drummond of Hawthornden

linguistic withdrawal from the religious and political strife which was the reality of the period. To support this is the fact that Scottish literature in the seventeenth century is otherwise best represented by a group of poets known as the Aberdeen Doctors, of whom the most famous is Arthur Johnston, who wrote in Latin a poetry which reflected Renaissance Europe's renewed devotion to the Classics. Such work was a final after-glow of the learned and courtly tradition in Scottish poetry, but it was no longer expressed in Scots. Thereafter, the folk poetry of the people continued to defy extinction, while the survival of literary Scots lay in the hands of the country lairds whose poetry was itself based upon the folk tradition. Such a one was Robert Sempill of Beltrees. The fact that the metre which he used in his mock elegy 'The Epitaph of Habbie Simson' was to earn the title 'Standard Habbie' among the poets of the 18th century revival, is indicative of the precedents which remained available to that revival.

(ii) The Ballads

Muir (p.114), in considering what he deems a decline in Scottish culture consequent upon the Reformation and the Union of Crowns, points to the loss of a 'whole response' to experience which had once been a property of both 'the Makars and the Balladists'. In as much as he means by this property the assumption that life is an inter-relationship between natural and supernatural levels of being, we can certainly recognise such a presence in the Ballads. The bases of many ballads are at least as old as the poetry of the medieval Makars. However, unlike the literary tradition, the ballads continued throughout the seventeenth century. The central factor permitting this continuity, and the most important point to be absorbed in connection with the Ballads, is that they are part of an oral, or non-literate culture. To be non-literate is not to occupy an underprivileged place in a literate world, it is rather to occupy another world altogether. David Buchan deals well with such matters. As he points out, where 'literary poems express a personal vision, ballads tell stories that express a community's outlook on life'. Moreover, particular to that expression 'is a kind of symbolic imagery whose roots lie in a now fragmented mythology'. The Ballads were based upon a symbolism which was part of a communal tradition. In the literate world however, change comes quicker, and literature reflects the change.

(iii) From Covenants to Enlightenment

Seventeenth century Scotland, marked by political and religious strife, persecution and an atmosphere hostile to creative expression, was transformed in the course of the 18th century, into a centre of the European Enlightenment. There was a time when this was wholly or predominantly attributed to the beneficial effects flowing to Scotland from the incorporating Union of Parliaments in 1707. Looking back beyond the seventeenth century however, it becomes clear that the Scottish Enlightenment had its roots in a centuries-old creative and intellectual tradition. Even in the difficult conditions of the 17th century itself, when the demotion of the Scots language undermined the literature of the nation, the intellectual heritage was continued in other areas. MacQueen outlines the situation well.

As was the case with William Drummond and Arthur Johnston, the continuation of such pursuits was largely an Episcopalian effort. However, by the beginning of the 18th century, the dogmatic zeal which had contributed greatly to the turmoil of much of the previous century came to be questioned by many Presbyterians, and as MacQueen notes, 'the reaction against Covenanting principles was one of the great formative elements in the Scottish Enlightenment.' Of course this was not universal. One of the most compelling advocates of traditional Calvinism, Thomas Boston, (1677-1732) produced his theological works in the eighteenth century. The traditional wing of the Kirk, who maintained a belief in mankind's total depravity, qualified only by the fact that we are arbitrarily predestined to salvation or damnation, came to be known as the 'Auld Lichts', in contrast with the 'New Lichts', amongst whom John Simpson, the Professor of Theology at Glasgow University from 1708 to 1729, and his successor, Francis Hutcheson (1729-46) were pioneers. The assertion by 'New Lichts' of man's innate goodness and of the possibility of universal salvation, was obviously contrary to the dogmas of the 'Auld Lichts' nor could it derive from such dogmas. Instead it sought a basis in the rationalism which was a central feature of eighteenth century European thought and of the Scottish Enlightenment. Such a theology encouraged an increased attention to the nature of the material world, and, together with increasing prosperity produced an environment conducive to the thought of David Hume, Adam Smith, William Robertson, Adam Ferguson, and many other 'Enlightened' intellectuals, discussed in Part I, Section 9 and Part III, Section 3.

(iv) The Eighteenth Century Cultural Revival

The improvements outlined above, and the re-emergence of Scottish letters which they facilitated, were not unnaturally accompanied by a renewal in the field of creative writing. In one direction, such literature reflected the predominance of England, and English, within the newly constituted Great Britain. The two most eminent ex-patriate Scots of the period are the novelist Tobias Smollett, (1721-1771), and James Thomson, (1700-1748), the poet of *The Seasons* and *The Castle of Indolence*. Both men spent their adulthood outwith Scotland and wrote in English - though for Smollett there was little linguistic alternative, there being no living tradition of Scots prose for him to use. Nevertheless, modern scholarship is making it increasingly obvious that both Smollett and Thomson need to be considered not only as Scottish writers, but as products of the Scottish Enlightenment.

In the other direction, there was a revival of interest in, and practice of, poetry in Scots, which reflected both a reaction against the dilution of Scottish identity, and a new respect for past tradition that the Enlightenment itself encouraged. Between 1706 and 1711, James Watson printed a *Choice Collection of comic and serious Scots Poems both ancient and modern*. The collection relied to a great extent upon the folk tradition and the literary expression of that tradition by country lairds such as Sempill. Allan Ramsay, (1684-1758) who had access to the *Bannatyne Manuscript* (perhaps the most important collection of medieval and Renaissance Scottish poetry), expanded and consolidated Watson's work by including in his own *Evergreen, a Collection of Scots Poems wrote by the Ingenious before* 1600, (2 vols, 1724) some Henryson,

Allan Ramsay

a good deal of Dunbar, Alexander Scott, and Montgomerie, and a number of their more shadowy contemporaries. Ramsay was also himself a poet. Many of his efforts seek to imitate the English Augustan style, but his poems in Scots are worth more attention. Pieces such as 'Familiar Epistles' or 'The Twa Books' or 'Lucky Spence's Last Advice' are both worthwhile in themselves and a bequest to his greater successors, Fergusson and Burns. They also indicate that while he might publish Henryson and Dunbar, his own work finds its roots in the popular poetry which had survived the demise of the medieval and Renaissance literary tradition, and this point holds true of Fergusson and Burns also.

On 2 January 1772, there appeared in *Ruddiman's Weekly Magazine* a poem in Scots entitled 'The Daft Days', by Robert Fergusson (1750-74). The stanza form is 'Standard Habbie' but as David Daiches (further reading) puts it, the language 'is not the patronising or nostalgic rural Scots or the antiquarian Scots of so many writers of Scots verse since the latter part of the seventeenth century.' Instead, it is 'an assured, balanced, confident Scots.' Over the next two years the *Weekly Magazine* published a steady stream of Fergusson's Scots poems. Many, like 'The Daft Days' (Yuletide) are vigorous chronicles of the seasonal celebrations which punctuated life in contemporary Edinburgh, while in 'Auld Reekie' he gives a portrait of the variety of life that might be encountered in the streets of the town in the course of a day. Elsewhere, his poetry displays his anxiety about the survival of the distinctive features of Scottish life, as in his 'Elegy on the Death of Scots Music' or 'The Ghaists', in which he laments the loss of Scotland's political and economic sovereignty. Throughout his short career Fergusson, like Ramsay, continued his imitations of the English Augustans, but he is less successful when imitating a foreign mode than when working with confidence from a Scots linguistic base. On the other hand, when working from that base, he can incorporate English and indeed classical material with the utmost fluency. As Daiches puts it 'Fergusson found a way of developing a poetic vocabulary larger and more versatile than either a limited regional Scots or a standard neo-classical English.' He established a whole new range of possibilities for Scots poetry. Many were taken up by Burns, whose debt to the Edinburgh poet was immense. Others, for example a certain urbanity of tone, remain distinctively Fergusson's own, and any discussion of his work must be overshadowed by the squandered potential involved in his tragic death in the Edinburgh bedlam at the age of twenty four. Fergusson was overcome by a religious melancholy centring on a conviction that the life celebrated in his poetry was incompatible with spiritual salvation. The views of the Enlightenment, and even the theology of the 'New Lichts' did not evolve from the traditional dogma, but rather existed in conflict with it, and this may throw some light upon Fergusson's dilemma. Certainly, a more positive response to a similar dilemma is a central feature in the poetry of Burns.

SAQs

1.   Consider the relationship between the Reformation and the Union of Crowns, with regard to their effect on Scottish culture.

2.   How do the areas in which the Scottish Enlightenment excelled relate to the conditions from which it emerged?

3.   What is new to Scottish literature in Fergusson's poetry?

FURTHER READING

D. Buchan (1972) *The Ballad and The Folk*.

T. Crawford (1979) *Society and the Lyric: a study of the Song Culture of eighteenth-century Scotland*.

D. Daiches (1964) *The Paradox of Scottish Culture*.

D. Daiches (1982), *Literature and Gentility in Scotland*.

D. Daiches (1982) *Robert Fergusson*.

J. MacQueen (1982), *Poetry and Progress: The Enlightenment and Scottish Literature*.

ROBERT BURNS

OBJECTIVES

You can consider Burns' poetry in relation to the following headings:

❂— influences and themes

❂— the poems

❂— Burns and the literary tradition

READING

Burns' *Poems*, Penguin selection, or Oxford University Press, complete, ed J Kinsley

Watson, Ch 5

Wittig, Ch VII, pp 199-220

Robert Burns

SOME MAJOR THEMES

(i)   Influences and Themes

The stylistic influences in Burns' poetry are essentially those inherited by Ramsay and Fergusson, with the important addition of the works of these poets themselves, especially Fergusson. Together with a variety of long established stanza forms, the popular tradition bequeathed a basis for satires and epistles, mock elegies and, of course, songs. Fergusson in particular demonstrated that these properties could encompass all that was new in terms of both language and content, including the influence of neo-classical English poetry. Turning to content, Crawford indicates the new themes that characterise Burns' work as follows.

Four great events colour all his life and work: the agrarian changes in eighteenth century Ayrshire; the American Revolution; the conflict within the kirk, which was a specific and local extension of the European 'Enlightenment'; and the French Revolution.

The agrarian reforms referred to (see Part I, Section 8) while improving the lot of many, displaced the cottar whose small holding had formed the lowest tier of the traditional agricultural hierarchy, creating a landless class for whom farming 'improvements' were disastrous. However far their situation related to such changes, farming life for Burns and for his family was seldom more than unmitigated and unrewarding toil. The depression and bitterness which Burns felt at these conditions is the other side of the hopes that he found in the American and the French Revolutions, and in the rationalism and benevolence of 'New Licht' theology. All these contributed to the democratic impulse which runs through his work. Conversely, the tyranny and greed through which the natural rights of the 'honest man' whom Burns extolled were undermined, are linked in his poetry with the hypocritical pretensions to spiritual (and material) preferment of those upholding the 'Auld Licht' position in the kirk.

(ii) The Poems

The hardship of life for the many finds early expression in Burns' work, most memorably in 'Man was made to Mourn.' But if 'Man's inhumanity to Man / Makes countless thousands Mourn', it also breeds, in the dispossessed, more anarchic sentiments. To read *The Jolly Beggars* is to gain a real feeling of the squalor and the energy existing in European society only a few years before the storming of the Bastille. Even ten years later, (1795-6) when the nature of European events had persuaded Burns to join the 'Dumfries Volunteers' - and to write a song with that title beginning 'Does haughty Gaul invasion threat' - his democratic instincts remained unshaken. Indeed, in the same year he gave that philosophy its anthem:

> *For a' that and a' that,*
> *Its comin yet for a' that,*
> *That Man to Man the warld o'er,*
> *Shall brothers be for a' that.*

The Epistles, as Crawford puts it, 'in their occasional and informal nature were ideal for the expression of a plethora of moods together with the transition between them.' Essentially Burns writes them as one honest man to another, the bond being mutual acceptance of the natural pleasures of humanity - sexuality and comradeship. The transition of mood is most often from the contemplation of such things to what, for Burns, is their opposite:

> *An honest man may like a glass,*
> *An honest man may like a lass,*
> *But mean revenge, an' malice fause*
> *He'll still disdain,*
> *An' then cry zeal for gospel laws,*
> *Like some we ken.*
> > *(Epistle to Rev John M'Math)*

Willie brewed a peck o' malt

Here Burns is referring to the 'Auld Lichts', those of the 'sighan, cantan, grace-proud faces' (same epistle), who stimulated his most brilliant satires. In the preceding section, we saw that the conflict between 'Auld Licht' dogma and 'New Licht' morality could be related to the instability that destroyed Robert Fergusson. Burns' more assured position is displayed by the fact that he could deal with this conflict itself, hilariously, in 'The Holy Fair'. Even in doing so he acknowledges that the 'tidings o' d-mn-t—n' delivered by the Calvinist preachers continue to hold an Ayrshire audience more effectively than the 'moral pow'rs an' reason' of the new men. But if, as the

'Auld Lichts' maintain, every aspect of human life is the property of the Devil, then a logical reversal suggests itself which distinguishes Burns' response from that of Fergusson, and which he expresses with superb effect in the 'Address to the De'il'. The converse of a Devil-ridden humanity is an extremely human Devil, the 'Auld Hornie' who might, as the poem suggests, find salvation himself if he mends his ways. Having thus confounded the idea that mankind is entirely reprobate, Burns turns upon the doctrine of predestination, in which the self-righteous find assurance. In his 'Address to the Unco Guid or the Rigidly Righteous' he poses the question 'what maks the mighty differ' between themselves and those they presume to be damned? The answer, he suggests, is merely the hypocrisy of the Godly, of which he gives the most memorable testimony in 'Holy Willie's Prayer'.

Willie's assumption of his own salvation and the damnation of his enemies is intimately related to his right to material eminence:

> But L—d, remember me and mine
> Wi' mercies temporal and divine!
> That I for grace and gear may shine,
> Excell'd by nane!

For Burns, the pretension to spiritual preferment which he sees as an aspect of traditional Calvinism, combines with the pretension to material preferment in denying the dignity and rights of ordinary humanity. Crawford suggests that Burns is at his most universal when his is most parochial - and when his opinions find expression in the context of the controversies of rural Ayrshire, such indeed is the result.

Burns excelled as a song writer, altering and expanding old lyrics or providing entirely new lyrics for traditional airs. In the songs Burns looked directly to the folk tradition with its perennial expression of the basic impulses of life conveyed, in the merger of words and music, at a level more immediate than that of the written word alone. It is difficult to speak of the merits of the songs without reference to the music, as the merit is in the totality. However, in song writing, as in verse epistle, comic narrative, and satire - to mention only the most clearly defined genres in which he worked - Burns' achievement is unquestionably of the first rank.

(iii) Burns and the Literary Tradition

The twentieth century has seen a re-assessment of Scottish literary history, that has centred on the re-discovery of the great poets of the pre-Union, pre-Reformation era. This has been entirely beneficial, not only because those writers deserve it, but also in rescuing Burns from his solitary eminence, and from the self-congratulatory world of the Burns cult. For Daiches he becomes 'the last brilliant flare up of a Scottish literary tradition that had been developing for centuries and that in the eighteenth century was in its final, disintegrating phase.' But earlier Muir had indicated a fundamental gulf dividing the consciousness of the medieval poet from that of Burns. There is something in this proposal and it is of importance to the study of Scottish culture as a whole. However, it can be grossly unfair to Burns and other writers on the wrong side of the medieval comparison, who tend to be discussed in terms of what they did not write, with the implication that what they did write is inferior. Much that Burns *did* write, in terms of his own time and his own intentions, is superb. Muir's treatment of Burns centres on 'Tam o' Shanter' which in contrast with the 'whole response to experience' of the 'Makars and the Balladists', he defines as 'a joke followed by an explanation'. This may be so. However, 'Tam o' Shanter' is unique, complex and supremely successful. Even in response to experience there is more internal logic than Muir will allow. Kate's prophecy that Tam will be:

> .... *found deep drown'd in Doon;*
> Or *catch'd wi' warlocks in the mirk,*
> By **Alloway's** *auld haunted kirk.*

echoes the predestined perdition which Calvinist fatalism imposed. As ever, Burns elaborates on this psychological condition to great comic effect. He also purges it, however, for Tam is ultimately neither drowned nor damned, but like the 'bardie' in the 'Address to the De'il' he manages to 'turn a corner jinkin' ',thereby bringing down the whole concept of predestination. Whatever the relative profundity of the world in which he found himself, here as elsewhere Burns' response to that world deserves to be considered on its own merit.

SAQs

1.   How accurate is it to say that Burns writes well in Scots but badly in English?

2.   Consider the merits and failings of 'The Cotter's Saturday Night'. How far is Burns' religious and linguistic heritage involved?

3.   Burns' nearest contemporary among major British poets is William Blake. Does their poetry have anything in common ?

FURTHER READING

T. Crawford (1960) *Burns: A Study of the Poetry and Songs.*

D. Daiches (1964) *The Paradox of Scottish Culture.*

D. Daiches (1966) *Robert Burns.*

D. Daiches (1982) *Literature and Gentility.*

J. MacQueen (1982) *Poetry and Progress.*

ENLIGHTENMENT AND FEELING 1746-1832

OBJECTIVES

This section aims:

✪— to outline the development and the impact, in Britain and internationally, of Scottish literary production between Culloden (1746) and the death of Scott (1832)

✪— to suggest a reading of Scott's *Waverley* in its broad cultural context

✪— to note Byron's Scottishness.

READING

Scott (1814), *Waverley*, edited with an introduction by Andrew Hook, Penguin 1972

Byron (1816), 'The Prisoner of Chillon' and (1823) 'The Island', in any complete *Poetical Works*

Muir, pp 75-109

Watson, Chs 5 and 6

SOME MAJOR THEMES

(i)   From Thomson to Scott

Between Buchanan and James Thomson (1700-1748), Scottish writing had no international reputation and little significance within Great Britain as a whole. The success of Thomson's *Seasons*, first published complete in 1730, was a portent. Since then the *success* of some Scottish writers, in Britain and internationally, and the *success* of publishers in exploiting genuine and spurious elements of Scottishness, Scottish history, Scottish landscape and Scottish heritage, have frequently dominated, sometimes to the point of sheer distortion, the development of literature in Scotland. While

Walter Scott

Conan Doyle wrote without much acknowledgement of his Edinburgh upbringing, Buchan in much of his writing sentimentalised *England*, and Englishness.

The philosophy of David Hume (1711-1776) did not, despite his international reputation, sell like hot cakes. However, he was able to live as a professional man of letters, enjoying great success with his *History of Great Britain* (1754-63). William Robertson (1721-1793), Principal of Edinburgh University, received the amazing sum of £4,500 for his second work of history. Both men wrote the formal, not-quite-idiomatic English which was the jargon of Scotland's Enlightenment - the literati studied style and elocution avidly and eschewed Scotticisms in both. Despite Hume's suspected atheism and Robertson's role as leader of the Moderates in the kirk, the works of these founders of modern historiography did not stir up controversy like *Douglas* and *Ossian*.

In 1756 *Douglas* was performed at the Canongate theatre in Edinburgh: a blank-verse tragedy, neo-classical in type, but based on an old Scots ballad. It was very well received - to the horror of the Presbyteries, which were scandalised by the fact that its author, John Home (1722-1808), was a minister of the Kirk. Home had to resign from his ministry and retreated to London, where he wrote more plays. *Douglas* was widely performed, read and quoted - its reputation as what we would call a 'modern classic' survived well into the nineteenth century.

But the success of 'Ossian' was still more momentous. Between 1760 and 1765 James Macpherson (1736-1769) published 'translations' in poetical prose purported to be from the Gaelic of Ossian, a bard of the third century AD. Their authenticity was soon challenged. Macpherson was a Gaelic-speaker and modern scholarship tends to condone his work as creative adaption of oral tradition. But it can justly be seen as a neo-classical invention, a typical product of 'Enlightenment'. In any case, for at least half a century many readers in Britain, Europe and America found 'Ossian' deeply moving and revered him as a Northern Homer. Through his influence on (amongst many others) Goethe, Blake, Wordsworth, Scott and Byron, Macpherson entered the mainstream of European literature. Highland Gaels had been reviled in the Lowlands and England as thieving barbarians. Macpherson began the process of rehabilitating them and converting them into picturesque 'children of nature'. He bestowed mystery and dignity upon their Gaelic traditions, and also paved the way for innumerable sentimental misconstructions.

'Sentiment' was very much in the air. Whereas Macpherson, unreadable as he seems now, was a genuine innovator, the next Scottish international best-seller, Henry Mackenzie (1745-1831), followed in the wake of recent fashion. His *Man of Feeling* (1771) was in the 'sentimental' mode pioneered by Sterne and Goldsmith. Burns wore out two copies of it and claimed he prized it next to the Bible. Mackenzie unwittingly returned the compliment when he was the first significant critic to hail

Burns, in his short-lived periodical *The Lounger* (1785-7). Despite international fame, he stayed in Edinburgh. Scott knew him and dedicated *Waverley* to him.

Finally, James Boswell (1740-1795) established biography as a best-selling art form with his *Life of Johnson* (1791). His journals, discovered in our own century, also display high literary quality, and his conflict with his father, Lord Auchinleck, intriguingly prefigures the Oedipal motif which haunts Scottish fiction from *Redgauntlet* to *Docherty*.

Scott's extraordinary career as a best-seller thus followed on the success of other Scots in reaching wide and expanding markets. *Pleasures of* Hope (1799) by a twenty-one year-old Glaswegian, Thomas Campbell (1777-1844) was a

Henry Mackenzie

meditative poem which brought its author instant fame - an important work in the general transition of taste to 'Romanticism'. But Campbell was swiftly overhauled by Scott (1771-1832), whose *Lay of the Last Minstrel* (1805) popularised the technical freedoms and lyrical freshness of Wordsworth and Coleridge while drawing on Scott's own profound involvement in Scottish history and folk tradition. It sold 21,300 copies in five years. *Marmion* (1808) and *The Lady of the Lake* (1810) consolidated his vast reputation as a poet. Then, in 1813 Scott was deposed by a twenty-five year-old Aberdeen-bred writer, George Gordon, Lord Byron. From 1813 till his death in 1824 Byron was by far the best-selling living poet - in four different years his sales exceeded the *combined* sales of the half dozen next most popular poets, dead or living.

Scott turned to fiction, with *Waverley*. The 'Waverley Novels' established the basis for 19th century European 'realism' in fiction, constructed a new sense of history for Western man, and helped inspire nationalist cultural movements almost everywhere *except* Scotland. But while admiring Scott's extraordinarily original synthesis of existing discourses, we should not ignore the abundance of tools provided for him by his recent Scottish predecessors. Hume, Robertson and such Enlightened theorists on Man and Society as Adam Smith, Adam Ferguson and John Millar helped him create simultaneously the historical novel and the societal novel. While Smollett,and in a different way, Burns, had provided vigorous examples of Scots speech in literature, Mackenzie's Anglophone hero of 'feeling' can be discerned behind such figures as Edward Waverley, and Boswell's characterisation-in-depth through dialogue may have helped Scott almost as much as the examples of Shakespeare and Fielding. Scott's 'realism' conditioned his handling of Gaelic Highlanders in *Waverley*, yet 'Ossian' is inescapably present - for instance when Flora McIvor sings to Edward.

All this said, the *Waverley* series could not have captivated the world without the existence in Scott's home city, Edinburgh, of a powerful, innovative, publishing industry.

(ii) Publishing and Reviewing

The 'Romantic' revolution in literary taste coincided, around 1800, with the industrialisation of publishing. Four 'great' publishers rose to dominate the world of books, meeting and *shaping* the demands of a large and growing British reading public. Constable and Blackwood in Edinburgh were a match, and often more, for Longman and Murray (an expatriate Scot) in London.

20 guineas had been a good payment for a novel in the late eighteenth century - now Constable and his rivals put up huge sums for narratives in verse and prose. Scott earned £10,000 a year by his fiction. Galt (Craig, p.297) did far less well, but Scott's prestige meant at least that Galt's 'Scotch Novels' became publishable.

Constable put up the money with which a group of brilliant young professional men founded the *Edinburgh Review* (1802). This became essential reading for every British person of the upper and middle classes with any pretensions to intellect and culture. Its print-run of 13,000 in 1814 was then much larger than that of the London *Times*! The *Edinburgh* was Whig in politics; Scott helped found a Tory, London-based rival *The Quarterly* (1809); then in 1817 *Blackwood's* emerged as a new Tory review in Edinburgh. (James Hogg's relationship with that journal is of great importance and interest.) Though their criticisms, often biassed and caustic, of the British Romantic poets are today the best-remembered feature of these journals, they covered all topics of serious interest and represented the vigour, as well as the not-infrequent cruelty, of the ambience of ideological struggle which surrounded Scott as he wrote his fiction.

Scott's death in 1832 decisively marked the end of Edinburgh's 'Golden Age'. But its demise had been portended by the shipwreck of Scottish publishing in the bank crisis of 1825, which had ruined Scott himself, and the retirement from the editorship of the *Edinburgh Review* of Francis Jeffrey in 1829 - the year in which Thomas Carlyle quit Edinburgh for London. Thomson had won success in London almost exactly a century before; the wheel had come full circle, and from 1830 on it would be difficult for a Scottish writer to gain recognition without exiling himself from his native land.

(iii) Waverley

The sneer that Scott 'only wrote fast for money' deserves to be laid to rest; the same can be said of Dostoevsky. The 'Waverley' series of novels can be seen as the last great performance of the Scottish Enlightenment, and the best of them deserve to be taken very seriously as achieved artistic expressions of ideological tensions. *Heart of Midlothian* was long regarded as Scott's masterpiece, but critical favour now tends to fall on *Waverley*, *Old Mortality* and *Redgauntlet*. There is general agreement that these four are at the core of Scott's achievement, together with his other novels of seventeenth and eighteenth-century Scottish history - *Guy Mannering*, *The Antiquary*, *Rob Roy*, *A Legend of Montrose* and *The Bride of Lammermoor*. All these, save *Redgauntlet*, had been published in five astonishing years, by 1819. Thereafter Scott turned with less (artistic) success to English history and to the Scottish and European middle ages. It is unfortunate that the stylised 'tushery' ('Gadzooks!') which mars the weakest parts of these fictions is still assumed by many to characterise Scott's entire output. *Waverley* and *Redgauntlet*, so far from being 'romances', are central to the development of fictional 'realism'. Look, for instance, at the masterly construction of the hamlet of Tully-Veolan in Chapter Eighth of *Waverley* (p 74). Nothing could be further from 'Brigadoon', or the Kailyard.

Yet strong feeling for Scotland and for its defeated Gaels informs the whole novel. In Scott's best fiction the unresolved tension between 'reason' and 'Enlightened' faith in progress on the one hand, and 'feeling' - above all 'feeling' for lost Scottish causes - on the other, is a constant source of interest and strength. He was 'romantic', in one sense of the word, in his attachment to Scottish traditions, yet can plausibly be accused of excessive pragmatism and undue distrust of imagination and feeling. This was a tension long present in Edinburgh literary culture. As Phillipson has written:

> 'Neither Hume nor Smith were fatalists. Nevertheless there is a fatalistic streak running through their concept of the Science of Man... Perhaps it was better for Scotsmen to resign themselves to the inevitability of change and a closer union with England and salve their patriotic consciences by remembering the glories of a bygone age. That, at least, seemed to be the teaching of Ossian ... the spokesman for a new, sentimental style of stoicism, which taught men to resign themselves to the inexorable forces of history'.

As Phillipson goes on to point out,

> 'Scott's heroes and heroines belong to the world of Hume's Science of Man. They are benevolent, sociable and honourable in their way, motivated by a desire to live at ease with themselves and society at large, yet often perplexed by the rival claims of the past, present and future'.

Waverley's very name suggests his uncertainty. The novel makes us nostalgic for the old Gaelic society, yet projects its passing as inevitable.

(iv) A Note on Byron

Byron (1788-1824) lived with his Scottish mother in Aberdeen till he was ten. In the 1930s the two most influential critics of the day pointed to the Scottishness of his poetry. Leavis proclaimed his affinity with Burns; Eliot noted the influence of Calvinism on his writing and claimed that he wrote English like an intelligent foreigner.

Whatever the merits of these particular views, Byron's verse, to be fully understood, has to be read in the context of Scottish cultural history. His favourite writer among his contemporaries, both in prose and verse, was Scott, but more basic than any direct influence from Scott or Burns was the 'secular Calvinism' of his cast of mind. Doubting God's existence, he nevertheless retained a predestinarian fatalism, a consciousness of the individual soul's aloneness, in a material universe which had replaced God as the aloof presence dominating human destiny. These emerge strongly in his powerful narrative, 'The Prisoner of Chillon'. His most important acknowledgement of his Scottishness is found in 'The Island', his last narrative, loosely based on the story of the mutiny on the Bounty. A young Scottish sailor is the only mutineer to escape death at the hands of pursuing justice. Byron associates his own love of Scotland with his sympathy for the cause of Greek freedom: both are related to the idea of 'paradise regained' in the lives of 'children of nature'. If Byron sentimentalised the Highlands, his use of them here was refreshingly far from 'Ossianic' or Scott-like fatalism.

SAQs

1.   Would it be fair to say that Scott's use of standard English, in narrative and in the speech of his hero and other respectable characters, serves to demote and to make seem quaint the language given to Scots speakers?

2.   Does Scott's novel really support his affirmation in his first chapter that human passions have been the same throughout history?

3.   Consider Byron's 'Prisoner of Chillon' alongside MacDiarmid's 'On a Raised Beach', comparing 'Secular Calvinism' in the two poems.

FURTHER READING

(a)   Context

J.H. Alexander (ed.) (1992) *The Tavern Sages. Selections from the 'Noctes Ambrosianae'.*

D. Craig (1961) *Scottish Literature and the Scottish People.*

A. Chitnis (1976) *The Scottish Enlightenment.*

J. Clive (1957) *Scotch Reviewers: The Edinburgh Review 1802-1815.*

H. Mackenzie (1967) *The Man of Feeling*, ed. B Vickers.

J. MacQueen (1982) *Poetry and Progress*.

J. MacPherson (1971) *Poems of Ossian*, introduced by J. MacQueen.

N.T. Phillipson and R. Mitchison, eds. (1970) *Scotland in the Age of Improvement*.

(b)   Scott

D.D. Devlin, ed.(1969) *Modern Judgements: Walter Scott*.

W. Scott (1817) *Old Mortality*, ed. A Calder, 1975.

W. Scott (1972) *Selected Poems*, ed. T Crawford.

(c)   Byron

A. Bold, ed.(1983) *Byron: Wrath and Rhyme*.

Byron (1980) *Complete Poetical Works*, ed. J.J. McGann.

A. Calder ed.(1989) *Byron and Scotland*.

A. Calder (1987), *Byron*.

T.S. Eliot (1957) On *Poetry and Poets*.

F.R. Leavis (1936) *Revaluation*.

SCOTT, GALT AND CARLYLE

OBJECTIVES

Having placed Scott in the context of the Enlightenment with Section 6, your aims here are:

❈— to look at *Redgauntlet* as a historical novel and as one of Scott's finest achievements

❈— to compare his work, especially his treatment of historical change, with that of John Galt, through a study of *The Provost*

❈— to note similar concerns in the work of Carlyle

READING

Scott (1824), *Redgauntlet*, preface and glossary by W M Parker, Everyman, 1958

Galt (1822), *The Provost*, ed with an introduction by I A Gordon, Oxford University Press, 1973

Carlyle (1971), *Selected Writings*, ed A Shelston, Penguin

Watson, Ch 6

SOME MAJOR THEMES

(i)   Redgauntlet

Redgauntlet can be seen as one of Scott's greatest works; not only by virtue of its plot - one of the best-constructed of the Waverley series - but also in terms of its exploration of the sense and implications of historical change. And by the device of double heroes, Darsie Latimer and Alan Fairford, Scott moves beyond the need for a passive hero as in *Waverley* to a clearer expression of his own conflicts and ambivalent attitude to the romance and violence of Scotland's past.

Certain features are immediately striking about *Redgauntlet* when compared with other important Scott novels. Firstly, very little of actual historical significance takes place: the novel is full of nonevents and anti-climaxes. Secondly, its main event, the return of the Pretender, is totally fictional. Such fictionality appears to allow Scott greater freedom to consider the power of the past over both his own and Scotland's present, to choose his own criteria for depicting historical change, and to embody this through elements of symbolism - an increasingly noticeable feature of his later work.

Nevertheless, the issues he confronts are familiar from his other novels. If you know *Rob Roy* and *Waverley* you will be able to view his explorations of Jacobitism in rather different contexts but all three novels attempt to discuss the imaginative threat it poses to the Enlightenment's

Gala day at Abbotsford by Sir William Allan.
Scottish National Portrait Gallery

philosophy of Reason. *Redgauntlet*, although based on a fictional incident, faces up to the challenge in a more direct way, since events are much closer to Scott's own time and experience. Although Redgauntlet is shown to be outmoded, a figure of the past (see his meeting with the Fairfords in Edinburgh for proof of this), Scott's characterisation gives him a potential magnificence. Unlike Fergus Mac-Ivor in *Waverley*, who is shown in full glory and then loses some of our sympathy, Redgauntlet is shown in glimpses from various perspectives and only by the end of the novel can he assume his full identity, with a tragic stature which makes him, according to Muir, Scott's 'one character of a more than purely practical heroism'. Yet it is important to notice that such heroism is finally realised in a situation which renders it impotent - the last moving scenes of the Pretender's departure. And despite his importance, events in the novel refute the concept of history which Redgauntlet represents - for his deterministic views on fate and destiny look at p.235. In contradiction to his view, history in the novel is revealed as a process of change and development, brought about through influences and decisions. Many of the characters and incidents illustrate this - the contrast of Alan Fairford's values with those of his father, the fact that neither Lilias nor Darsie are Catholics, the decision of King George to leave Charles to escape. And you may also notice a host of smaller details such as the Fairfords' move to a new town house, the new methods of fishing brought in by Joshua Geddes to upset the traditional rural ways, and those characters who are trying to maintain the status quo and forget the past - not just types like Provost Crosbie who weigh the effects of the past in financial terms but also men such as the young Jacobite nobleman advocating 'caution to ourselves and to our families'.

Such an approach favours Enlightenment attitudes and allows Scott to represent the conflicting mood of his times - to give, as the Hungarian critic Lukacs put it, 'living embodiment to historical-social types'. Of course, the novel is also a clear embodiment of dichotomies of which Scott was aware in his own person. Darsie and Alan appear initially to embody this disjunction between the attraction to romance and the use of reason, but in terms of the novel's narrative structure Darsie is portrayed as increasingly disillusioned with the dangers of romance. Though retaining the Redgauntlet horseshoe mark on his brow, he signals the family's assimilation into civil society, so he can be viewed merely as Scott's acknowledgement of the appeal which romance has for the imagination. However, in terms of the writing in the novel, of actual emotional engagement, Redgauntlet emerges not only as the strongest character but also as a representative of the very real threat of violence, of an alternative which cannot be denied although it may be ignored.

Such a threat is reinforced by the actual power that the past may have over the present, as the use of ballads in the novel illustrates. 'Wandering Willie's Tale' and the songs of the blind fiddler indicate the influence of memory. It is Darsie's knowledge of the code of the Ballads - his retention of a particular, aesthetic form of Scottishness - which enables him to escape his imprisonment with Wandering Willie's help, and to go on into the new, Anglicised future. Ballads also point to an awareness of ideas and experiences which cannot be rationalised, through use of the supernatural as subversion of the status quo. Yet the novel contextualises such threats by emphasising its own fictionality in the conclusion of Dr Dryasdust. Such framing is a common device in Scott's novels and serves spuriously to authenticate a tale while simultaneously distancing it from the author's self.

Finally, Scott's use of language is worth considering - especially in a comparison with Galt. Scots is used to point to the past; it belongs to the traditions of Wandering Willie and his wife, and to the older representatives of both sides in the conflict, about to be superseded by the young. You might consider the speech of Saunders Fairford, Peter Peebles and Maxwell Pate-in-Peril in this context, comparing it with the anglified language of Darsie and Alan. The conflicts of past and present, order and barbarism are everywhere in the novel - even the Solway area serves much the same function as the Highlands in *Waverley*. And although the intruder from the past, Father Bonaventure, returns to exile at the end, it is worth thinking about whether this resolution accommodates the issues brought to the surface through the force of the novel's images.

(ii) Galt: The Provost

Although most critics now recognise Scott as a serious novelist expressing a particular view of historical processes in his interpretation of contemporary Scotland, for most of the nineteenth century he was popularly regarded as a producer of exciting, romantic adventure stories: Muir's discernment of 'a very curious emptiness' behind the imaginative richness of his novels is, in part, a reflection of this view.

Turning from Scott to Galt, it becomes immediately apparent that the latter could not have suffered from the same kind of misinterpretation.

In his *Autobiography* (1833), John Galt said of his writings:

They would be more properly characterised, in several instances, as theoretical histories, than either novels or romances. A consistent fable is as essential to a novel as a plot is to a drama, and yet those, which are deemed my best productions, are deficient in this essential ingredient... I do not think that I have had numerous precursors in what I would call my theoretical histories of society, limited, though they were required by the subject, necessarily to the events of a circumscribed locality.(pp.219-220)

John Galt by Alfred, Count d'Orsay.
Scottish National Portrait Gallery

A major element of Enlightenment thought was its reaction against Thomas Hobbes' theories of self-interest. He had argued (for example, in his *Leviathan* (1651)) that man acted always and only for selfish reasons, and, consequently, that public good was merely accidental. By contrast, Enlightenment philosophers in general held that self-interest and social amelioration did not occasionally coincide but were indissolubly linked, so that the history of mankind was one of human action consistently resulting in the improvement of both personal and social conditions. Since evidence from all periods of civilization was recognised not to be extant, the term 'theoretical history' was coined to describe works (such as Adam Fergusson's *Essay on the History of Civil Society* (1767)) which argued in these terms.

In claiming that his books should also be classified as 'theoretical histories', Galt is drawing attention to the role which he would wish *Annals of the Parish* (1821) and *The Provost* (1822) to be seen to be attempting. As a young man in Irvine and Greenock in 1797, he had been a founder of a literary and debating society through which he had developed a keen interest in the thought of his day that was not displaced by his commercial and legal adventures in London (from 1804), his more dramatic activities as a commissioner of the Canada Company (which included founding of the town of Guelph, Ontario, in 1827), nor even his imprisonment for debt in 1829.

Both of these books trace the development of a small Scottish community between 1760 and 1810, the *Annals* describing events from the perspective of the minister, the Reverend Mr Balwhidder, who points out that this is precisely the period of the personal reign of George III. Its secular companion, *The Provost*, is an investigation of the intermingling of personal and private interest as motives in achieving the improvements in the life of Gudetown, as seen by shop-keeper and three-times leading civic dignitary, James Pawkie. You may wish to look particularly at the variety of ways in which Pawkie derives personal benefit from instigating and/ or managing such public affairs as the enclosure of public land, the repairs to the kirk, the alterations to the local markets, the provision of new housing, the raising of a local militia and the renovation of the school.

But be careful to notice the changes which occur in Pawkie's attitude as the narrative proceeds. Writing from the end of his involvement in public life, he is concerned to show the developments in public morality which have occurred in the transition from eighteenth to nineteenth century and from a rural, agricultural community towards a more urban, incipiently industrial society. He repeatedly emphasises that getting personal advantage from public position is a natural motive; yet he is also aware that Mr M'Lucre's activities would no longer be acceptable, and regards the point as of sufficient importance for him to devote the whole of Chapter XXIII to a dissertation on the subject:

... it seemed to be the use and wont of men in public trusts, to think they were free to indemnify themselves in a left-handed way, for the time and trouble they bestowed in the same. But the thing was not so far wrong in principle, as in the hugger-muggering way in which it was done, and which gave to it a guilty colour, that by the judicious stratagem of a right system it would never have had. ... I have endeavoured, in a manner, to be governed by the spirit of the times in which the transactions happened, for I have lived long enough to remark, that if we judge of past events by present motives, and do not try to enter into the spirit of the age in which they took place, and to see them with eyes with which they were really seen, we shall conceit many things to be of a bad and wicked character, that were not thought so harshly of by those who witnessed them, nor even by those who, perhaps, suffered from them; while, therefore, I think it has been of great advantage to the public to have survived that method of administration in which the like of Baillie M'Lucre was engendered, I would not have it understood that I think the men who held the public trusts in those days a whit less honest than the men of my own time.

There is, of course, a certain element of irony in Pawkie's plea for historical relativism. In apparently seeking our understanding for M'Lucre's morality, he is also asking that his own estimation of himself as an honest man be upheld by a later audience whose standards would have advanced to the point where Pawkie would seem intolerably corrupt. Galt had to use a personal narrator to draw the reader into sufficient sympathy to achieve an understanding of the processes which he wanted to illustrate, not as abstract notions but as explanations of the life of very ordinary - and often quite unattractive - people.

Galt does not always use personal narrators in this way: *Annals of the Parish* may be the record of Mr Balwhidder, but *The Entail* (often held to be his most impressive novel) employs a more common strategy of impersonal narration. Yet Galt deserves credit for at least being willing to experiment with different techniques. Although the inconsistencies of Mr Pawkie's narrative - for instance, in the dating of his periods of office - suggest nothing more sinister than the decline of memory of facts and figures with age (and perhaps less business acumen than Pawkie would claim), nevertheless Galt perhaps stands closer to Hogg than to Scott in his open attitude to what fiction might attempt.

Scott's novels undoubtedly won great regard for the use of Scots; yet Muir argues that it was the kind of regard paid to a restricted dialect and so reflected the doomed situation of the language. Coming from the west of Scotland, Galt not only uses a much more consistent and thorough-going form of Scots, one which seems far more confident in its maintenance of non-English forms and vocabulary, but employs it at many registers and across the entire spectrum of social class. From local Lairds and Westminster MPs, lawyers, doctors, ministers and provosts, to vagrants, petty criminals and 'natural' idiots, his characters not only talk and write in Scots but do so in a highly effective way. This might be seen as idealisation by a Scots language fanatic: yet the fact that Pawkie's narrative uses English quite happily when it suits the particular circumstances suggests not only a disparity between Edinburgh and the rest of the country, but also a certain amount of linguistic naturalism in Galt's work.

Although Galt's novels were safe from being seen as rollicking adventures and nothing more, this did not secure them from attacks on other, equally ill-founded premises. Galt commented that his 'histories' were 'limited... necessarily to the events of a circumscribed locality' (*Autobiography*, p 220). His work can be described in ways which led him for many years to be seen as a prototype of the later Kailyard school of fiction (see Section 10). For example, he wrote as an exiled Scot about small Scottish communities set in the past. But modern criticism has rediscovered the vast difference in attitude between his writing and that of Barrie, Crockett and the like. At the simplest level, they wrote sentimental stories in which change was decried as anathema, the only agent to threaten the cosy consensus of places such as Thrums; while Galt's writings are intellectual investigations precisely of the nature of change, a process that was to him so exciting and invigorating that he devoted entire novels to exposing its political operations.

Thomas Carlyle by Helen Allingham. Scottish National Portrait Gallery.

(iii) A Note on Carlyle

Critics of English literature have often written of Carlyle as the first in a tradition of Victorian 'sages': men of letters whose criticism of the society in which they lived helped create and shape the selfconsciousness of the English and Scottish bourgeoisie in the nineteenth century. But Carlyle's fascination with the society in which he lived, with the rules by which it could be discerned to be developing, and with the degree to which the individual may determine his own actions and affect the alteration of the process of change, can all be seen as developments of the Enlightenment attitude towards society, as exemplified particularly in the idea of 'theoretical history'. Carlyle's major histories (especially the *French Revolution*, 1837) may deal with more dramatic events than those of Gudetown. His 'heroes' (itself a concept owing much to his own study, *On Heroes and Hero Worship, and the Heroic in History*, 1841) may be figures, like Frederick the Great (1858-65),who are considerably grander than Provost Pawkie. But the themes of Carlyle and Galt are identical, and the form of the seminal *Sartor Resartus* (1830-1), with its multiple narration and intrusively interpretative narrator, may owe more to Scott's Dryasdust and Hogg's 'Editor' than to any abstract impulse to experimentation.

Finally, note should be taken of a growing consciousness of the work of Susan Ferrier. A great friend of Walter Scott, her work centres on the gently satirical observation of contemporary social mores. See what you think of *Marriage*, 1818, *The Inheritance*, 1824, and *Destiny*, 1831.

SAQs

1.   In what ways does Muir's omission of Galt from *Scott and Scotland* affect his case for the Reformation's achieving the dissociation of Scottish sensibility?

2.   Compare the treatment of family life in any Scott novel with that in *The Provost* and *The Entail*, and with that in *Auld Licht Idylls*.

3. Discuss the functions of 'Wandering Willie's Tale' in the context of *Redgauntlet*.

4.   In what ways do Scott and Galt differ in their use of detail to indicate social change?

5.   Consider the suggestion that Carlyle's style is 'un-English' - or at least was so when he first wrote.

FURTHER READING

(a)   Biography

D. Daiches (1971) *Sir Walter Scott and His World*.

E. Johnson (1970) *Sir Walter Scott the Great Unknown*.

J.G. Lockhart (1848) *Life of Sir Walter Scott*.

D. Mack, ed. (1972) *Hogg's Memoirs of the Author's Life and Familiar Anecdotes of Sir Walter Scott* (1834).

(b)   Criticism

D. Brown (1979) *Walter Scott and the Historical Imagination*.

T. Crawford (1982) *Walter Scott*.

F.R. Hart (1966) *Scott's Novels: The Plotting of Historic Survival*.

R. Mayhead (1968) *Walter Scott*.

G. McMaster (1981) *Scott and Society*.

A. Welsh (1963) *The Hero of the Waverley Novels*.

Galt

I.A. Gordon (1972) *John Galt*.

C.A. Whatley ed. (1979) *John Galt, 1779-1839*.

Carlyle

I. Campbell (1974), *Thomas Carlyle*

J. Holloway (1953), *The Victorian Sage*

A. LaValley (1968), *Carlyle and the Idea of the Modern*

Ferrier

W.M. Parker (1965) *Susan Ferrier*.

JAMES HOGG

OBJECTIVES

Your main objectives in this section should be:

✽— to place Hogg against the background of his time

✽— to compare the narrative techniques used in his various fictions

✽— to concentrate in some detail on *The Private Memoirs and Confessions of a Justified Sinner*

READING

Hogg (1824), *The Private Memoirs and Confessions of a Justified Sinner*, ed J Carey, Oxford University Press, 1969

Watson, Ch 6

Wittig, Ch VIII(2)

James Hogg

SOME MAJOR THEMES

(i)   Background

Hogg was influenced both by his contemporaries (see section 6) and by traditional forms of literature.

(a)   'The Ettrick Shepherd'

Born in a remote district of the Borders in 1770, James Hogg spent his early life working as a shepherd. Writing verse from his twenties, he began to move in the literary circles of the time when, using his wide knowledge of local tradition and folk-tale, he helped Walter Scott with the latter's collection of Border Ballads. The cultural centre of the day was, of course, Edinburgh, and Hogg soon moved there to set up his own literary journal; yet one can see from the writings of resident 'literati' that he was never fully accepted by this group. His style was more robust than the mode of writing currently fashionable, and his frequent use of country ballads and tales of the supernatural was misinterpreted as literary naivety by the sophisticates of Edinburgh. However, Hogg himself did much to enhance the impression that he was a rustic - on a much-acclaimed visit to London he insisted on wearing shepherd's garb of plaid and bonnet - and seems to have found a certain security in playing the innocent or clown. This personal trait has a parallel in his work; he frequently attempts to conceal his own controlling presence, to efface the element of artifice by hiding his own literary awareness behind a tone of simplistic bewilderment.

(b) The Folk Tradition

Hogg achieved fame almost overnight with the publication of *The Queen's Wake*, a book of verse, in 1813. Although much of the subject matter of these poems will seem slight to us today, the most interesting adopt, or at least imitate, the language of the medieval Makars. 'Kilmeny' and 'The Witch of Fife' provide very different examples of this, one lyrical, the other humorous. The latter also shows the strong influence of traditional balladry in both its stanza form and its phrasing:

> *Ye lee, ye lee, ye ill womyne,*
> *Se loud as I heir ye lee,*
> *For the warst-faured wyfe on the shores of Fyfe,*
> *Is cumlye comparet with thee.*

This reprimand, from a witch to her husband, also indicates that Hogg, like Fergusson and Burns, delighted in the verve and grim humour of traditional Scots comic verse. A love of the traditional, combined with a Border upbringing, accounts for another major feature of Hogg's work: his interest in diablerie and the supernatural. Compare him with Scott in this respect, and note how far removed Hogg is from the 'reason' of the Enlightenment, a distance which often allows his work greater scope. Scott is clearly attracted to the supernatural but always constrains his interest within the contexts of society and of his plot. 'Wandering Willie's Tale' remains only an echo of the themes of *Redgauntlet*. But in Hogg's *Basil Lee*, a short picaresque novel of 1820, fantastic events play an essential part in the plot, in order to mock the conventions of 'normal' society. In *The Brownie of Bodsbeck*, a tale of the Covenanters, Hogg uses the supernatural to reveal the absurdity of demanding earthly allegiance to one sect or another, when the real concern of the majority of ordinary people lies with the unknown, with the far greater polarities of life and death. Use of fantasy in this way subverts the authority of dominant power structures - you may like to compare Hogg's treatment of the conflict between Covenanters and Royalists with that of Scott in *Old Mortality*.

(ii) Narrative

Much of Hogg's fiction may seem alien to us, partly because of his radical mixing of genres and traditions. Yet we should not suppose that the various elements were simply thrown together through the literary ignorance of a rustic genius; even today the shifts in tone and interplay of forms carry significance for the reader. In

The Three Perils of Man, he takes as a subject the siege of Rochester Castle, adopts the style of High Romance, and through this parodies the self-indulgence of aristocrats, placing it in direct contrast with the vigorous local dialect of those who actually fight the battles. As in most of Hogg's work, such speech forms are used to indicate common-sense and sincerity, thus providing a standard for moral judgement. Into his epic form Hogg also weaves a tale of magic and the supernatural, used to imply a wider moral and spiritual dimension and revealing the arbitrary nature of man's earthly combats - although the significance of this device is concealed by the highly conventional 'story-telling' format. One further feature worth noting in this work is Hogg's habit of disclaiming all responsibility for his fiction. The traditional form creates an impression of autonomy, reinforced by the author continually pointing out that the story was told to him by 'Simon the Curate'. Asserting the tale's fictionality in this way, he emphasises his role as being one of selection alone, so it is left to the reader to search for further implications in the narrative. *The Three Perils of Man* is over-long and, at times, clumsy but it is worth a quick glance, as its technique can be seen repeated to greater effect, and in more refined form in Hogg's best known work, *The Confessions of a Justified Sinner*.

(iii) The Private Memoirs and Confessions of a Justified Sinner

Although receiving little recognition until acclaimed by André Gide in 1947, this novel is now considered a classic expression of the Scottish religious psyche and of fanaticism in general. Published in 1824, the novel experiments with narrative through its division into three parts. After an Editor's narrative which relates the story of a young fanatic who murders his brother and mother, committing all kinds of evil in the name of God, secure in the belief that he is justified by Faith alone, the novel then moves to the Confession itself. An account of events from the Sinner's point of view is given, sanctimoniously explaining the good reasons behind his actions, all undertaken on the advice of a mysterious 'Friend' who subsequently appears to gain possession of his soul. The third section contains a strange concluding note from the 'Editor' - an attempt to analyse and document the 'truth' of events, which fails miserably. The novel's main purpose is clear - the manipulation of ideas of supernatural forces and demonic possession in order to push to an extreme the concept of justification by faith alone, thereby revealing its absurdity. But note too that diablerie is used in such a way as to occlude the real nature of events; no single truth can be found. As readers we are left in a position of even greater uncertainty than the final Editor's. So the tale achieves significance on several levels. As Gide commented, 'The personification of the Demon in Hogg's book is among the most ingenious ever invented, for the power that sets him in action is always of a psychological nature; in other words, always admissible, even by unbelievers'.

In building up conflicting interpretations of the story, Hogg's exploitation of narrative forms is therefore of the utmost importance. The first Editor's narrative is reasoned, tolerant and at second hand, making no attempt to explain the tale's obvious mysteries. In contrast, the following Confession revolves around the tension created between the narrator's complacency about his position of grace, and the subtle clues given to the stranger's identity which, combined with the apocalyptic imagery of the last few pages, suggest the torment awaiting the Sinner. Although this section carries the plot further forward, its details do not always coincide with the Editor's. Another strand of narrative set within the Sinner's tale clarifies the novel's basic premise; the tale of 'the deil at Auchtermuchty' reveals that evil can assume the guise of religion. With the Sinner submitting to external as well as internal pressures of evil, the Confession ends on a note of emotional climax. So you may be surprised by the cooling effect of the following conclusion, again setting the reader at a distance. But this section adds an important dimension to the novel by drawing our attention to the Editor's refusal to recognise the extremes leading to such events, and to his futile application of reason. Hogg even mocks his (and our) predicament by introducing himself as a character - the shepherd who refuses to help the 'literati' elucidate the truth; 'I hae mair ado than I can manage the day, far by ganging to hack up hunder-year auld bones'. And although both bones and manuscript are discovered, they shed no light on the situation. We are left only with the Editor's feeble explanation of the Sinner; 'in short, we must either conceive him not only the greatest fool, but the greatest wretch on whom was stamped the form of humanity; or that he was a religious maniac, who wrote and wrote about a deluded creature, till he arrived at that height of madness that he believed himself the very object whom he had all along been describing'. We could all continue to offer explanations in this vein as to the contents of the novel. But the form of the whole is more significant. The framing narrative shows that the novel is not only an account of religious fanaticism but also a study of man's attempts to rationalise aspects of the psyche which cannot satisfactorily be accommodated within his consciousness: one may choose to use Religion as the Sinner does, or to follow the Editor's use of Reason. The novel therefore explores far wider issues than the perversions caused by Calvinist indoctrination. Although Hogg must receive credit for his development of traditional Scots ballads and his preservation of Scots dialect, he must also be acknowledged to be a sophisticated manipulator of the forms of fiction, exploring far beyond parochial contexts.

Rosslyn Chapel and Castle, Midlothian. From an engraving by a contemporay of Hogg.

SAQs

1.   To what extent can we see Hogg as typical of his age? (A comparison with Scott and Galt may be useful.)

2.   Discuss Hogg's use of language in light of the various influences on his writing.

3.   Assess the advantages of Hogg's methods in his presentation of the Devil. (Comparison might be made with Lockhart's *Adam Blair*, with 'Thrawn Janet' and with 'The Tale of Tod Lapraik' (in *Catriona*), both by Stevenson.)

FURTHER READING

(a)   Works by Hogg

D. Gifford ed. (1972) *The Three Perils of Man*.

D. Mack ed. (1970) *James Hogg Selected Poems*.

D. Mack ed. (1972) *Memoirs of the Author's Life and Familiar Anecdotes of Sir Walter Scott*.

D. Mack, ed. (1976) *The Brownie of Bodsbeck*.

(b)   Criticism and Biography

A. Gide (1947) Introduction to Cresset Press edition of *The Private Memoirs and Confessions of a Justified Sinner*.

D. Gifford (1976) *James Hogg*.

D. Groves (1988) *James Hogg: The Growth of a Writer*.

N. Parr (1980) *James Hogg at Home*.

L. Simpson (1962) *James Hogg. A Critical Study*.

ROBERT LOUIS STEVENSON

OBJECTIVES

In this section your objectives will be:

- ✪— to examine Stevenson's approach to fiction
- ✪— to think about the ways in which he uses various fictional techniques to convey the major themes in his novels through surveying his novels, but concentrating on *The Master of Ballantrae*.

READING

Try to read at least *The Master of Ballantrae* (published with *Weir of Hermiston*) Everyman paperback 1978, and if possible *Dr Jekyll and Mr Hyde, The Merry Men and other tales*, Everyman paperback 1980. Watson, Ch 6

SOME MAJOR THEMES

Robert Louis Stevenson (1850-1894) was the most widely read and important Scottish writer, in verse as well as in prose, of the late-Victorian era. Reacting against Edinburgh, his home city, living in exile, he nevertheless carried forward traditional and recent preoccupations

Robert Louis Stevenson.
Scottish National Portrait Gallery

in Scottish writing from Scott and Hogg to Doyle and Buchan - and also to other 20th century Scottish fiction.

(i) Stevenson's approach to fiction

'Life is monstrous, infinite, illogical, abrupt and poignant; a work of art, in contrast, is neat, finite, self-contained, rational, flowing and emasculate,' Stevenson wrote in 'A Humble Remonstrance', his famous reply to Henry James on the nature of the novel. This remark draws attention to Stevenson's emphasis on stylistic competence, but it also focuses on a more fundamental aspect of all his work - his awareness of fiction's artifice and his determination to exploit divergences between literary resolutions and realist solutions to life. The problems he sought to resolve were primarily of a moral nature, exploring the distance between real and ideal. 'To every view of morals,' he stated, 'there are two sides: what is demanded by the man; what is exacted by the conditions of life'. ('On Lay Morals'). His fictions are permeated by a consciousness of the limitations of his medium which forces him to seek liberation through experiment with genres and through manipulations of the interplay between text and reader.

(ii) Stevenson's fictional techniques

(a)   Experiments with form

A quick glance over the range of Stevenson's work will show his interest in different genres. His affinity for the Romance form is immediately noticeable but within this area he experiments. *Treasure Island*, a boy's adventure story, incorporates archetypal images of the quest, of flight and of conflicts between good and evil, epitomised by the opposing surrogate father-figures of Doctor Livesey and Long John Silver. Despite the simplicity of the plot, the tale is centred around the very ambiguous character of Silver, whose force of personality compels us to assess our own moral sympathies. Similarly, in *Kidnapped* images reverberate beyond their mere plot significance - the blind beggar, the spiral stair leading nowhere, even the friendship of David Balfour and Alan Breck - and are used to explore basic moral dichotomies as well as Stevenson's own complex relationship to his Scottish past. Stevenson's belief in the 'quality of the brute incident' is an important factor in his story-telling, put to its most sophisticated use in the adventures of *The Master of Ballantrae*. Again he deals with conflict between opposing figures - the Master and his brother Henry - to test the validity of conventional moral judgements. He expands this into an assessment of Scottish identity. Taking as its excuse the Jacobite cause, the contention between the aristocratic brothers can only be resolved in a primitive a historical setting: the wastes of America. Reduced in humanity, wearing animal skins, their mutual destruction ensures that only MacKellar, their middle-class, middle-of-the-road retainer returns to Scotland, assuming control over the decaying aristocracy of the house of Durrisdeer.

Stevenson also experimented with the currently fashionable mode of Gothic romance, especially in the short stories, which show his craftsmanship at its best. *Dr Jekyll and Mr Hyde* (although its significance has been oversimplified to the point of extinction by countless retellings on stage and screen), *Markheim* and *The Merry*

Men all investigate the nature of moral motivation and identity, of concepts of duality, in addition to their skilful exploitation of conventional adventure motifs of murder, mystery and buried treasure. Stevenson defended lack of subtlety in incidents of plot by arguing, 'It is only by some bold poetry of thought that man can be strung up above the level of everyday conceptions to take a broader look upon experience or accept some higher principle of conduct'. ('On Lay Morals'). His finest example of this theory in practice may be *The Ebb-Tide*, co-written with Lloyd Osbourne, which uses an exotic, almost fantastical setting to assess the reality of man's reactions when confronted by moral absolutes.

(b)   Narrative

Treasure Island and *Kidnapped* adopt the convention of a naive, inexperienced but trustworthy narrator, thus focusing attention on the significance of the events themselves. In contrast, *Dr Jekyll and Mr Hyde* and *The Master of Ballantrae* both make radical experiments with narrative form. *Jekyll and Hyde's* framework of narration by Utterson contains at least three more narratives by apparently similar characters - Enfield, Lanyon and Jekyll himself - all attempting in different ways to justify their actions and their chosen vices, thus providing a realistic amplification of the central fantasy's horror. The continual reappraisal of our own judgements which such an approach creates in us as readers is also very much a feature of *The Master of Ballantrae*. There we are forced into an uneasy reliance on MacKellar's biased narration, and into suspecting the soundness of his moral judgement. And in *The Ebb-Tide* Stevenson openly exploits authorial shifts of sympathy, with each character in turn becoming the repository of invested values - an approach which has more in common with today's post-modernist fiction than with the realism of his contemporaries.

(c)   Use of Scots

A third type of experiment which Stevenson made in his fiction draws deeply on the Scottish folk tradition. *Thrawn Janet* and 'The Tale of Tod Lapraik' (in *Catriona*) combine narrative in Scots with a reliance on folk-tales of the supernatural. Stevenson's delight in the vigour of the language and in the vivid incidents of the ballad tradition can also be seen as a major influence on his last, unfinished, novel, *Weir of Hermiston*. Once again the focus is on divergence - in this case between the power of rural legend and tradition, and the severity and strength of Enlightenment Edinburgh. Lord Hermiston and Kirstie represent polarities for the passive hero, Archie, and both have now been assimilated into our culture as archetypes of the Scottish imagination. (Both Kirstie and Weir speak in Scots, placing them very much in Scotland's past as opposed to Archie's present - in *The Master of Ballantrae*, James resorts to speaking in Scots when he wishes to remind his family of childhood affection, again in the past). Although the language of *Weir of Hermiston* is an indisputable achievement there has been much debate over the novel's general value and its significance for Scottish literature. Since the novel is unfinished, it is up to each reader to decide whether it signals the descent into the Kailyard or whether it could have provided Stevenson with an opportunity of changing the course of the Scottish novel. Certainly, subsequent writers were eager to borrow from Stevenson's subject matter but few appear to have been much influenced by his deeper assumptions about the nature of the fictional medium.

SAQs

1.   In what ways can Stevenson be seen as transposing specifically Scottish concerns to other contexts in his fiction?

2.   Why do you think Stevenson appears to have reserved narrative in Scots for treatment of supernatural material? Does the language gain or lose by this?

3.   How does the relationship between the two brothers in *The Master of Ballantrae* reflect Stevenson's interest in duality? You might like to consider also *Kidnapped* and *Jekyll and Hyde*.

4.   Stevenson once wrote, 'Man's one method, whether he reasons or creates, is to half-shut his eyes against the dazzle and confusion of reality' ('A Humble Remonstrance'). Is his obvious fascination with style an advantage or disadvantage in his treatment of reality?

FURTHER READING

(a)   Works by Stevenson

R.L. Stevenson, Introduction by R. Sale (1981), *Treasure Island* and *Kidnapped*.

R.L. Stevenson and L. Osbourne (1894), *The Ebb-Tide*.

(b)   Biography

M. Black (1994) *Robert Louis Stevenson*

J. Calder (1980) *Robert Louis Stevenson: A Life Story*.

J.C. Furnas (1952) *Voyage to Windward*.

F. McLynn (1993) *Robert Louis Stevenson: A Biography*

J.A. Smith, ed. (1948) *Henry James and Robert Louis Stevenson*.

(c)   Criticism

J. Calder, ed. (1981) *Stevenson and Victorian Scotland*.

D. Daiches (1947) *Robert Louis Stevenson*.

E. Eigner (1966) *Robert Louis Stevenson and the Romantic Tradition*.

F.R. Hart (1978) *The Scottish Novel*, Ch 9.

THE KAILYARDS AND REACTIONS

OBJECTIVES

Through looking at novels produced in the late 19th and early 20th century, your objectives in this section are:

✿— to discuss the nature and origins of 'Kailyard' literature

✿— to trace the development of a reaction against its conventions

READING

MacLaren (1895), *Beside the Bonnie Briar Bush*, Albyn Press 1977

Douglas Brown (1901), *The House with the Green Shutters*, Mercat Press 1983

Watson, Chs 6 and 7

SOME MAJOR THEMES

(i) The Kailyard

In 1926, Hugh MacDiarmid wrote of the literary phenomenon since known as 'The Kailyard': 'The disease has never been properly diagnosed, and although its evil effects have been recognised and certain steps have been successfully taken to abate them, it is still working widespread, if subterranean mischief'. Nearly fifty years later his comment can still be taken as representative of critical attitudes towards this phase in our national literature, which retains a distinct literary identity of a clear sociological significance.

(a) Literary Identity

'Kailyard' was the name given by the critic W H Miller, in 1899, to a group of novels written and published under the auspices of William Robertson Nicholl, a Free Church Minister and Editor of the influential *British Weekly* magazine. Three major authors contributed to the establishment of this style - James Matthew Barrie, Samuel Rutherford Crockett and John Watson, who wrote under the name of Ian MacLaren. Their work was obviously characterised by its subject matter - rural life in Scotland - but even more so by authorial attitude, consisting of a tone of sentimental nostalgia and the continual evocation of bland harmony. An old Scots song, used as a frontispiece in MacLaren's novel, *Beside the Bonnie Briar Bush*, provided an image of static domesticity which ideally designated the style:

There grows a bonnie briar bush in our kailyard
And white are the blossoms on't in our kailyard

The works of the three authors differ. Crockett tends towards the whimsical in his best known work, *The Lilac Sunbonnet* (1894), MacLaren favours pathos, and Barrie uses a more austere style for his lamentations over the passing of a way of life in *A Window in Thrums* (1889) and *Auld Licht Idylls* (1888). But all develop the same stereotypes of the self-sacrificing mother, the stern-but-just father, the 'lad o' pairts'(the son who gets on in the world), the innocent and 'bonnie' daughter, grim but amusing village kirk-elders and, at the centre of the novel, the community itself - frequently isolated in its condition of stasis by snowstorms or the surrounding hills. Read *Beside the Bonnie Briar Bush* - and you will easily recognise images used to depict Scotland today in the pages of the *Sunday Post* and *People's Friend*. The most alarming aspect of the Kailyard was its complete dominance over the literary markets of the time. Not only was very little else being written about Scotland, but the genre was immensely successful in commercial terms. Its appeal was increased by the growing numbers of expatriate Scots, and by the current vogue for 'Balmoralism' as established by Queen Victoria.

S. R. Crockett (Midlothian Libraries)

Two other writers whose work relates at times to the Kailyard School are Margaret Oliphant, in such novels as *Effie Ogilvie*, and *The Minister's Wife*, (sentimental but interesting on female perspective) and George MacDonald, in *David Elginbrod*, *Alec Forbes* and *Robert Falconer*. Elsewhere, both writers are remembered for their works of fantasy, a response considered in Part III, Section 4.

(b)   Sociological Significance

Much has been written about the Kailyard - most of it vituperative in tone - but only in recent years has research been undertaken into the causes of the phenomenon's success and the significance of its effect on Scotland. Ian Carter has come up with a plausible explanation of Kailyard ideology in economic terms, suggesting its role in dealing with the social consequences of the final triumph of agrarian capitalism. Based on an ideology of community, Kailyard literature emphasised harmony between landowner and tenant farmer in direct contradiction to the social tension created by the declining function of peasant modes of production within capitalist agriculture. Carter's argument that Kailyard novelists were essentially concerned with decline is supported by Christopher Harvie's assessment of the novels' religious themes. Gently mocking the fanaticism of the Free

Margaret Oliphant by J. M. Oliphant.
Scottish National Portrait Gallery.

Church and its splinter groups - see, for example, Crockett's depiction of 'the Marrow kirk' - the Kailyard writers advocated a more liberal theology, again with the emphasis on harmony. Critical approaches along such lines have proved more fruitful than those which attempt to understand the cultural influences on the Kailyard, as such ventures inevitably over-centralise its importance and literary value. Admittedly, the seeds of Kailyard themes can be seen in the work of previous Scottish writers; Scott, for example, could be described as sharing something of Kailyard nostalgia, Henry MacKenzie's *Man of Feeling* invokes a similar sentimentality though within a very distinct cultural context, and John Galt frequently takes as his subject the life of a small rural community (and his imitator, D.M. Moir can be seen as having a more definite and adverse influence on the Kailyard through his novel *Mansie Wauch* [1828].) But in general, such writers were prepared to face up to the complexities and contradictions of their themes, whereas the Kailyard writers sought to impose an all encompassing ideology of 'feeling' on their material, to exploit emotion rather than explore it. Turning now to novels which consciously departed from this type we should be aware of similarities as well as differences, if we are to avoid imposing a false line of development on this period.

(ii) Reaction against the Kailyard

Strong links can be drawn between the Kailyard novels and those most commonly seen as constituting a reaction against them - George Douglas Brown's *The House with the Green Shutters* and J MacDougall Hay's *Gillespie* (1914). Each novel deals with the life of a small community and, as MacDiarmid put it, the treatment is 'the same thing disguised as its opposite'. However, both novels make a conscious effort to shock the reader accustomed to Kailyard sentiment, by destroying harmony and inverting stereotypes. Now the mothers are either slatterns or drunkards, the fathers are greedy boors and the sons weak and foolish. And in George Douglas Brown's villagers, the 'Bodies' of Barbie, we can see a masterly extension into malevolence of the Kailyard's local gossips. Both novels, moreover, provide detailed analysis of the implications of social and economic change. In *The House with the Green Shutters* the suffering of Gourlay can be seen as a result of his refusal to acknowledge external economic progress, ignoring the fact that his business is becoming outmoded. This situation is reversed in *Gillespie* in which the character of the title exploits the forces of economic change in his role as a capitalist entrepreneur. Both novels are considerably more melodramatic than any Kailyard novel, which indicates their

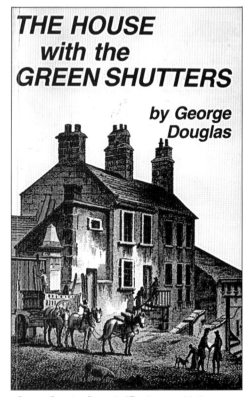

George Douglas Brown's "The house with the green shutters". The Mercat Press edition, 1983.

intention to encompass more complex psychologies and events. *Gillespie* consciously presents the religious psyche; *The House with the Green Shutters* shows the influence of Greek tragedy. Finally, both novels attempt to integrate the Scots language into the text rather than using it only in dialogue and thus labelling it 'quaint' in the Kailyard fashion.

But it cannot be simply assumed that these novels heralded the rebirth or salvation of the Scottish novel. Both are fine works but still ignore the dimensions of urban experience, and despite their social awareness, neither acknowledges Scotland's growing industrial work force. Still very much tied to the form which they were attacking, they failed even to explore very deeply the peculiarities behind the Kailyard phenomenon. Yet novels exist within the Kailyard tradition which use that form to explore important aspects of rural society. *Johnny Gibb of Gushetneuk* (1870) by William Alexander provides an early example, while J Bryce's *The Story of a Ploughboy* (1912) and Lorna Moon's *Doorways in Drumorty* (1926) represent very different variations of this approach. It is also important to remember that in discussing this time we are talking about the age of James and Conrad, moving into the period of Joyce and Lawrence - and to note that since Stevenson no similar technical innovations had appeared in the Scottish novel. Only with Lewis Grassic Gibbon's A Scots Quair do signs of formal development appear. In this trilogy Gibbon uses his distance from the Kailyard to deal with a wider range of rural experience. He can parody the Kailyard yet mockingly acknowledge its assimilation into Scottish culture:

> So that was Kinraddie that bleak winter of nineteen eleven and the new minister, him they chose early next year, was to say that it was the Scots countryside itself, fathered between a kailyard and a bonny briar bush in the lee of a house with green shutters. And what he meant by that you could guess at yourself if you'd a mind for puzzles and dirt, there wasn't a house with green shutters in the whole of Kinraddie. (**Sunset Song**)

SAQs

1.   Discuss the various ways in which *Beside the Bonnie Briar Bush* uses sentiment.

2.   Is it a fair comparison to see Kailyard novels as the equivalent of today's popular romances, or do they possess greater significance?

3.   Compare the use of Scots in a Kailyard and anti-Kailyard novel.

4.   Does *The House with the Green Shutters* show any advance on the sexual stereotyping of *Beside Briar Bush*?

FURTHER READING

(a)   Comparative Novels

J.M. Barrie (1911) *Peter Pan.*

A.J. Cronin (1931) *Hatter's Castle.*

V. Jacob (1922) *Tales of my own Countryside.*

L. Moon (1929) *Dark Star.*

(b)   Criticism

G. Blake (1951) *Barrie and the Kailyard School.*

I. Campbell (1981) *The Kailyard. A New Assessment.*

I. Carter (1976) 'Kailyard: The Literature of Decline in Nineteenth Century Scotland', *The Scottish Journal of Sociology*, vol. 1, no. 1.

C.M. Grieve (1926) *Contemporary Scottish Studies.*

F.R. Hart (1978), *The Scottish Novel.*

Hugh MacDiarmid

OBJECTIVES

Your aim in this section is to gain understanding, through a chronological survey covering his hugely voluminous writings, of:

❂— MacDiarmid's philosophical, political and aesthetic principles in leading the 'Scottish Renaissance' movement from the early 1920s

❂— the balance of influence in his poetry between the traditions of Scottish literature and contemporary developments in European modernism.

READING

The Hugh MacDiarmid Anthology (1972), ed. M. Grieve and A. Scott.

Muir, especially pp. 21-2, 110-4

Watson, Ch 7

Wittig, Ch X

SOME MAJOR THEMES

(i)   MacDiarmid and the Renaissance

We have already seen, in the novels of Douglas Brown and MacDougall Hay, how the Kailyard image of Scotland was beginning to come under attack in the early years of the twentieth century. About the same time, writers such as Marion Angus, Violet Jacob and Lewis Spence were experimenting with verse in Scots, attempting to extend its range of reference beyond the 'pawky' humour of the parochial newspaper versifiers. But it was only with the appearance of this declaration from Christopher Murray Grieve in 1923 that there materialised the elements of something more than a negative reaction:

> We base our belief in the possibility of a great Scottish Literary Renaissance, deriving its strength from the resources that lie latent and almost unsuspected in the Vernacular, upon the fact that the genius of our Vernacular enables us to secure with comparative ease the very effects and swift transitions which other literatures are for the most part unsuccessfully endeavouring to cultivate in languages that have a very different and inferior basis. Whatever the potentialities of the Doric may be, however, there cannot be a revival in the real sense of the word - a revival of the spirit as distinct from a mere renewed vogue of the

letter - unless these potentialities are in accord with the newest and truest tendencies of human thought.
'A Theory of Scots Letters', 1, **Scottish Chapbook** (1923), p. 182)

Although the introductions in the *Anthology* will familiarise you with the general pattern of Grieve/MacDiarmid's life and work, they do not make sufficiently clear his essential role as the chief theoretician, propagandist and practitioner of the Renaissance movement. Perhaps partly because he had served in Salonika rather than on the Western Front, Sgt Grieve returned to Scotland with an awareness of 'small Nationalism' that was in no sense isolationist. ('If there is ocht in Scotland that's worth ha'en/ There is nae distance to which it's unattached...', *To Circumjack Cencrastus*.) Moreover, as repulsion against the horrors of 1914-18 grew in the post-war period, there was a

C. M. Grieve ("Hugh MacDairmid") by Robert Heriot Westwater. Scottish National Portrait gallery.

general loss of faith in notions of uninterrupted, evolutionary progress through time, reflected in MacDiarmid's insistence that Scots could be in the vanguard of 'the newest and truest tendencies of human thought' if they would rediscover their 'true' history and tradition. (The slogan of the *Scottish Chapbook* in 1923, 'Not Tradition - Precedents!',had become 'Not Burns -Dunbar!' by the time of *Albyn* in 1927.)

Armed with these twin notions, MacDiarmid began to report on a major Scottish Renaissance. *The Scottish Chapbook* was only one of several short-lived magazines (including *The Scottish Nation*, *The Northern Review* and, in the forties and fifties, *The*

Voice of Scotland) which Grieve founded, financed, edited and published, and in which, along with his *Northern Numbers* anthologies, many of the original productions of the Renaissance made their first appearance.

In *Scott and Scotland*, Muir argues that the regeneration of Scottish culture can result only from unification, through the repair of the 'dissociation of sensibility' which he holds to have destroyed the organic society he attributes to pre-Reformation times. In part this is a response to MacDiarmid's espousal in the twenties of the principle of continuing revolutionary dialectic on every level - aesthetic, political, intellectual - in both personal and social life. Following Gregory Smith's idea that the continual clash of opposites is the essential characteristic of the Scottish psyche ('The Caledonian Antisyzygy', *Scottish Literature: Character and Influence*, 1919), he does not try to evade the conflicts of identity common to the Scottish experience between the polarities of Highland/Lowland, Nationalist/ Internationalist, Catholic/Protestant, Gaelic/ Scots and English, spiritual/material, Royalist/Republican. Rather, MacDiarmid discovers in the dynamics of flux a more profound and liberating philosophy:

> *I'll ha'e nae hauf-way hoose, but aye be whaur Extremes meet - it's the only way I ken*
> *To dodge the curst conceit o' bein' richt*
> *That damns the vast majority o' men.*
>
> **(Drunk Man, p 27)**

Such inconsistent extremism was often exasperating to MacDiarmid's contemporaries (as the history of his expulsion from both Nationalist and Communist parties shows), and the slow growth of his literary reputation both within and outwith Scotland is indicative of a similar lack of responsiveness in the critical establishment to the challenge posed by his unorthodoxy. He has faith in the power of human beings to improve their own condition:

> *Oh, it's nonsense, nonsense, nonsense,*
> *Nonsense at this time o' day*
> *That breid-and-butter problems*
> *S'ud be in ony man's way*
>
> **('Second Hymn to Lenin', p 193)**

His exploration of that condition in the most profound metaphysical terms ('He canna Scotland see wha yet/ Canna see the Infinite/ And Scotland in true scale to it') can often seem, like the contemporary modernist writing of Yeats, Eliot and Pound, dauntingly difficult. ('Glasgow 1960', p 285, comments satirically, and 'Direadh III', p 226, more directly, on his own hopes of a Scottish intellectual revival.) But MacDiarmid does not offer only dry ratiocination:

> *Reason ser's nae end but pleasure*
> *Truth's no' an end but a means*

To a wider knowledge o' life
And keener interest in it.

(A *Drunk Man, p* 39)

(ii) The Poetry

(a) The Early Lyrics

The poems of *Sangschaw* (1925) and *Penny Wheep* (1926) were the first to show Grieve's principles in practice. Using any word from any regional dialect or any historical period (through Jamieson's *Etymological Dictionary of the Scots Tongue*), MacDiarmid's first experiments in 'synthetic Scots' are remarkable for their power to tackle universal themes in a few, highly lyrical lines. They bring together an essentially modernist aesthetic - based on the Imagist idea of 'an intellectual and emotional complex in a moment of time' - with Scottish language and rhythmical patterns, and cultural markers such as the predominantly rural context of the poems' settings. 'The Bonnie Broukit Bairn', for instance, mixes notions of lacrimae rerum, the glitter of Edwardian society ladies and the tear-stained face of a street urchin; and 'Empty Vessel' draws on the new Einsteinian notions of flexible light, the archetypal ballad figure of 'The Cruel Mother' (and Wordsworth's reworking of it in 'The Thorn') and the lost past symbolised only by a small cairn.

(b) A Drunk Man Looks at the Thistle

If the lyrics make reference to Pound's work of the Edwardian era, A *Drunk Man* reflects another major aspect of European modernism: it is a long poem structured by the 'stream of consciousness' technique. It has been argued that by being an almost unwritten language for over two hundred years, Scots has become predominantly a spoken language, particularly suitable for monologue or dialogue. Certainly it is the persona of the drunk man that holds this poem together. An infrastructure of interconnecting symbols (such as the thistle and the rose, the tree and the sea serpent, man and woman) develops throughout the poem (see Roderick Watson's essay 'The Symbolism of A *Drunk Man*' in Glen [Further Reading]) and, like the intricate rhythmical patterning, helps create a unified artifact of which the most profound theme is the difficulty, if not the impossibility, of integration. But look, too, for the ways in which MacDiarmid develops and extends the skills shown in the lyrics: the passage '0 wha's the bride...' on p. 42, for instance, considers the virgin birth (among other things) through the question-and-answer pattern of the Scots peasant balladry in a way that elicits a quite unconventional response.

(c) Later Work

The paucity of the selection from MacDiarmid's later work (over some 50 years) in the *Anthology* suggests not only his amazing productivity, but also the failure of critics to respond to his later developments. 'On a Raised Beach', however, does give some indication of his refusal to stop experimenting with language, and his willingness to rework English as he had renovated Scots. The poem's concern with fact (for instance, in the opening verse paragraph) reflects MacDiarmid's ambition to attain 'a poetry full of erudition, expertise, and exstacy' ('The Kind of Poetry I Want', p. 223). In searching for this he completed a number of long poems in both English and Scots (*To Circumjack Cencrastus*, 1931, *In Memoriam James Joyce*, 1955) as well as experimental prose 'autobiographies' (the early *Annals of the Five Senses*, foreshadowing *Lucky Poet*), and produced a constant stream of short poems (such as 'At My Father's Grave', 'Of John Davidson', the 'Hymns to Lenin' and 'Crystals Like Blood') which alone would give him claim to be recognised as a major poet.

SAQs

1. Do the 'translations' from European writers in A *Drunk Man* constitute any more than a token 'internationalism'?

2. What are the political and aesthetic implications of MacDiarmid's invocation of the Border Ballads? How does this usage compare and contrast with Muir's reliance on them as a critical standard in *Scott and Scotland*?

3. How would you defend MacDiarmid's later poetry against a charge of intellectual elitism?

FURTHER READING

The Complete Poems of Hugh MacDiarmid (1978), ed. M. Grieve and W.R. Aitken

H. MacDiarmid and L. Grassic Gibbon (1934), *Scottish Scene*

A *Drunk Man Looks at the Thistle*, Annotated edition, (1987), ed. K. Buthlay

A. Bold (1988) *MacDiarmid*.

K. Buthlay (1964) *Hugh MacDiarmid*.

K. Duval and S. Goodsir Smith, eds. (1962) *Hugh MacDiarmid: A Festschrift*.

D. Glen (1964) *Hugh MacDiarmid and the Scottish Renaissance*.

D. Glen, ed. (1972) *Hugh MacDiarmid, A Critical Survey*.

P.H. Scott and A.C. Davie, eds. (1980) *The Age of MacDiarmid*.

R. Watson (1985) *Hugh MacDiarmid*.

LEWIS GRASSIC GIBBON

OBJECTIVES

Focussing on the major work of Lewis Grassic Gibbon, your aims in this section will be:

✪— to assess A *Scots Quair* as a significant development of the Kailyard/anti-Kailyard debate

✪— to look at Gibbon's linguistic innovations

✪— to view the trilogy in light of the subsequent development of the Scottish novel, its features and themes.

READING

Grassic Gibbon (1934), A *Scots Quair*, Pan edition 1982

Watson, Ch 7

Wittig, Ch X

SOME MAJOR THEMES

(i)   Reaction against the Kailyard

Section 10, on Kailyard literature, deals with the tradition in which Lewis Grassic Gibbon wrote A *Scots Quair*. Links with that genre are most readily found in the first novel of the trilogy, *Sunset Song* - and perhaps it is an indication of Scottish taste and expectations that this volume remains by far the most popular. It is set, like the Kailyard novels, in an enclosed rural community and, following in the steps of anti-Kailyard literature, the author reveals the savagery behind the apparently harmonious facade. However, there are also some major differences. Gibbon's use of a central experiencing consciousness, Chris, enables him to articulate her personal awareness of the hypocrisies and dualities inherent to that society, but also permits him to create in the reader a strongly sympathetic identification with her. By moving within the consciousness of a character encapsulating many of the novel's central issues, he also ensures a means of transcending these problems on an imaginative level. Chris acquires a symbolic significance extending far beyond the immediately obvious - 'Chris Caledonia, I married a nation!' (*Cloud Howe*)

In contrast to that image of the split consciousness of contemporary Scotland embodied in Chris, Gibbon also develops a new means of presenting 'the folk' - not just as the inhabitants of Mearns communities in the early twentieth century but as a body of people reaching back beyond traditions to encompass all those who have worked the land since the dawn of history. He gives this mass a distinctive voice which can be heard at the beginning of each section in the trilogy, and a coherent image as represented by the standing stones and ruined monuments which appear on each landscape. But the past is not Gibbon's only, or main, concern; the trilogy also displays a far greater awareness of general social change, and its economic, political and spiritual implications, than any of the

Leslie Mitchell ~ Lewis Grassic Gibbon (Midlothian Libraries)

Kailyard or anti-Kailyard novels previously considered. By following Chris's transition from village, to small town, to city, the reader moves with the social shifts of the period.

(ii) The Language Question

In *The House with the Green Shutters* and *Gillespie* you may have noticed how their authors attempted to integrate Scots vocabulary into the text. Gibbon takes their aims one step further by creating a prose style which emulates the rhythms, grammar and phrasing of spoken Scots yet remains intelligible to those unfamiliar with the dialect. Gibbon's problem with the language was similar to that of his contemporary, MacDiarmid, but rather than creating a synthetic Scots - which was perhaps more suited to the density of poetry - he adapted Standard English to the oral style of the Mearns 'speak', pulling readers in through his frequent use of the 'you' construction which refers either to the folk, to Chris or to us as readers. This flexible style permitted him to make changes in tone from one book to another without losing the consistency essential to convey the concept of a united and tradition laden proletarian peasant consciousness. In Kinraddie the folk voice is that of a basically well-disposed gossip;

in Segget it becomes ill-informed and actively malevolent; and in Duncairn it is swallowed up in the greater diversity of an urban consciousness. By *Grey Granite* the voice of Chris, which has continued to move in and out of the folk voice, finally retreats into silence as she becomes like a stone, transformed into part of the countryside. In this third novel the voices of the lower middle-classes and of the media acquire greater authority, attempting to discard Scots and to assume the affectations of the ruling classes. But a movement in the opposite direction is begun by Ewan who assimilates his educated voice with that of the workers, the despised 'keelies', and, like Chris, retreats into nonverbal articulation - the unintelligible growl raised by the strikers on their march. The novel makes language an integral part of its themes. Gibbon's concern with language, of course, was very much a feature of the age in which he lived, and may be related to Modernist attempts at creating private languages to convey more than English apparently holds; in this respect Gibbon provides an interesting comparison with James Joyce. Yet his work can also be linked to MacDiarmid's and T S Eliot's in its more general concern with the ultimate failure of communication itself, in which there is no alternative to silence. In Chris and Ewan he provides two different aspects of the solution found at the end of *A Drunk Man Looks at the Thistle* and *The Waste Land*.

(iii) A Development in the Scottish Novel

You will have realised by now that the same themes recur in many of the Scottish novels which we have discussed, and that most arise from real or presumed features of Scotland that have been assimilated into our culture and built on by its literature. Gibbon was very conscious of the power of such myths (note his remark quoted in section 10) and used the trilogy to explore their bases, in some cases creating his own alternative versions.

(a)   History

Gibbon had an extremely idiosyncratic view of history - for more information about his Diffusionist theories see Douglas Young's *Beyond the Sunset* (Further Reading) -but the *Quair* does not show the same obsession with concepts of a Golden Age as can be found in other novels such as *The Thirteenth Disciple* (written under his own name, James Leslie Mitchell). Scotland's concern with history can be viewed as the attempt to escape from its own past, or as the desire to carve for itself a genuine place in history (see Craig's article, Further Reading). In his trilogy Gibbon translates such dualities into a concern with the conceptual boundaries of time. Chris, for example, experiences temporal lapses, movements into another dimension, thus transcending time's limitations. Her perception of time becomes increasingly spatial rather than linear, until she reaches a point where she need no longer justify her particular place in history. If Chris sees herself as a stone, being pushed, Ewan again offers an alternative, incorporated in the image of pushing the stone up a hill. His desire is to change history's course, not by adapting to, and struggling with the present, as does Chris's second husband, Robert, but by sweeping away past and present, by shaping the future. Chris and Ewan provide different answers to time and history, one on an imaginative, the other on a practical level, one mythical, the other revolutionary.

(b) The Land

Although parts of *Sunset Song* in particular show strong links with Scottish traditions of pastoralism - the land presented as a solace and as an a temporal absolute - the *Quair* also depicts the land as a drain on man's resources, and its cultivation is revealed as exploitation of man's labour. Chris's father is clearly destroyed by the land; the short stories in A *Scots Hairst*, 'Clay' and 'Greenden', carry this theme even further. Only in its impartiality does the land possess real virtue. It is such an essential disregard for humanity that Chris finally attempts to reach, and that Ewan, the archaeologist and plunderer of the land's lessons, also tries to follow.

(c) Women

Chris is an unusual figure in the Scottish novel in that she is not presented either as a pure and self-sacrificing mother, nor as a down-trodden wife - both common stereotypes. In A *Scots Quair* women are portrayed as sharp, percipient, independent and possessing considerable power in the community. Nevertheless, Chris is still a source of wisdom and strength, an idealised image in the romantic tradition. Moreover, despite her power and knowledge, the solution she offers at the novel's conclusion is passive, compared with Ewan's more active stance.

(d) Future Developments

Themes emerging from A *Scots Quair* will be encountered again and again in studying subsequent developments in the Scottish novel (section 14). Important issues raised by Gibbon include the effect of the First World War as a force of disintegration on communities, the alienating effects of the city, and the problems of adapting from rural communities to an urban, industrialised life-style. In the *Quair* two strands can be seen which represent the two main ways of dealing with such issues in novels which followed. One option is pastoral regeneration; adopting the myths of the land, going back into history in search of some significance for the future. The land, and life on the land, are offered as a source of escape (although, as in the case of the Clearances, it may be an avenue of liberation which is under threat). It becomes the material for rebuilding myths, creating a reassuringly cyclical view of history. Not surprisingly, the majority of novels about Highland life tend to follow this format. Alternatively, *Grey Granite* indicates the potential of urban, industrial experience in general, and working class life in particular - although it is arguable whether Gibbon ever really resolves the intrusion of rural consciousness into city life. Many writers have attempted to follow Gibbon's example in spite of the difficulties he encountered, but most have been unable to free themselves from the sentimentalising and paternalistic ethos of Kailyard literature, continuing to impose old and unsuccessful techniques on new situations. Part of their failure must be attributed to the fact that the only solution they could envisage for their gloomy depictions of city life was individual escape. Lewis Grassic Gibbon's more radical vision allowed him to portray a society from which a whole class could escape, unafraid of the kind of changes this would entail. *Sunset Song* is still credited as, artistically, the most successful part of the trilogy, but it is also least threatening to the status quo. In *Cloud Howe* and especially in *Grey Granite* Gibbon was dealing with increasingly complex social structures, hitherto scarcely discussed in fiction, and therefore had to forge new tools and new techniques for approaching such constructs.

SAQs

1.   Do you see Chris Guthrie as being more significant for A *Scots Quair* in the context of myth or in her personal and social roles?

2.   How accurate is Raymond Williams' description of *Sunset Song* as 'a classic statement of the dissolution of the peasantry', and can this be extended to the *Quair* as a whole?

3.   To what extent do the various 'voices' develop in the course of the trilogy, and how does Gibbon maintain a consistency of tone?

FURTHER READING

(a)   Works by Gibbon

L.G. Gibbon (1967) A *Scots Hairst*.

L.G. Gibbon and H. MacDiarmid (1934), *Scottish Scene*.

J.L. Mitchell (1936) *The Thirteenth Disciple*.

(b)   Biography

I.S. Munro (1966) *Lewis Grassic Gibbon*.

(c)   Criticism

A. Calder (1982) 'A Mania for Self-Reliance', *The Uses of Fiction*, ed. G. Martin and D. Jefferson

C. Craig (1979) 'The Body in the Kitbag', *Cencrastus* 1.

G. Trengrove (1975) 'Who is You? Grammar and Grassic Gibbon', *Scottish Literary Journal*, vol 2, no 2.

R Williams (1973) *The Country and the City*.

D. Young (1973) *Beyond the Sunset*.

THE MODERN SCOTTISH NOVEL

OBJECTIVES

This has to be a selective general survey. Your objectives are:

✺— to look briefly at the situation of Scottish fiction writing today

✺— to study major developments in the Scottish novel since the 1920s through concentrating on several significant trends.

READING

Gray (1981), *Lanark*, Canongate

Gunn (1937), *Highland River*, Arrow Books 1982

Kelman (1989) *A Disaffection*

McIlvanney (1975), *Docherty*, Mainstream 1983

Spark (1961), *The Prime of Miss Jean Brodie*, Penguin 1980

Watson, Ch 7

Alasdair Gray's "Lanark". Granada edition, 1982.

SOME MAJOR THEMES

(i) The Scottish Situation

Burdened perhaps by the international reputation and commercial success of Sir Walter Scott, suffering even more from the adverse legacy of the Kailyard, the Scottish novel has been slow to develop in any coherent pattern. Falling behind the Modernist developments of the early 20th century in England and abroad, it failed even to gain much recognition by building on the social realism fashionable in the 1950s. Within Scotland the novel's development has been somewhat overshadowed by the flowering of Scots poetry in the Renaissance period. (See sections 11 and 14.) It seems to face a problem peculiarly related to Scottish experience. In an article on 'The Beatnik in the Kailyard', Edwin Morgan expresses the nature of the dilemma:

> *There are patterns and meanings in modern Scottish life, but writers who are most conscious of their Scottishness are often afraid to look for them, in case the vivid image of*

the truth should overturn their notions of what 'Scottish' ought to mean.

Apart from this problem of subject and outlook, a limited audience for 'Scottish situations' makes the commercial success of our novelists highly unlikely. So any study of their work is further complicated by a lack of material in print, and many major texts are unobtainable, except through public libraries. The novels listed above have been suggested because all are still in print; although they are fine works in themselves, they would most usefully be read against a background of other novels mentioned below.

(ii) Patterns of Development

(a) Urban Experience

Thinking back on the work of Lewis Grassic Gibbon (section 12) you will remember the ways in which he attempted to deal with the kind of urban, industrialised experience that had become the norm for a large part of Scotland's population. Although it is arguable whether he fully escaped from a rural consciousness, even his degree of success was not readily followed, despite a growing tradition of 'Glasgow novels'. Long and McArthur's *No Mean City* (1935), co-written by an aspiring novelist and a journalist, although still popular, contains an uneasy mixture of sensationalism and documentary detachment. That novel highlights a real problem for the novelist with such subject matter - where should the author place himself with regard to his material, and what value should he place upon it? George Blake, for example, attempts to capture an industrialised consciousness in *The Shipbuilders* (1935), but cannot avoid creating a sentimental, paternalistic relationship between his working class hero and a shipyard owner, embodying a special relationship denied to their fellows. In Fred Urquhart's *Time Will Knit* (1938), which views Scottish city life through the eyes of an American visitor, the tone of description is unmistakably patronising. In Edwin Muir's *Poor Tom* (1932), the central character cannot escape the author's desire for a rural sensibility in his approach to the city. None of these succeed in penetrating proletarian consciousness as well as Gibbon.

Gibbon, of course, possessed an advantage in his use of language, which created the novel's unity. Most other novelists have been distanced by their own language from their characters. Even heavy use of Scots in dialogue often only emphasises the contrast with an anglicised prose in descriptive writing. Sidney Goodsir Smith offered an idiosyncratic solution in *Carotid Cornucopias* (1947), by creating his own language, but such a solution limits readership. Perhaps the most successful novel in overcoming this difficulty is McIlvanney's *Docherty*, which openly acknowledges it. Despite passages of purple prose, the novel establishes the central character in the context of those around him. Even the obituary of Tam Docherty is expressed in the terms of his contemporaries:

Slowly as they stood shrugging off the night wind they began to realise they had a clear view of Tam.

Their sense of him had hardened. They began to talk themselves towards it.

'Jesus Christ a helluva man fur the size o' him.'... 'If the wee man walked doon the street the noo, you wid ken. The wee cauld bit in the pit o' yer stomach.' 'He wis a hert'...

They were the right men to judge him - his peers. They knew the hardness of his experience because it was theirs too. They could appreciate what he had tried to make of it. With their words they sketched out some sense of a life built out of all these small moments.

(p 323)

And in a similarly tentative way, McIlvanney builds a picture of life in the industrialised West of Scotland. Yet *Docherty* remains an achievement very much on its own.

However, by the 1960s a new concern with the nature of their problems was evinced by several writers. The number of one novel novelists proved that a problem stated was not necessarily a problem solved. Concluding scenes of fantasy in George Friel's *Mr Alfred M.A.* (1972), mock the schoolteacher/ writer figure's failure to understand the language of his urban environment as the failed attempt of a rational mind to comprehend the threat of incipient anarchy. In *From Scenes Like These* (1968) Gordon Williams solves the problem of distance between a thinking hero and his environment by having Dunky Logan simply reject thought, and this is symbolised by his move from football played to spectator and hooligan. In *The Dear Green Place* (1966) by Archie Hind, the central character, himself a novelist, defines the problem:

In lieu of all the artistic extravagance, the menace, violence and horror which had been the experience of so many European writers, in Scottish life there was only a dull blot, a cessation of life, a dull absence, a blankness and the diminution and weakening of all the fibres of being, of buildings not blown up but crumbling and rotten, of streets not running with blood or rivers of fists but wan puddles...

But no solution is found, and the novelist finds that he can only write about his home town in a historical context. Alan Sharp's *A Green Tree in Gedde* (1965) held out some hope by using innovative techniques to confront directly the burden of the past, the desire for present security paradoxically coupled with longing for historical glory, epitomised by recurring graveyard scenes, but its sequel, *The Wind Shifts* (1967) failed to fulfil such promise and the intended trilogy has never materialised. However, one more recent novel, reflecting all the concerns mentioned above, has received acclaim as a major development in fiction. Facing up to the problem of subject matter - 'if a city hasn't been used by an artist, not even the inhabitants live there imaginatively' - Alasdair Gray wrote in *Lanark* an epic which deals with Scottish urban experience on the levels of both realism and fantasy, transforming it into a valid expression of more universal concepts. By introducing the novelist as a conjuror into the final section of the novel Gray bypassed the distance between author and characters. Through a proliferation of such devices, a willingness to innovate, and a respect for the past, he promoted a wider recognition that the Scottish experience can be seen and expressed in imaginative terms. The problems of contemporary urban reality are also memorably treated in James Kelman's A Disaffection, (1989), in a mood that is suggested by his title.

(b) Novels of Regeneration

Douglas Gifford, in a round-up of Scottish novels points to two main groups: satirical/bleak and predominantly urban, and regenerative/ rural/historical. Such a division is perhaps slightly imbalanced, since the novels mentioned above are trying to create a positive response to modern experience, not merely to satirize it, and looking at the novels of Neil Gunn, Ian Crichton Smith, even George Mackay Brown, you may notice a difference in subject matter but not necessarily one of aim. In their basic concerns, their explorations of the influence of the past, their search for means of responding to the present, they are very similar to those writers choosing modern, urban life as their material.

If, despite this, we are to see such rural/historical writers as a group, Neil M Gunn is undoubtedly the most important, and Highland River is the novel containing the fullest expression of his philosophy, with its celebration of creativity as integrated with the environment, and its analysis of the search for wholeness through attempting to come to terms with the forces of history. The Silver Darlings (1941) and The Serpent (1943) offer variations on this theme. For writers wishing to turn to the Scottish past, the Highland Clearances possess obvious symbolic value (see History Guide, section 10). Neil Gunn's Butchers Broom (1934), Fionn MacColla's And the Cock Crew (1945) and Ian Crichton Smith's Consider the Lilies (1968) are worth comparison for the different ends to which they put the same issue. Interesting, too, is Greenvoe (1972), George Mackay Brown's version of a modern Clearance as big business hits an Orkney island. One final variation on the theme of the land can be found in the return from city to country, exploring the tensions between them through the experience of a single character. Gunn's The Drinking Well (1947), Eric Linklater's White-Maa's Saga (1929) and Magnus Merriman (1934), and Fergus Lamont (1979) by Robin Jenkins, all treat this subject with varying degrees of cynicism and facetiousness, which seems to imply that regeneration through the land is only possible today in the realms of literary myth.

(c) The Innovators

Several major novelists, abandoning such obviously realist modes of writing, have refused to adopt either approach as set out above. Robin Jenkins, one of Scotland's most prolific novelists, uses aspects of the Scottish scene, both urban and rural, but is more deeply concerned with the metaphysics of moral issues - as revealed in *The Cone-Gatherers* (1955) and A *Would-be Saint* (1978). Nor is he afraid to translate his concerns into a context outwith Scotland - as *Dust on the Paw* (1961) and *The Holy Tree* (1969) show by their success. Similarly, although *The Prime of Miss Jean Brodie* is Muriel Spark's only Scottish novel (well worth reading for the subtlety which can be discerned behind the apparent creation of a Scottish stereotype), her concern with Calvinist concepts of predestination and with the identity of self are expressed through other locations in *The Ballad of Peckham Rye* (1963), *The Mandelbaum Gate* (1967) and *The Abbess of Crewe* (1974). James Kennaway, another writer who abandons specifically Scottish scenes, appears to have benefitted less from the change; his most confident works deal with upper middle-class life in Scotland - *Tunes of Glory* (1956) and *Household Ghosts* (1961).

(d) Conclusion

If you are interested it would also be worthwhile to consider writers as diverse as John Buchan, Compton MacKenzie, Ian MacPherson, Giles Gordon and Naomi Mitchison, assessing their places in the pattern of the novel's development. Hart's *The Scottish Novel*, despite its rather tedious plot summaries, is a useful source of background information for further reading - even if you don't agree with his very definite categorisations. Nor should Scotland's short story writers be forgotten - Ian Crichton Smith, George Mackay Brown, Dorothy K. Haynes, and Elspeth Davie have all proved themselves in this form, while Alan Spence and Brian McCabe are promising newcomers.

SAQs

1.   How has a consciousness of the past influenced the modern Scottish novelist's response to the present? (You may wish to focus on one writer.)

2.   From your own reading, would you say that the problems of Scottish novelists differ radically from those of their English or American counterparts?

3.   Is discussion of a 'pattern of development' a justifiable approach to the Scottish novel, or does it impose a false organicism? (It may be useful to think of *Scott and Scotland* in this context.)

FURTHER READING

F.R. Hart (1978) *The Scottish Novel*.

I. Murray and R. Tait (1984) *Ten Modern Scottish Novels*

G. Wallace and R. Stevenson (eds.) (1992) *The Scottish Novel Since the Seventies : New Visions, Old Dreams*.

E. Morgan (1974) *Essays*.

MODERN SCOTTISH POETRY

OBJECTIVES

The aim of this section is to examine, in the light of MacDiarmid's example and influence:

✪— the choice of language; and

✪— the attitude towards tradition in modern Scottish poetry, making special reference to the work of Sidney Goodsir Smith, Robert Garioch, Norman MacCaig and Edwin Morgan.

READING

Goodsir Smith (1975), *Collected Poems 1941-1975*

Garioch (1983), *Collected Poems*

MacCaig (1985), *Collected Poems*

Morgan (1990), *Collected Poems*

Watson, Ch 7

SOME MAJOR THEMES

(i)   The Choice of Language

Muir argues that 'the prerequisite of an autonomous literature is a homogeneous language' (p 7): perhaps the most immediately striking characteristic of modern Scottish poetry is precisely its heterogeneity of language. MacDiarmid's legacy has not consisted of dogmatic pronouncements on the necessity of any one language or style of writing, but rather of cultural and linguistic self-confidence such as Scotland has lacked since well before the time of Burns.

It is not just that MacCaig has felt free to use English ('My ancestry's Gaelic... My language is English') while Garioch, Smith and Morgan have used Scots regularly in their work. Consider the huge range of types and registers of Scots that are used now. It extends from Garioch's Edinburgh colloquialism, as in 'I'm Neutral':

> ('*Last nicht in Scotland Street I met a man*
> *that gruppit my lapel - a kinna foreign*
> *cratur he seemed; he tellt me, there's a war on*

atween the Lang-nebs and the Big-heid clan.' p 126)

to the Latinate mock-seriousness of his 'Did ye see me?'
('I'll tell ye of ane great occasioun:
I tuk pairt in a grand receptioun.
Ye canna hae the least perceptioun
hou pleased I was to get the invitatioun.' p 127).

Morgan can suggest the vocabulary and rhythms of Glasgow patois (in 'Good Friday', for instance), as comfortably as he uses 'standard English' ('In the Snack Bar', 'Trio'); while Goodsir Smith, encountering MacDiarmid after arriving in Scotland from a childhood and adolescence spent in New Zealand, mastered synthetic Scots and used it for a wide variety of poems, from the political 'Ballat of John Maclean' to the love elegies of *Under the Eildon Tree.*

The point is illustrated again, from a slightly oblique angle, by Morgan's experiments with form ('The Clone Poem', 'The Loch Ness Monster Poem', 'Canedolia', for instance) and his essays in 'concrete poetry'. While MacDiarmid's early lyrics released writers from the inability to use Scots, his later verse fostered the continuation of an experimental attitude towards language as a whole, such as survives in post-modernist writing in England only among 'regional' and working-class writers like Tony Harrison, whose 'Them and Uz' shows him still fighting for a freedom to parallel that won by Scots for their own language against the southern standard.

Edwin Morgan (Photograph by Kevin Low)

(ii) The Attitude to Tradition

Again, contemporary poets show great diversity - resulting from renewed confidence -in their approach to traditions of subject matter and form.

Under the Eildon Tree, for instance, is cast in the form of a sequence of poems charting the progress of a love affair; but within this traditional shape, Goodsir Smith discusses not only the development of a particular relationship, but the interrelation of varying ways -including the literary - of interpreting experience, and the relative value of differing types of experience. Conventional notions are brought smartly up to date, as the love-sick swain is transmuted into 'Sidney Slugabed Smith', opposed as the epitome of bourgeois indolence to 'Uncle Joe' Stalin's rhetoric:

For Knox has nocht on Uncle Joe
And Oblomov has nocht on Smith
And sae we come by a route maist devious
Til the far-famed Aist-West Synthesis!
Beluved by Hugh that's beluved by me...

Thus are the michtie faaen,
Thus till the end o' a michtie line,
Dunbar til Smith the Slugabed
Whas luve burns brichter nor them aa
And whas dounfaain is nae less,
Deid for a ducat deid
By the crueltie o' his ain maistress.   (V)

MacCaig's poetry has often been compared to that of the metaphysical school of English seventeenth century writers in its startling imagery ('Toad': 'Stop looking like a purse') and the quality of intellectual speculation to which it leads (see 'Antique Shop Window'). But the sequence of 'Poems for Angus', with its use of Miltonic and Tennysonian allusion in 'In Memoriam' as part of a series drawing predominantly on MacCaig's Highland sensibility, illustrates the ease with which he assimilates various and varying traditions.

Garioch's work can be quite explicit in its reference to Scottish traditions of writing: 'Embro to the Ploy' continues the long series of poems in celebration of festive days which includes 'Christ's Kirk on the Green' and 'The Jolly Beggars', while 'Dr Faust in Rose Street' seems to draw more on the Scottish familiarity with the supernatural and the satanic (as exemplified in 'Tam o' Shanter') than on Marlowe or on Goethe. The classical allusions of 'Sisyphus' are thrown into a new light by the use of Scots as Garioch reworks the myth for his own time and situation.

Translation from foreign poetry has gained in popularity in Britain since the war, as evidenced by the work of such writers as Tomlinson and Davie. MacDiarmid's 'translations' in A *Drunk Man* gave a special emphasis in Scotland to the practice, recovering the mediaeval attitude that Scots was as suitable a language in which to render foreign as well as native poetry as any other: Henryson's *Fables* and Douglas' *Aeneid* stand as literary models, in attitude if not in form, behind Garioch's translations from the Italian poet Giuseppe Belli. Morgan's versions of Mayakovsky, *Wi the Hail Voice*, continued the explicit harnessing of revolutionary politics and modernist poetry which MacDiarmid had propagandised for Scotland:

Nicht haurdly gane: day loups up:
and ilka morn loup wi't
folk to CENTGEN
folk to GENCOM

folk to COMPOLIT
folk to POLICENT -
hooses skail, offices fill,
till wow! the papers rin like watter...
   ('*Mayakovsky's Anecdote*')

Perhaps more than any other, Morgan seems to have accepted MacDiarmid's notion of all-inclusiveness as object and ambition. His poetry ranges freely, in the words of the title of one of his volumes, 'From Glasgow to Saturn', and his energy, productiveness and drive towards the new represent most concisely the influence which MacDiarmid has had.

SAQs

1.   Does the heterogeneity of these poets' works prevent their being considered part of an autonomous Scottish tradition?

2.   What critical standards can be applied to translations into Scots to get the reader beyond the state of being merely dazzled by their novelty?

3.   Is there a conflict between the political attitudes expressed by these poets and the arguable 'elitism' of their experimental approach to language and form?

FURTHER READING

Critical material on contemporary writers obviously lags behind as each new publication alters the perspective on an individual's work. Essays on the writers looked at closely here have appeared in literary magazines (*Akros*, *Chapman*, *New Edinburgh Review*) and you may like to look particularly at the following:

D. Campbell (1981), 'Interview with Robert Garioch', *Cencrastus* 6

J. Hendry and R. Ross (eds.) (1990) *Norman MacCaig: Critical Essays.*

M. McCulloch (1993) *Edwin Muir: Poet, Critic and Novelist.*

K. White (1983), 'Morgan's Range', *Cencrastus* 12.

There are of course, many other contemporary poets whose work you should look at for a fuller idea of the range and character of Scottish poetry today, including Mackay Brown, Dunn, Fulton, Graham, Leonard, Lochhead, Mackie and Crichton Smith.

GAELIC LITERATURE

OBJECTIVES

Gaelic is currently spoken by about 80,000 of the 5 million inhabitants of Scotland. Most users of this guide will have difficulty in dealing with poetry in translation, and differences in culture are expressed by the three languages and traditions of writing in Scotland, so Gaelic literature has been given a separate section. However, you should be alert to the reciprocal influence of all three strands of literature. Gaelic writing has impinged on the Lowlands in more subtle ways than merely by providing the 'inspiration' for the 'Ossian' poems of the 18th century.

The aims of this section are:

✪— to sketch the historical position of poetry in Gaelic society; and

✪— to examine the development of a 'new' style of Gaelic writing since the 1930s.

READING

The Gaelic poetry in Watson's *Poetry of Scotland* can be augmented by:

Jackson, (ed.) (1951), *The Celtic Miscellany*.

D. MacAuley (1976), *Modern Scottish Gaelic Poems*.

D. Thomson (1990), *An Introduction to Gaelic Poetry*.

Watson, Chs 5 and 7

SOME MAJOR THEMES

(i) The Gaelic Tradition

By the 5th century, Gaelic-speaking people from Ireland had settled throughout the Highlands and Islands of Scotland. Although isolated communities did exist elsewhere (for instance, in the south-west until the 17th century), this area formed a distinct cultural unit which took its lead in politics, social custom and law not from Edinburgh but from Ireland. Ruled by the 'Lord of the Isles' (the leader of Clan MacDonald), the society maintained the Celtic attitude towards the importance of an oral tradition which was serviced by members of the castes of bards and poets. The bards were regarded as the inferior order, specialising in the composition of panegyrics for great men, while the poets were accorded an almost religious status as visionaries and seers. They acted as the historians of the society, and were patronised by the leading families. After the Norman movements into Scotland in the 12th century, the Gaelicisation of families such as the Grants, Gordons and Frasers added elements of the courtly love lyric to the native tradition.

The most obvious characteristic of Gaelic poetry is the codification of the diction in sets of images. This trait reflects the oral nature of the tradition and the role of poems in reinforcing the sense of that continuing tradition, especially at the dangerous time of a leader's death. Poets would often go to considerable lengths in listing not only the ancestors and contemporaries of the person in question, but all his political and social allegiances as well.

Beside this intellectual tradition, there was also a more popular form of oral composition, perhaps more similar to the Border Ballads than to any other aspect of Scottish poetry, although completely lacking the Ballads' supernatural concerns. Surviving in the working songs such as those which accompanied the waulking of tweed, they often lack much logical or linear progression and seem to have been part of a female sub-culture, composed and transmitted in wholly female contexts.

The disintegration of this Highland culture following the risings of 1715 and 1745 might well have destroyed Gaelic poetry. The idea of the society held by those outwith the Highlands was thereafter very much a backward-looking stereotype. But Alexander MacDonald's publication in 1751 of his first book of secular poems greatly extended the scope of writing in Gaelic. A university-educated man fully aware of modern developments, he encouraged not only individual writers such as Rob Dom, Duncan MacIntyre and Donald Buchanan, but also the work of anthologising a previously unwritten literature, which culminated in the publication from 1776 of a series of collections by his son Ranald MacDonald.

The nineteenth century Clearances continued the attack on Highland society: but the methods used were not confined to physically unsettling the people. The Scottish Society for the Propagation of Christian Knowledge and the Free Church of Scotland had been carrying out widespread educational programmes in Gaelic, but the Education Act of 1872 made it obligatory that all education be in English, without making any provision for the teaching of the language in preparation for its use as a medium for instruction. Consequently, many Gaels developed neither a satisfactory grasp of English nor literacy in their despised native language, and writers adopted a very defensive, often isolated position which reflected the situation of their culture (see the work of Mary MacPherson, William Livingstone, John Smith of Lewis).

(ii) 'New' Gaelic Writing

As in Lowland Scottish writing, the First World War proved the catalyst of a new approach. MacAuley's introduction deals well with the stylistic aspects of this (such as the exploitation of Gaelic's rich metrical resources and the use of rhyme and assonance). The 'Renaissance' encouraged a renewed confidence in Gaelic - as in Scots - for its own sake, and a determination that it need not be parochial in subject matter or attitude. Sorley Maclean's work, even in the translations which he makes himself as 'cribs' to the Gaelic, will stand comparison in range, seriousness and lyrical power with that of, say, Yeats ('The Blue Rampart', 'The Cry of Europe'); and poems such as 'Death Valley' and 'Highland Woman' show the ease which he feels in tackling subjects set both in Scotland and abroad. Perhaps 'Heroes' best reflects the Renaissance

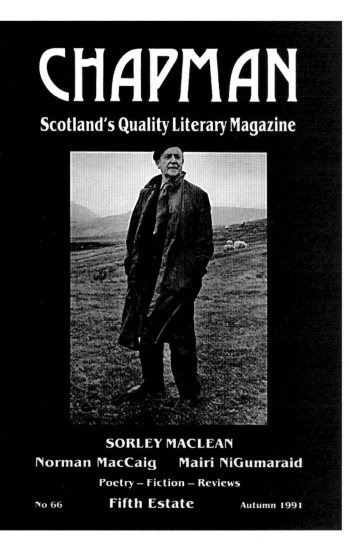

principle of combining 'Scottish' and 'International' themes in its drawing on the panegyric tradition in a freshly ironic manner:

> I did not see Lannes at Ratisbon
> nor MacLennan at Auldearn
> nor Gillies MacBain at Culloden,
> but I saw an Englishman in Egypt.
>
> A poor little chap with chubby cheeks
> And knees grinding each other,

pimply unattractive face -
garment of the bravest spirit.

He was not hit "in the pub
in the time of the fists being closed",
but a lion against the breast of battle,
in the morose wounding showers.   (1.1-12)

'Clan Maclean', 'The National Museum of Ireland' and 'Palach' reflect a willingness to engage with highly sensitive political material. In this, too, Maclean acknowledges the influence of MacDiarmid.

Other modern writers (Thomson, Crichton Smith, Campbell Hay) have developed their own styles, suggesting a further parallel with the diversity of approach taken by writers following MacDiarmid in Scots and English.

SAQs

1.   Examine the symbolism of Maclean's 'The Woods of Raasay'. How far does the use of such techniques depend   upon knowledge of specific cultural patternings, and does this result in parochialism?

2.   What evidence of the oral nature of the Gaelic tradition is discernable in *Modern Gaelic Poetry*?

FURTHER READING

M. Chapman (1978) *The Gaelic Vision in Scottish Culture*.

G. Campbell Hay (1981) *Mohktar is Dubhgall*.

F. MacFionnlaigh (1980) *A'Mheanbhchuileag: The Midge* (English translation, *Cencrastus* 10, 1982).

O *Choille Gu Bearradh* (*From Wood to Ridges*), Collected Poems of Sorley Maclean in Gaelic and English, (1989).

Sorley Maclean: Critical Essays, ed R. Ross & J. Hendry (1986).

A. Macneacail (1986) *A Seachnadh: The Avoiding*.

J. MacInnes (1981) 'Sorley Maclean and the Evangelical Background', *Cencrastus* 7.

I. Chrichton Smith (1981) *Selected Poems 1955-80*.

D. Thomson (1981) *Creachadh na Clarsaich: Collected Poems 1940-80*.

SCOTTISH DRAMA

OBJECTIVES

The aims of this section are:

✪— to examine - very briefly - how Muir's thesis might apply to the history of Scottish drama; and

✪— to survey developments in theatre since the publication of *Scott and Scotland*

READING

Bridie (1978) *Mr Bolfry*, ed. J.T. Low.

Lindsay (1989), *Ane Satire of the Thrie Estaites*, ed. Roderick Lyall.

MacGrath (1982), *The Cheviot, the Stag and the Black, Black Oil*; (1981), *Blood Red Roses and Swings and Roundabouts*; (1981), *A Good Night Out: Popular Theatre, Audience, Class and Form*.

SOME MAJOR THEMES

(i)   Pre-1936

Muir's strategy in *Scott and Scotland* is to use poetic tragedy as the identifying marker of a 'mature' literature. His inflated statement that such drama is 'a unique act of self-consciousness, perhaps the most comprehensive act of self-consciousness outside of mystic contemplation' (p 28) distracts attention from the implicit premise of his attack on Scottish literature: which is that only in England can we find the paradigmatic development of a national literature, and consequently we must judge any other tradition inferior by the degree to which it fails to match the pattern set by English writing: since Scottish literature does not have a drama to match that of the Elizabethans, it is condemned to perpetual infantilism. This chapter of *Scott and Scotland* is particularly rich in examples of Muir's method of simply accumulating statements, rather than *arguing* any logical connection between them, and is a good one to read several times in order to make yourself aware of exactly what Muir is doing.

But however suspect Muir's touchstones may be, it remains the case that Scottish drama was badly retarded from the time of the Reformation.

Very little textual evidence of pre-16th century drama has survived. Dunbar and Lindsay both mention the 'farses and plesand plays' performed at the court, but records of the one complete work which we do have, Lindsay's *Satire*, by mentioning outdoor performances at Cupar and Edinburgh, suggest that there was not too rigid a division between this work of 'literature' and such popular medieval traditions of drama as the miracle plays.

The supposition is supported by the circumstances of the General Assembly's 1575 ruling. Calvinists had many doubts about the morality of art: but drama seems to have been held to be particularly suspect, since it depended upon people pretending to be other than they really were - a species of lying which could only have its origins in the Father of Lies, Satan, himself. Although Knox was at first willing to use plays as vehicles of anti-Catholic propaganda, in 1575 the Assembly issued a general prohibition of 'clerk-plays or commedies based on canonical scriptures' which seems to have led to the cessation of drama for many years.

Sir James Mathew Barrie by Sir William Nicholson.
Scottish National Portrait Gallery.

There was only intermittent theatrical activity. In 1756, John Home's *Douglas* was premiered in Edinburgh and met with an enthusiasm such that one member of the audience was prompted to cry, 'Whaur's yer Wullie Shakespeare noo?'. But even this success was marked by an unusually long run that amounted only to 6 days, and Home continued his career in London.

This drift to the south continued to be the rule for Scots of theatrical ambition, amongst whom Barrie was as popular for his sentimental plays as for his novels (*Peter Pan* being far outpaced by the kailyardy *Margaret Ogilvie* in the opinion of his contemporaries).

Meanwhile, the indecorousness of the stage was beginning to lessen as a public scandal in Scotland. There was a great growth of amateur dramatic societies whose activities probably helped create an audience for the professional theatre, although Hutchison (Further Reading) argues that they may have inclined towards a kailyard view of Scotland when not ignoring the situation of their own society completely. Between the wars, groups such as the Scottish National Players and the Unity Theatre Company attempted to apply the principles of the Renaissance to the theatre. MacDiarmid had always argued for the establishment of a National Theatre to parallel the role of the Abbey in Ireland, and these groups of dedicated professionals not only attempted to open audiences to foreign drama but also to make it possible to discuss the urban condition of most Scots.

Plays such as *The Gorbals Story* and those revived in the 7:84 Company's 'Clydebuilt' series achieved much success, although the companies which created the climate in which they might be written were unable to last long against the financial pressures of the commercial theatre.

(ii) Since 1936

The first Edinburgh International Festival was held in 1947. Though it has always been primarily a music festival, its 'Fringe' did help to foster an audience which would take drama seriously.

The Traverse Theatre Club in Edinburgh was founded to provide a venue for experimental theatre that would be open for more than the statutory three weeks of the summer binge. In the fluctuations of its artistic policy, there have been periods when emphasis was placed on encouraging Scottish writers, whether they wanted to create realistic drama or to attempt something more avant garde. Tom McGrath is probably the archetypal Traverse playwright, having co-authored *The Hard Man* with Jimmy Boyle and gained great success with the wordless *Animal*. Though the Traverse remains unique in its dedication solely to *new* drama. Glasgow, with the Tron Theatre and 'Mayfest', also provides outlets for fresh activity.

Such seriousness of attitude has undoubtedly affected the 'commercial' theatre (now mostly run by local authorities). The work of 'James Bridie' (1888-1951) was essentially middle-class in its concerns and settings, and reflected the middle-class lack of awareness of nationality in as much as each play might be set in any developed Western European country. (Even *Mr Bolfry* could be easily transposed to Geneva.) But this strain of writing has produced some playwrights who credit their situation with more significance: Donald Campbell's *The Jesuit* and *The Widows of Clyth* are probably the strongest examples. However, local theatres still take more money when English vehicles for popular TV personalities hit the boards than when indigenous material is produced, and stress on the need to get 'bums on seats' was responsible for many of the difficulties of the Scottish Theatre Company founded in 1979.

In aiming to tour rather than set up a single 'National Theatre', the STC were attempting to draw on the principles (and the success) of the most effective development in drama in the 70s, the small, politicallycommitted companies. 7:84 with The Cheviot had got people who would never dream of going to the theatre' to enjoy plays: and in John MacGrath's words,

> the kind of theatre which 7:84 has done a great deal to establish in Scotland is there to represent the realities of working-class life and history directly to working-class audiences, without translating it into the language of the middle-class theatre which has dominated our stages since the 1890s. It has its roots in the popular tradition of entertainment, and it takes the values of the working-class very seriously.

Clydebuilt, p 5

Cheviot drew on the ceildh, the music hall and the drawing-room vignette. Later plays have involved elements from working mens' clubs organisations, TV and film cliche, and direct didactic address. The continued success of the group and its offspring (Wildcat) and allies (Communicado, Borderline, Theatre Workshop) has opened up a new kind of experimentalism which is often more *interesting* in its commentary on contemporary life than the more extravagant reaches of the Glasgow Citizens or the Traverse. But the latter, under Jenny Killick's direction, has recently earned local and wider acclaim for its exciting productions of new plays from Scotland by John Clifford, Chris Hannan and Tom McGrath. Finally, John Byrne's extraordinary six part *Tutti Frutti*, seen on BBC TV in 1987 surely proves new inspiration for Scottish drama.

SAQs

1.   Compare and contrast the works of Bridie, Barrie and Shaw.

2.   Look at the role of song in *The Cheviot*. Can it be related to Muir's view of the Border Ballads?

3.   Consider the degree of 'realism' in *Blood Red Roses*.

FURTHER READING

The plays of J M Barrie (1918-38).

'James Bridie' (1930) *Tobias and the Angel*; (1933), *A Sleeping Clergyman*.

J. Byrne (1974) *The Slab Boys Trilogy*; (1987) *Tutti Frutti* (book of series).

D. Hutchison (1977) *The Modern Scottish Theatre*.

H. MacMillan (1974) *The Sash*.

R. McMillan (1974) *All in Good Faith*; (1978), *The Bevellers*.

A. Reid (1950) *The Lass wi the Muckle Mou*.

PART 3:
SOCIETY &
CULTURE

Aberlemno Stone, Aberlemno Churchyard, Angus

INTRODUCTION

Part III is designed to provide links between the previous two parts of this volume dealing with history and literature, so that you can give some consideration to the inter-relationship of historical and literary material. The views expressed may not always coincide with those of the set reading, but this should encourage you to seek your own balanced assessment. Though space is limited, the definition of culture is widened to touch on art, architecture, philosophy and music. We hope this will help your appreciation of chronological relationships between attitudes and events.

CULTURE AND HISTORY BEFORE 1560

OBJECTIVES

You can see that Part I begins with the Reformation period, centring on the crucial year, 1560. This is somewhat later than the starting point of Part II, which begins with the emergence of literature in Scots, subsequent to the long Wars of Independence, in the mid-14th century (though some initial remarks on earlier Gaelic and Latin cultures are included). To answer this, the present section indicates some of the relationships between pre-1560 culture and its historical context. We also acknowledge briefly some earlier cultural and historical inter-actions, under the following headings:

✿— Celtic and Latin Scotland to 1286,

✿— The Wars of Independence,

✿— Late-medieval and Renaissance Scotland.

SOME MAJOR THEMES

(i)   Celtic and Latin Scotland

In Part II we saw that cultural traditions in both Gaelic and Latin already existed before the lowland Scots tongue emerged as a cultural medium. Indeed, it could be said that the earlier history of Scotland is really the inter-action of these two traditions - later to be qualified profoundly by the assertion of the lowland vernacular.

Smout opens by suggesting that the coming to power of Malcolm Canmore in 1057 saw the beginning of a new era in Scottish history. Malcolm himself, like his predecessors was a Celtic monarch, and at the time of his accession Celtic remained the dominant influence upon Scottish life. Of the early Celtic peoples whose gradual integration formed the basis of his kingdom, the most mysterious are the Picts. They left no written record. Instead, we find reference to them in chronicles of the Gaels, British, Romans, and Angles. Something of their life style and art can be seen in the many carved standing stones that survive, on which are repeated a series of symbols that continue to confound interpretation. Remarkable stone brochs scatter their territory to the north of the Forth-Clyde line - and it was many centuries before such permanent building was again taken up.

To the south were British peoples, speaking an early form of the language that we now call Welsh. To the east was a tribe who called themselves the *Gododdin*, whose territory is said to have stretched from the Forth to the Wear, and whose main stronghold, *Din Eidyn*, was translated by the Angles as *Edinburgh*. In the course of the seventh century this territory gradually fell to the Angles invading from the south (whose drive north was finally halted by the Picts at the battle of Nechtansmere, in 685). However, part of the process which saw the subjection of the Gododdin is recorded by one of their bards in a long poem bearing their name. Poetry is not history, but the events to which the poem refers coincide broadly with chronicle accounts of the period. It seems that the king of Gododdin assembled an army, mainly of Britons, but including Picts and Scots, for a crusade against the heathen Anglo-Saxons, whose invasions from the south had been encroaching on British territory since the fifth century. The army feasted at Din Eidyn until the time seemed propitious, but on riding south was confronted by a much larger force of Angles at Catreath (Caterick). The Celtic army was annihilated but for the bard Aneirin, who survived to elegise, individually and collectively, the men of Gododdin. Thus in the Lothians the Britons were displaced by the Angles from Northumbria. To the west, the British kingdom of Strathclyde remained intact. With its capital at Dumbarton and its territory stretching into what is now north-west England, Strathclyde too had its closest linguistic links with the Britons to the south, though the bond was weakened as these were forced back to the mountains of Wales by the Anglo-Saxons. Another of the great Welsh bards, Taliesin, was a Strathclyde Briton. However, to the north of Strathclyde the other linguistic branch of the Celtic peoples, the Gaels, had established themselves, and it was this people and their language that proved the dominant force in moulding Scotland in the immediate future.

Coming and going between Ireland and the west of Scotland had occurred since earliest times, but in the course of the fifth century the Irish visitors, the Scots, consolidated at the expense of the Picts, establishing the kingdom of Dalriada in what is now Argyll. Closely related to its sister kingdom in Northern Ireland, Dalriada brought the Scottish mainland within the scope of great poetic tradition of the Gael. Simultaneously, the arrival of St Columba saw the spread of Celtic Christianity with its particular wisdom and beauty that is recalled in great illuminated scriptures, such as the Book of Kells which was created at Iona. The peculiar contribution of the Celtic church to the survival of Christianity can hardly be over-stated, at a time when all Christendom was prey to successive waves of marauding pagan tribes. For example, in the Middle Ages the abbey at Cluny in central France would emerge as the centre of the European monastic tradition. But Cluny was itself established by monks from a tiny monastery in Franche Comte which had been founded by Irish missionaries in the sixth century. Nearer home, Christianity had made initial inroads in Roman times through the mission of St Ninian in Galloway. From there, the mission had spread to Ireland, and it was now brought back across the Irish Sea by St Columba and his followers. From Iona, the monks carried their faith to the Picts as well as to the Angles of Northumbria. The resultant common ground greatly facilitated the process of integration.

In 843, the Scot, Kenneth mac Alpin, not without a degree of coercion, gained acceptance as ruler of a United Kingdom of Picts and Scots north of the Forth Clyde line known as Alba. Around 1014, Malcolm II defeated a Northumbrian army thereby securing the lands between the Forth and the Tweed. In 1034, his son Duncan, the king of Strathclyde, also succeeded his father as king of Alba. The three Celtic peoples together with the Angles of the south-east were then part of a single kingdom. Indeed, the Scottish crown would long continue either to hold or lay claim to much of Cumbria and Northumbria. To the south then, everything within the present border was by now part of the Scottish domain. To the north and west things were far less certain. In these centuries the Vikings were raiding, and later colonising in Scotland, Ireland and England. In Scotland, the Norsemen took and held the northern and western islands as well as Sutherland and Caithness. In reality, these far flung territories would fairly rapidly lose any deep connection with the Norwegian crown. Indeed this is also partially true of the relationship with the Scottish crown that regained the northern mainland by the end of the twelfth century, and was ceded the Western Isles in 1266.

Such was the situation as the first thousand years of the Christian era came to a close. Territorially, an entity approximating to our idea of Scotland had emerged. Within its boundaries however, there was as yet no such thing as a consciously Scottish people. The inhabitants of the Lothians were predominantly of Anglian stock, to the north and west there was a Norse presence, and within the majority Celtic population, there were, as we have seen, three distinct peoples, though the Gaelic influence had become the dominant one. Moreover, as Smout suggests, after the coming of Malcolm III, Celtic Scotland was itself to face a new challenge.

In 1068 Malcolm married the Saxon princess Margaret, and her arrival saw the beginning of a new phase of external influence which increased throughout the reigns of their sons and grandsons. Margaret's own time and influence was limited, but her establishment of a Benedictine monastery at Dunfermline indicated the start of a process whereby the unique features of the old Celtic church would be sacrificed to orthodoxy with the rest of Christendom. Christianity on a wide basis had come to Scotland and the north of England with the arrival of Columba and his disciples from Ireland. A generation later a mission from Rome, led by Augustine, spread from the south of England. The need to decide between divergences in practice, centrally with regard to the dating of Easter, were debated at the *Synod of Whitby* in 663 when the king of the Angles opted to follow the Roman practice. The Celtic monks withdrew to Iona. However, while the Scottish church differed from the rest of Europe in these matters, it was really a question of local custom, growing from isolation - an isolation increased by the encirclement of the Vikings in the eighth and ninth centuries - than any conscious dispute.

Thus isolated, the general form of the Celtic church continued untouched by European developments. The Celtic church was essentially monastic, its *Celi De*, or servants of God, (commonly *Culdees*) following spiritual 'rules' like other monks though often leading solitary eremitic lives. Unlike the continental orders, withdrawn from everyday life within their cloisters however, the Culdees were free to go abroad in the community. On the other hand, unlike secular clergy, they had not done much by way of developing things on a territorial and hierarchical basis. It was such anomalies that Margaret and those who followed her sought to remove. Margaret was a Saxon. However, her attitudes cannot simply be thought of as English influence. England itself was still at this time an ethnic melting pot. Indeed, the date of her flight to Scotland and subsequent marriage is indicative of the arrival in England, and soon in Scotland too, of a source of more widespread influence, the Normans.

The Scottish kings who succeeded Malcolm III, until the demise of the last of the line of 1286, were sympathetic towards the Norman arrivals, and their reigns saw the allocation of lands to Anglo-Norman incomers on a large scale, particularly in the lowlands. The Norman institutions were also imported all of them contributing to the creation of a more structured society. In the secular area, life began to take the hierarchical shape of Feudalism, while the establishment of burgh towns saw trade emerge in regularised form. The creation of territorial bishoprics, and of parishes within them had a similar organisational effect upon the church. In the secular field, the old Celtic tribal values for the most part managed to achieve a compromise with these new forces in the lowlands. In the highlands of the north-west however, Celtic traditions continued intact. In the church, Culdee ways were not suppressed, but they were allowed to die out. Old Culdee monastic communities were gradually superceded by new Continental orders, particularly Augustinian canons, who simultaneously adhered to a monastic rule, and served the spiritual needs of the lay community, at St Andrews for example, or Holyrood, and thus most closely resembled the Culdee manner. Elsewhere, fully enclosed orders, particularly the Cistercians who became established at

Dundrennan, Sweetheart, Newbattle and Melrose - to name but a few - were introduced. A glance at a map of religious foundations will suffice to convey the scale of this expansion of the European monastic orders. But note that this was European rather than English expansion and not a crusade against the Celtic church. The new orders were also new in Europe - the Cistercians, Augustinians, Premonstratensians and Tironensians, were founded in the twelfth century as expressions of spiritual renewal throughout Christendom, just as the Franciscan,

Dominican and Carmelite friars would be in the thirteenth century. The debt that Christendom owed to the Celtic west was noted. But there was also much that the Celtic west could gain from Christendom. Anyway as Smout puts it:

> 'Until the end of the thirteenth century Scotland was ruled by a succession of unusually able kings, the descendants of Malcolm Canmore and St Margaret, all of whom held the values of European Christendom more dear than the traditions of Celtic Alba whence they sprang'.

Architecturally, the period and its preoccupations have left many reminders. The feudal system involving the delegation of lands from the king downwards in return for service, called for the maintenance and protection of these lands at every level. Major strongholds such as Edinburgh and Stirling had been utilised from earliest times, but this need saw the proliferation of castles, at first wooden 'motte and baileys' - but gradually replaced by stone buildings which still mark the Scottish landscape.

More beautiful, and more culturally important are the cathedrals, churches and abbeys. Here, we must note the immense significance of such establishments as they functioned in their own day. The religious men and women who came to occupy them represented a considerable intellectual and moral core, at once Scottish - the successful assertion of independence against the claims to superiority of Canterbury and York, whereby the Scottish church was made a 'special daughter' of Rome was a crucial pre-requisite in the later struggle for general independence - and in full communion with the best of European thought. It would be quite wrong to present the period from the accession of Malcolm III in 1058 to the death of Alexander III in 1286 as being one of unqualified benevolence and prosperity. There are many negative sides to it. Racially, and therefore culturally, the influx and influence of an Anglo-French aristocracy in the lowlands could not but be resented, and at times resisted by the Alban Celts. On the other hand no real sense of Scottish identity had yet formed, and perhaps this influx was yet another factor contributing to the evolution of that identity.

At all events one cannot but remark on the lengthy continuity which the period presents. A glance at the extended reigns of most of the monarchs involved, (Alexander I - 17 years, David I - 29 years, Malcolm IV - 12 years, William the Lion - 49 years, Alexander II - 35 years, Alexander III - 37 years) contrasts sharply, not only with the carnage consequent upon the demise of their line, but also with the chaotic statistics of the Stewart dynasty. It would be fair to couple this continuity with a process of cultural and material expansion and an atmosphere of relative peace,and the fact that it is expressed in the great religious foundations of the borders, suggests more than that areas fertility. There must have been limited concern for the vulnerability of such investment to English aggression. Of course the period saw sporadic war with the English, but significantly, for the most part, it concerned the disputed ownership of Northumbria and Cumbria.

Ultimately these areas went to England, but it was really only thereafter, and for centuries to come, that the fertile border valleys and their great abbeys would become the easy prey of English aggression.

Yet these most enduring monuments of the medieval period are at once the most readily accessible. Centuries of English mayhem, reforming zeal, neglect and the fact that they supplied ready made masonry have left most of the great ecclesiastical buildings of the Middle Ages in ruins. Those that survive sufficiently to be in use, have normally been adapted to presbyterian worship, and have often been restored in a way detrimental to the original. Moreover, little of the internal furnishings and decoration such as woodwork, wall-paintings, tapestry and sculpture, survive - though the quality of what does, implies the scale of the loss. Yet enough remain: in the ruins of the great cathedrals and abbeys to form the basis of a fascinating study that gives a better insight into the period and a more lively appreciation of its complexity and achievements.

The medieval cathedral followed a basic building pattern, within which the particulars, and idiosyncrasies of the designers can be interpreted. Thus, in recognising the balance between pattern and particulars we have the basis of a mode of comparative study. On a more ambitious scale still perhaps, the layout of the major abbeys, which were in a sense self-contained university towns, in the same way adhere to a general design formula, though each has its own specific character. Moreover, the remains of different abbeys preserve different aspects of the abbey complex, so that in visiting the various sites you will understand a different piece of the whole. The HMSO booklet, *Scottish Abbeys*, gives you a good idea of the basic pattern, and indicates the strong points of some of the sites. It also supplies details of the dates and the particulars about the specific religious order connected to each abbey. Having read this you could visit one with the *specific* HMSO booklet describing the remains, in order to investigate the particular variety within the general order. In the process, this interesting pastime might develop your appreciation of the achievement and dedication of a very different age.

The accidental death of Alexander III at Kinghorn in 1286, and the subsequent loss of his only direct heir, the 'Maid of Norway', plunged the country into a misery of invasion and subjection that only ended with the victory at Bannockburn in 1314. Even then, though the integrity of a newly conscious Scottish nation was established, the reality of English power would remain a fact of life for centuries, until, it could be said, Scotland had become everything that England wished it to become. If this is so, the feeling that a better time had passed away with the events of 1286 has significance beyond the immediate consequences. In order to appreciate the cultural achievements of this period we must look to Celtic and to Latin. However, one oft-quoted fragment of early Scots poetry does provide a haunting memorial to the passing age:

Sen Alexander our king wes deid
That Scotland left in luve and lee,
Away wes sonse of aill and breid,
Of wine and wax, of gamin and glee.
The gold wes changit all in leid,
The frute failyeit on everilk tree.
Christ succour Scotland and remeid
That stad is in perplexitie.

(ii) The Wars of Independence

There were thirteen claimants to the vacant crown, most of them, including the main contenders, Robert Bruce and John Balliol, Anglo-Normans who also held lands in England of the English king. This circumstance, and the relatively cordial atmosphere that had existed between the two countries hitherto, prompted the Scots to invite Edward I of England to arbitrate over the torturous and potentially chaotic matter of succession. Edward however, immediately applied the situation to his plans for the annexation of anything he could annexe, in this case Scotland. The condition that he attached to his acceptance of the role of 'honest broker' was that the chosen candidate should acknowledge that he hold the lands and crown of Scotland of his feudal superior, namely the English king. The spiritual and temporal community in Scotland dismissed this pretention at once. It was however accepted by the contenders, including not only the successful Balliol, but also Bruce his disappointed rival.

Balliol's position was from the outset untenable. His 'overlord' Edward made humiliating demands which could not but undermine the Scottish king's authority. Most of the Scottish nobility had in any case favoured Bruce. Among the councils of the wise the whole idea of feudal subjection to England was unthinkable, particularly among the clergy, who had long since fought and won against English pretensions to ecclesiastical authority. Resentment was widespread among the population at large, and it is thus significant that this found focus with the emergence of a country gentleman from Paisley, Sir William Wallace. The bickering and willingness to capitulate by Anglo-Scottish nobles helped to articulate the sense of nationality among the population, and before the upheaval was over that nobility would itself have to choose which side of the Tweed it acknowledged.

In combination with a force led by Andrew de Moray, Wallace's army gradually regained from their English garrisons most of the strongholds north of the Forth-Clyde. The climax of the campaign came with the defeat of a large English army at

Stirling Bridge, and the capture of the castle in 1297. But defeat followed a year later at Falkirk, and Wallace's career ended in London with horrendous butchery. The struggle in Scotland continued with Robert Bruce, (the grandson of the original claimant) having eliminated John Comyn (the heir to Balliol's claim), leading the protracted campaign of resistance which culminated in the battle of Bannockburn in 1314. Military and political skirmishing continued for a decade and more, but after the rout at Bannockburn, Scotland always held the upper hand. By 1328, the independence of the Scottish kingdom had been formally acknowledged by the English, and the legitimacy of Bruce's kingship, and that of his heirs, approved by the Pope.

The experience of the Wars of Independence, in gradually bringing the disparate peoples of Scotland together against a common foe, did much to develop a common sense of nationhood. So much so in fact, that the celebrated *Declaration of Arbroath*, written probably by the abbot of Arbroath, Bernard de Linton (in Latin) to put the Scottish case to the Pope, is one of the most eloquent statements of national integrity ever written, ending in the famous assertion:

> *... as long as but a hundred of us remain alive, never will we on any conditions be brought under English rule. It is in truth not for glory, nor riches, nor honours that we are fighting, but for freedom - for that alone, which no honest man gives up but with life itself.*

Essentially, the Declaration voices the rights of the Scottish community. One of those rights is to choose "the Lord Robert" as its "Prince and King", and indeed the document itself enumerates the many ways in which Bruce had won the right through his actions. Perhaps in consideration of the feudal bargaining which began the whole business, the following remarkable qualification is included:

> *... Yet if he should give up what he has begun, and agree to make us or our kingdom subject to the King of England or the English, we should exert ourselves at once to drive him out as an enemy and a subverter of his own rights and ours, and make some other man who is well able to defend us our king...*

The proviso hardly applied to the hero-king Robert I, but the future would show the sense of such an attitude, as when Bruce's own son, David II, who had been captured by the English at Neville's Cross in 1346, and had been ransomed by his people for an economically crippling amount, suggested that, in order to be quit of the ransom payments, an agreement should be arrived at whereby the English king would succeed to the Scottish throne. Needless to say, the Scottish parliament rejected this proposal.

From Bruce's death in 1329, until the arrival of James I in 1424, Scotland was deprived of effective leadership, a prey to English interference, and when that abated to internal strife. The minority, and the personal reign of David II, saw almost as much destruction by Edward III as had been wrought by his grandfather. David died without heir, and the crown passed to the High Steward, the husband of his step-sister and first of the Stewart line, Robert II. This coincided with the beginning of a period of dynastic upheaval in England which eased the pressure from that direction. However, such was the weakness of both Robert II and his successor Robert III that this was only replaced by an era of internal anarchy as the great families elbowed for influence and control.

If we seek continuity and progress in this period we must look to the Church. One such development was the establishment of a university at St Andrews in 1412. Hitherto, Scottish scholars had for the most part attended the university at Paris. This was a time of schism in the church with two, and at one point three claimants to the Papacy, and different nations acknowledging different candidates. At first France and Scotland supported the same pope, but when France shifted allegiance, the disagreement virtually obliged the Scottish masters and students to withdraw from Paris. The dispute was temporary, but it was sufficient to see the displaced scholars establish a centre of learning under charter from Henry Wardlaw, bishop of St Andrews in 1412, which was solemnised by a papal Bull in 1414. Continental universities had produced Scots for service in the Church at home and abroad for centuries. Indeed the teachers at the new Scottish universities (Glasgow was founded by Bishop Turnbull in 1451, Aberdeen by Bishop Elphinstone in 1496), continued to study and teach on the Continent as well. But the establishment of home universities to which they could return, greatly accelerated the spread of ideas.

From the church too, the first identifiable author in Scots literature emerges. Both in language and content Archdeacon Barbour's *Bruce* gives expression to the heightened sense of identity, and independence of spirit that the long struggle with England had forged in the Scottish people.

The troubles were not all past however. Barbour was writing at a time when the unity of purpose that the Wars of Independence had created had all but dispersed, so that threats from without and dissention within continued to menace and impoverish the people. The nostalgic element in Barbour's poem, stressing the need to return to the values that had secured independence, is a subject to which, as in Holland's *Howlat* or Hary's *Wallace*, circumstances would cause the Scottish poet to return.

(iii) Late Medieval and Renaissance Scotland

The royal line that died with Alexander III had ruled by hereditary right, and Bruce in turn was finally acknowledged by all for his service to the nation. Conversely, to the nobility at least, the Stewart succession was no more than the result of a lucky marriage. Some questioned their right to the throne, and certainly rejected the right of such a dynasty to interfere or impose on other noble families on their own lands. This, together with weak government, created the anarchy that continued virtually unabated till the crowning of James I in 1424, on his release from eighteen years of English captivity on the payment of yet another ransom. The new Stewart set about asserting his authority, exiling or executing those who threatened it, either by their actions or by having an equal claim to the throne. Stewart assertion and noble resistance long continued to be the pattern of existence of the great, and morally there seems little between the two.

When James I was killed in 1437, his murderers had grounds for claiming to have killed a tyrant. But few of the general population agreed, for, whatever else, a strong ruler meant better order, and progress and prosperity required order. The personal reigns of James I, James II, and even the impractical James III, were in this respect preferable by far to the long periods of minority rule and disputed regencies that came between them. As elsewhere in Europe however, progress and prosperity did accelerate, perhaps reaching its most self-confident phase in the reign of James IV. But, ending as it did in the disaster of Flodden, the nation's well-being would thereafter be overshadowed by its vulnerability.

The material expansion of the fifteenth century was accompanied by intensified artistic activity. In the centres of growth, the trading burghs, merchants and craftsmen erected beautiful churches such as St Michael's in Linlithgow, St John's in Perth, and the church of the Holy Rood in Stirling. The nobility commissioned collegiate churches, of which the chapel at Roslin is perhaps the most elaborate example. Despite later destruction, survivals like the van der Goes altarpiece from Holy Trinity church in Edinburgh, or the choir stalls in St Salvators in Aberdeen attest to quality or the internal furnishings. There is evidence too of the tradition of intricate church music and song with which such buildings echoed. The most accomplished composer whose music has survived is Robert Carver, who flourished in the earlier part of the sixteenth century. It is only now that the quality of Carver's Renaissance music is being recognised, and a ten part mass of his has been successfully revived. Finally, the period also witnessed a great flowering of Scottish poetry.

To a tradition that started with the epic strains of Barbour's *Bruce*, James I added the language of courtly love and of Boethian philosophy with the *Kingis Quair*. A philosophical tone is a feature of much medieval poetry. We see it again later, particularly in Gavin Douglas's *Palice of Honour* and in his great *Eneados*, while in the fifteenth century itself, we have Henryson's *Orpheus and Eurydice* and of course the *Testament of Cresseid*. Of special interest to us here, are the poems in which Henryson applies his learning to the world around him, the *Moral Fables*.

Again in medieval fashion, Henryson's main concern is with 'eternal verities', and his view of his world is primarily concerned with its relationship to those verities. Hence the fable form, the worldly context of the 'taill' followed by the eternal definition of the "moralitas". Having said that, some interesting insights into fifteenth century Scotland still emerge.

Every class of society is to be found in the *Fables*. For example *The Uplandis Mous and the Burgess Mous* contrasts the poor countrywoman with her aspiring middle-class sister in a way that pokes fun at the latter's accumulation of privileges and self-esteem.

> *This rurall mous into the winter-tyde*
> *Had hunger, cauld, and tholit grit distres;*
> *The uther mous that in the burgh can byde,*
> *Was gild-brother and made ane fre burges -*
> *Tol-fre als, but custum mair or les,*
> *And fredome had to ga quhairever scho list,*
> *Amang the cheis in ark, and meill in kist.*

The lion, in *The Lyoun and the Mous* could well be read as a criticism of James III:

> *Ane potestate, or yit ane king with croun -*
> *Quhilk suld be walkrife gyde and governour*
> *Of his pepill - that takis na labour*
> *To reule and steir the land and justice keip,*
> *Bot lyis still in lustis, sleuth and sleip.*

The ills springing from this absence of strong government are referred to repeatedly in the *Fables* - the breakdown of law, and the consequent oppression of the poor by the unrestrained "wolves".

> *The pure pepill this lamb may signifie -*
> *As* **maill-men,** *merchandis and all laboureris, (tenant farmers)*
> *Of quhome the lyfe is half ane purgatorie*
> **To wyn with lautie leving as efferis;** *(trying to earn an honest living)*
> *The wolf betakinnis fals extortioneris*
> *And oppressouris of pure men - as we see -*
> *Be violence or craft in facultie.*

The Wolf and the Lamb

Essentially, might is right, and its right is upheld by "fals perverteris of the lawis". This is the case even in the consistory, the ecclesiastical court which is the setting of the *Scheip and the Doig*, and where the innocent sheep is duly condemned:

> *Seis Thow not Lord, this warld overturnit is,*
> *As quha wald change gude gold in leid or tyn?*
> *The pure is peillit; the lord may do na mis;*
> *And simonie is haldin for na syn.*

Even in Henryson's day, the Church was not without a taint of corruption that would contribute to the Reformation crisis in less than two hundred years time. "Simonie", the sale of Church offices, was at the heart of the problem. But at this early stage in the process, Henryson's perception of the problem is very different from that of the Reformers. For him, the essence of the business is the effort of the temporal power, the crown, to impose its authority over the Church in the selection of religious appointments. The years that followed would increasingly see noble favourites and illegitimate royalty endowed with bishoprics and abbacies and the wealth that went with them, so that despite outstanding exceptions, the Church was pretty corrupt by the middle of the sixteenth century. But from Henryson's viewpoint, the corruption comes, not from the Church itself but from outside interference in an institution whose independence should be sacred.

Thus in *The Parliament of Beistis*, when a lion-king whose description parallels the Scottish monarchy commands all creatures to attend his parliament and submit to his authority, only the grey mare fails to turn up and is therefore in contempt of court. When the king's ambassadors, significantly the wolf and the fox, seek to force her to appear, she defies them, and by implication him. "The moralitas" describes the temporal ruler in terms of his flaw - his assumption that all can be reduced to his, temporal terms:

> *The lyoun is the warld be liknes*
> *To quhome loutis baith empriour and king,*
> *And thinkis of this warld to get incres.*

The mare is that which is beyond his terms, and defies his attempt to reduce her to those terms. Ultimately, she is the Church herself:

> *The mere is men of contemplation,*
> *Of Pannance, walkand in the wildernes,*
> *As monkis and other men of religioun*
> *That Presis God to pleis in everilk place.*

This is a simple example of the spiritual qualification of temporal reality which is everywhere often in more complex ways, the basis of Henryson's social criticism. But short of that, there are as indicated many contemporary references in the *Fables*. If what has been mentioned is for the most part serious, such is the nature of conditions referred to It should not obscure the fact that the *Fables* are often funny, especially in the delightful touches with which Henryson gives personal character to his animals. The social criticisms provide a corrective to the catalogue of cultural achievement that marks the period. At the same time, Henryson poetic mastery, and the wealth of learning that clearly supports his work expresses the extent of that achievement.

A generation later in the nation's capital, William Dunbar's poetry continues to convey the close proximity of refinement and squalor. He wishes the king's return to Edinburgh:

> That sone out of your panis fell
> Ye may in hevin heir with us dwell,
> To eit swan, cran, pertrick, and plover,
> And every fische that swymis in rever;
> To drynk with us the new fresche wyne
> That grew upoun the rever Ryne,
> Fresche fragrant clairettis out of France,
> Of Angers and of Orliance,
> With mony ane cours of grit dyntie:
> Say ye amen for cheritie.
>   (A Dirige)

This is that same town described in "To the Merchants of Edinburgh":

> May nane pas throw your principall gaittis
> For stink of haddokis and scattis,
> For cryis of carlingis and debaittis,
> For fensum flyttingis of defame.

Later in the same poem, Dunbar voices a social and moral criticism reminiscent of Henryson:

> Your proffeit daylie dois incres,
> Your godlie workis les and les;
> Through streittis nane may mak progres
> For cry or cruikit, blind and lame:
> Think ye not schame,
> That ye sic substance dois posses
> And will nocht win ane bettir name?

All told, the Scotland of James IV presents a mixture of grotesquery, glitter and genuine excellence, at times conveying a dilution of medieval ideals, at others expressing the vigour of the Renaissance. If Dunbar's poetry (and that of his younger contemporary Gavin Douglas) indicates something of the latter, it also rails against the debasement of those ideals, and as a whole it supplies a vivid impression of the end of an age.

In 1513, an awesome percentage of the adult male population was destroyed at Flodden. England did not immediately invade, life went on, and in that sense the school of thought that indicates the limits of the catastrophe has a point. Nevertheless, it could be argued that thereafter, via the Reformation, the Union of

Crown and the Union of Parliaments - albeit they coincided with certain Scottish interests -Scotland had little option but to move in the direction dictated by London, or be punished. The so called 'Rough Wooing', of 1544-45, could be seen as a heightened expression of a longer term situation.

Such vulnerability did not however stifle creative and intellectual life. The Church could still produce a scholar like John Major, whose *History of Greater Britain* was published at Paris in 1521. After yet another period of regency the new king James V sought to bolster the rule of law by establishing a supreme College of Justice in 1531, while in another direction, his reign saw great architectural activity, with the palaces at Falkland, Holyrood, Stirling and Linlithgow acquiring tone of the Renaissance. In literature, the tradition was continued pre-eminently by Sir David Lindsay. The matter of Lindsay's greatest work, *Ane Satyre of the Thrie Estaitis* is clear from its title.

Criticism, in what is at the same time a very comic play, is aimed at those traditional oppressors of the poor, the lords spiritual and temporal, and the burgesses.

> *As for our reverent fathers of Spirituality,*
> *They are led by Covetice, this carl, and Sensuality,*
> *And as ye see, Temporality has need of correctioun,*
> *Whilk has lang time been led by Public Oppressioun.*
>
> ...
>
> *Lo, here is Falset and Deceit weill I ken,*
> *Leaders of the Merchants and silly craitsmen.*

While the nobility and the merchants accept correction, the lords spiritual defy their critics, and it is clearly this last group that are most seriously satirised. The corruption continued. But the shift in perspective which separates Lindsay's response from that of Henryson is a telling one, which indeed relates to the demise of the medieval social order. That is to say, the source of correction to which the play implicitly appeals is the crown - the more so in the light of the precedent recently supplied by Henry VIII. In a sense this looks not to the correction, but to the culmination of a process that Henryson had recognised in his day, whereby the corruption of the Church was seen to stem from the ambition of the crown itself. Indeed this royal, and by extension national assertion, and the related decline of a united Christendom, is a central concern in any study of Reformation and Renaissance Europe.

In any event, until his death soon after another crushing defeat from the English at Solway Moss (1542) James V maintained the link with Rome, as did his queen, thereafter the Regent, Mary of Guise (their daughter, the future Queen Mary, being one week old). From then until 1560, France and England disputed the Scottish soul. Throughout the 1540's the armies of Henry VIII wrought periodic devastation in Scotland. In reaction, Mary of Guise sought the assistance of French troops and in 1558 her daughter Mary married the dauphin. Meanwhile a Protestant England required a Protestant Scotland, and but for the reign of Mary Tudor, Scottish reformers found succour and support there. In 1560 a group of Scottish noblemen, the Lords of the Congregation, most of them either political enemies of the crown, or seeking to gain from the redistribution of church lands, allied themselves against the regent in a conflict that ended, a month after the death of Mary of Guise, in

Mary of Guise, attributed to Cornielle de Lyon.
Scottish National Portrait Gallery.

the Treaty of Edinburgh and a triumph for the Protestant party. And yet the profundity of this historical watershed, not only in the religious sense, but with regard to consequent relationships with England is probably clearer to us now than at the time. Changes within the church were, at first, relatively gradual. In 1561, a Catholic queen was to return from France. In Latin, the greatest of Scottish humanists George Buchanan was at work, while in Scots Alexander Scott, a poet probably in sympathy with the Reformers, could welcome the Catholic queen in terms of moderation and reconciliation that envisage a continuity that in fact was not to be:

> This guid New Yeir we hoip with grace of God
> salbe of peax, tranquilitie and rest:
> this yeir sall rycht and ressone rewle the rod,
> quhilk sa lang seasoun hes bene soir supprest:
> (Ane New Yeir Gift to the Quene Mary)

REFORMATION AND UNION: SOME SPECIAL CULTURAL EFFECTS

OBJECTIVES

The preceding section included some elementary description of the sequence of historical events, because we were dealing with a period prior to that covered by Part I. The questions considered now relate to events that fall within the scope of that Guide. The remaining sections should therefore be correspondingly brief, being concerned only with aspects of the intellectual and cultural response and reaction to these events. In the present section we can consider how such matters relate to:

❂— the Reformation, and the course of religious controversy,

❂— the Union of Crowns, the Union of Parliaments and the growing relationship with England,

❂— some remarks on 17th century domestic architecture.

SOME MAJOR THEMES

(i)   Reformation and its aftermath; some cultural effects

In Part II, reference is made to Sir Richard Maitland's commentary on the Reformation period:

> Quhair is the blythnes that hes bein
> bayth in burgh and landwart sein,
> amang lordis and ladyis shein,
> daunsing, singing, game and play?
> Bot now I wait nocht quhat thai mein:
> all mirriness is worne away.

Of Maitland, MacQueen in his introduction to *Ballattis of Luve* writes:

He wrote during the troubled personal reign of Queen Mary and in the midst of the Reformation, a movement historically inevitable, no doubt, however far the social and artistic consequences went towards destroying Scottish culture and civilization.

A stark statement, and one which can perhaps be counter-balanced by the argument that sees the logical emphasis in Calvinist theology as evolving the cast of thought that would see Scotland excel in the eighteenth century 'Age of Reason'. In fact we need to acknowledge both positions, but MacQueen's point does remind us that to take one direction involves the abandonment of another. At any rate, it is difficult to see the period from Reformation to Enlightenment as one of cultural continuity. Smout, (171-184) attempts it. In doing so though, he has to look either to early examples -citing Montgomerie, the Catholic poet of James VI's court - or very late ones - the scientific enquiries of secular minds after the Restoration. What signs of intellectual life he finds in between come almost invariably from the Episcopalian stronghold of Aberdeen and its university. There is indeed a profound connection between Calvinism and the nature of the eighteenth century Enlightenment, but it is not entirely one of straightforward progression. The second half of Smout's chapter, "The Persecution of Witchcraft" is enough to alert us to this.

In the years immediately after 1560, there remained some room for creative activity. The intensity of the new puritanism, and the extent of its control, really came into its own with the arrival of Andrew Melville in 1574. Even then, the court continued to provide some haven for the poet until 1603. Thus, Queen Mary could accommodate the reforming tendencies of Alexander Scott, while the Catholic, Alexander Montgomerie, was the major poet at the court of James VI. Already though, there were signs of cultural decline. In the preceding section there are some lines from Henryson's *Parliament of Beistis*. If your own version differs from this, it is because it has been based on a text that has been altered in accordance with reforming principles. Similarly, in Dundee, the Wedderburn brothers were producing *The Gude and Godlie Ballats* in which 'profane', which is simply to say secular, songs are cobbled, not without incongruity, into hymns. Alexander Hume, who had written the marvelous "Of the Day of Estivall" in his youth, turned to the production of "sacred songs where the richt use of poesie may be espied". In the introduction already mentioned, MacQueen notes that Alexander Scott's poetic decline can be traced as his religious fervour increased.

It is crucial, of course, to acknowledge the idealism and elevated intentions of many of the most enthusiastic reformers. Our secular age has negative assumptions about all things puritanical. But we must recognise that at its noblest, the presbyterian programme sought to establish the City of God on earth, a society that would be a true human reflection of the will of the Creator. Nevertheless, such a programme does seem to have been contrary to the continuation of the cultural traditions of the nation. Beyond obvious factors such as censorship, a distrust of beauty, and the fact that a people with a vision of the *Civitas Dei* simply have different priorities, there does seem to be a deeper, perhaps psychological break with the cultural past in the Calvinist definition of existence.

The very form of Henryson's *Moral Fables* could be taken as an illustration of the medieval assumption that existence is an inter-relationship between the everyday human world, and the higher spiritual reality. It is an assumption that is implicit in all the art and literature of the age. Human imperfection ensures that there is a tension between the two, but it was this tension that Christ's sacrifice had reconciled, and that the symbols and the sacraments of the medieval church continuously restated. As a result, human existence both temporal and eternal could be viewed positively, and expressed thus in cultural terms. In a way, the precision of Calvinist theology seems to have struck at the heart of this accommodation. Mediation, other than Christ's original sacrifice, could not be countenanced. The artistic symbols of such mediation were pulled down, the sacraments were dismissed or downgraded, by extension, the assumption hitherto at the heart of the cultural tradition was denied. Logic and enthusiasm evolved a religious absolutism worthy of saints. But how, in psychological terms, was human imperfection to be catered for, and what place could there be for the artist and the poet, where that which was not sacred was profane.

Hawthornden on the River North Esk, Midlothian.

As we saw, the removal of the court in 1603 further weakened the cultural position in several ways. Religious fervour coupled with political strife culminated in civil warfare that with varying intensity typified much of the seventeenth century, with the apocalyptic fervour of the more extreme Covenanters a major feature of the period. Amid the chaos, the literary tradition lingered in the Latin of the Aberdeen Doctors, and the slightly forced English of Drummond of Hawthornden. Thus, what cultural life remained was largely an Episcopalian effort, and we tend to think of that quarter when we seek evidence of moderation and sense in an inordinately intolerant century. But a closer look at the issues might qualify this conclusion. It will be recalled that the essential political aspect of the Reformation, in Scotland as elsewhere, was that it saw the establishment of a state church. We may shudder at Melvillian ideas of theocracy, a state ruled by the church, but at the same time we can sympathise with Presbyterian defiance of the pretensions of the state, in the person of the monarch, to church leadership, as accepted by the Episcopalian and Anglican systems.

Henryson noted the tendency as early as the fifteenth century, and indeed in resisting it, Covenanters and Catholics, such as John Ogilvie, were strangely united in martyrdom at the hands of Episcopalian authorities. All in all, the issues and values of the period are complex and far removed from us, and any modern interpretation which illustrates the righteousness of any particular cause, is quite simply a distortion. On the other hand, it should be perfectly possible to recognise the various virtues in presbyterianism, Episcopalianism and Catholicism. Doing so, the differences might cease to be points of contention and begin to be valid aspects of a single heritage.

Having said that, Calvinist theology was the most important psychological influence upon Scottish life in the century and a half after the Reformation, and the cultural effects of this have been indicated. However, in the course of the eighteenth century Scotland witnessed a great intellectual flowering. This too, in its way, was coloured by the Calvinist experience. But we will look at this in the next section.

(ii) The Union of Crowns, the Union of Parliaments and the growing relationship with England

Frae bank to bank, frae wood to wood I rin
Owrhailit with my feeble fantasie,
Like til a leaf that fallis from a tree,
Or til a reed owrblawin with the wind.
Twa gods guides me: the ane of them is blin,
Yae, and a bairn brocht up in vanitie;
The nixt a wife ingenerit of the sea
And lichter nor a dauphin with her fin.

Unhappie is the man for evermair
That tills the sand and sawis in the air;
But twice unhappier is he, I lairn,
That feedis in his hairt a mad desire,
And follows on a woman throu the fire,
Led by a blin, and teachit by a bairn.

Mark Alexander Boyd (1563-1601) is a relatively minor figure in the annals of the older Scots poetic tradition, writing at the very point of its extinction. He wrote mainly in Latin, but his one sonnet in Scots is sufficient to stun the mind as to how such a subtle, complex medium, partaking of all the shared heritage of European literature, could in a generation be rendered obsolete by the political ambition of the Stewarts. The general direction of events thereafter, is outlined in Part II Section 4. What learned writing continued during the seventeenth century was voiced in Latin or English. In Scots, the most famous and influential poem of the century is Robert Sempill's "Habbie Simpson".

Written probably about forty years after Boyd's sonnet, it is introduced thus:

The Epitaph of Habbie Simson
Who on his drone bore mony flags;
He made his cheeks as red as crimson
And Babbed when he blew his bags.

There had always been a legitimate place for such verse. But we are met with little else for nigh on a century so that when Fergusson and Burns, poets of genius, sought to revive literary Scots, they did so, not only in defiance of the English linguistic ascendancy, but also effectively unconscious of the great literary tradition that had existed before the Union of 1603.

Though generally unpopular, it is no doubt the case that the incorporating Treaty of Union of 1707, loosely coincided with the beginning of a period of economic expansion, which found obvious illustration in the efforts of the gentry in imitating the ways of their more sophisticated English neighbours. We can too easily perhaps take this as a simple matter of cause and effect. Scottish poverty relative to England immediately prior to the Union was doubtless exaggerated by the worst century of civil strife since the time of Bruce - a comparison for the year 1507 would be far less stark for example. At the same time, Scottish prosperity before the Union was actively thwarted - see Part I, Section 6 - until such times as Scotland's position had been arranged to English satisfaction, and in the face of Scottish opinion, by the political settlement of 1707.

We can nevertheless understand that in these circumstances a poet such as James Thomson might see himself in a British context, and write his very considerable poetry in English. Conversely we can see the linguistic preference of Fergusson and Burns as a reaction against the political demise of Scotland, and the accelerated dilution of national identity that this implied. For Fergusson, writing in the early 1770's, it is still very much the central political question.

Black be the day, that e'er to England's ground
Scotland was eikit by the Union's bond.'
    ("The Ghaists")

There are many more powerful statements of a similar sentiment in Burns - "Parcel of Rogues", to go no further. Overall though, his tone is elegaic. His Jacobite sympathies are sentimental - as he is himself aware - while his political concerns are radically complicated by the revolutions in America and in France. However, given the linguistic pressures involved, political relationships with England since 1603 have had the most profound implications for the Scottish writer, as the poets of the eighteenth century revival demonstrate.

(iii) A Note on Architecture

The seventeenth century was a lean time for the arts in general. The conditions outlined in (i) above would have an even more obviously detrimental effect on visual arts such as painting and sculpture than on literature. However, this might be an appropriate time to note some architectural developments. Most of the architectural references in section I of this booklet related to religious establishments, since the most impressive monuments to medieval buildings are of this order.

There is little of note in that field in the period we are considering here, but the trends in secular architecture are not without interest. Most of the royal palaces were in existence before the Reformation, and indeed were already marked by Renaissance influences, but expansion continued during the seventeenth century - at Holyrood Palace for example - so that they can

Edinburgh Castle

be thought of in the present context. Elsewhere, the period shows change, as well as what could be seen as the culmination of some particularly Scottish architectural forms, both in the country tower houses and the tenements of Edinburgh. Life remained sufficiently risky to discourage the development of the equivalent of the Tudor mansion in Scotland. On the other hand, gunpowder had long since rendered the awesome defensive buildings of the Middle Ages obsolete. There was little point in having twenty-foot thick walls anymore, though the need for doors and windows defendable by a few inmates remained. The result was the sort of combination of features that are known as Scots Baronial. Meanwhile, the stone tenements being erected in Edinburgh - Gladstone's Land is a good example - in their own way reflected aspects of the same style. However, in the course of the century that was to follow, architecture, along with every other aspect of Scottish life and culture was to be profoundly re-defined.

ENLIGHTENMENT AND ROMANTICISM 1746-1832

OBJECTIVES

Your aim here is:

✸— to consider how the cultural advances of the period relate to the historical situation from which they emerged,

✸— to try to grasp the essential tone of the Enlightenment by looking at one or two major figures,

✸— to look at some of the ways in which the spirit of the period manifested itself in art and architecture.

SOME MAJOR THEMES

(i)   The Roots of Enlightenment

Bearing in mind the qualification registered in the preceding section, it is nevertheless the case that the economic opportunities available to Scotland expanded after 1707. Trade, production and wealth were on the increase, thus enhancing the lifestyle and leisure of the Scottish middle class, whence most of the major figures of the eighteenth century would emerge. At the same time, an understandable reaction against religious extremism, likewise served to turn the mind towards the business of the material world. This trend of event was not unique. As in Scotland, so in England and the Continent, the seventeenth century had seen religious fervour fight itself to a standstill. Likewise, the eighteenth century Enlightenment was a European experience, and not particular to Scotland. The remarkable thing about events in Scotland is rather a matter of degree. On the one hand there is the exceptional intensity of seventeenth century puritanism, and the consequent cultural dearth on the other, there is the unique achievement, in virtually every field of thought, of eighteenth century Scotsmen. As we know, this was once defined simply as the benevolent effects of the Union of Parliaments. But it has been pointed out that this distortion arises from restricting our comparison to the preceding century. If we take the longer view we recognise that the Scottish Enlightenment was but the resumption of a much older intellectual tradition, albeit the tone of this latest expression was influenced by the Calvinist experience in the intervening period.

As to the effects of that influence, and firstly in relation to material conditions, we must acknowledge Max Weber's famous thesis suggesting, as its title indicates, a relationship between *The Protestant Ethic and the Spirit of Capitalism*. While Smout rightly qualifies this proposal he concludes thus:

> We are not claiming that Calvinism 'caused' economic growth: all it did was to ensure that when the opportunity came for that growth, after many other preconditions had been fulfilled, the Scots would be a nation psychologically well equipped to exploit the situation to the full.

Essentially, the Calvinist years promoted a seriousness of purpose and self-discipline ideally suited to the exploitation of economic opportunities in a later, more secular age. If this in turn facilitated cultural growth then by extension Smout can conclude that:

> if we take the long view of Scottish history it does become difficult not to believe that Calvinism contributed certain things which could hardly help but favour the expansion of economic activity and the enrichment of cultural life.

The other area in which Calvinism could be said to have prepared the ground for the Enlightenment is in the field of education. An emphasis on education and on its expansion is a feature of Scottish society long before the Reformation. However, the Reformers continued this policy with renewed vigour. Of course, this was largely promoted by the need to ensure the establishment and maintenance of the reformed religion. Such was the principal end of the schools, while, with the exception of Episcopalian Aberdeen, the universities languished under Calvinist orthodoxy. Thus says Smout:

> Whatever the material condition of the middle and upper classes, and of the universities, it is hard to imagine that a cultural golden age could have come into being in the chilling religious atmosphere of the seventeenth century. ... Thanks to the very strict control that the presbyterian system of church courts from the kirk-session to the General Assembly exercised over the minutiae of national and parish life before 1712 it either destroyed or came near to destroying the Scottish tradition in poetry, painting, music and drama.

This account could seem to sit uneasily with the preceding extract from Smout, and yet both statements are accurate enough in their own terms. To begin with, an education system existed that a more liberal society might exploit. Beyond this, it could be said that Calvinism, with its distrust of mysticism, and its emphasis upon a logical approach to religion, promoted a tone of thought that would feel the need to rationally consider the propositions emerging from philosophy and the natural sciences, even where these challenged Calvinist orthodoxy itself. Thus in the course of the eighteenth century a group of liberal Presbyterian theologians established themselves in the Scottish universities, centring their beliefs on the all benevolent creator that reason and science seemed to perceive. By extension, the period saw a people long skilled in logical argument, gradually released upon the entire field of intellectual inquiry. The results were indeed remarkable.

We shall now look briefly at some of them. Before doing so however, we should make mention of the legacy of the Calvinist years. If liberal 'New Licht' theology had joined the Age of Reason, the truths of orthodoxy continued to be maintained by traditional 'Auld Licht' Calvinists, though the power of the latter had obviously begun to decline. Given the rigid conclusions of these truths - a reprobate world qualified only by an arbitrary predestination - there had always been a tension between them, and the muddled reality of human life. The new theology saw the need to accommodate that reality. In doing so, it could be said to have formalised the tension, so that while Calvinist tradition lingered, the new men lived, conscious that by the terms of their own religious background their attitudes stood condemned.

We find illustration of such tensions in the writers who re-emerged at this period. Possibly the most stark example is the contrast between the convivial world of Robert Fergusson's poetry, and the spiritual despair in a bedlam to which it led. We should not make too much of this perhaps, but it could be noted that the shadow of a similar religious melancholia can be found widely among Scottish writers of the period, from Bothwell and Hume, to Burns and Byron. More fruitfully, on the resumption of Scottish writing, the psychological contortions which the dichotomy between Calvinist ideals and human reality could promote, provided a subject area that would be richly exploited - from Burns' "Holy Willie" and the "Unco Guid", to Hogg's *Justified Sinner*, several of Stevenson's stories besides *Jekyll and Hyde* itself, and even as an aspect of the wider historical and cultural tensions in Scott's fiction.

(ii) Enlightenment: the Age of Reason

From references in Parts I and II, as well as the surveys contained in the set texts - Ferguson and Smout, Wittig and Watson - it will be clear that Scottish culture in the eighteenth century excelled in many areas. Setting aside literature and the visual arts, important original work was done in history, in various scientific and social scientific fields and in philosophy. Perhaps if we are to strike the keynote of the period however, we should look to the last mentioned, philosophy, in that it is the discipline that most squarely faced the theology that had dominated the preceding era, and in doing so, sought to replace it with a principle of inquiry and experiment that was the impetus behind the wider intellectual burgeoning. The rejection of Calvin and the espousal of rationalism by the university theologians themselves, was probably the crucial factor facilitating change. Men such as William Robertson, the principal of Edinburgh University and Francis Hutcheson, the professor of moral philosophy at Glasgow typified the shift. In a sense though this mating of rationalism and religion contained unforeseen implications for the latter. A greater thinker, David Hume, was to subject religion to a rational investigation of such an intensity as to seriously question the foundations, not only of traditional dogmas, but of rational religion itself.

Hume's major philosophical work, A *Treatise of Human Nature*, was published in 1739, followed by *Essays Moral and Political*, 1741-2. He then turned to history for a time, but came back to philosophy to re-define the terms of his original *Treatise* in a series of E*nquiries* and *Dissertations*, between 1748 and 1757. It is not possible here to cope with such complexities. However, in an earlier Open University course on T*he Enlightenment* (Units 8-9 Hume's Enquiry concerning Moral Principles, p.58), Stuart Brown points to the following telling statement in that E*nquiry*:

> Men are now cured of their passion for hypotheses and systems in natural philosophy, and will hearken to no arguments but those which are derived from experience. It is full time that they should attempt a like reformation in all moral disquisitions; and reject every system of ethics, however subtle or ingenious, which is not founded on fact and observation.

As Brown continues:

> These statements tell us something about Hume's perception of the intellectual climate of his time and how he saw his own work in relation to it. A new spirit of inquiry had been started by. Francis Bacon (1561-1626) and brought to fruition in physics by the great work of Isaac Newton (1642-1727). Hume's ambition was to accomplish for the 'science of man' what Newton had accomplished for physics.

This gives us some idea of the scope of the project Hume set himself. He was careful to stress that in his study of man, he did not seek the kind of absolute truths that form the bases of mathematics. The imperfection of human nature made such an end inappropriate. But what he did propose, was an investigation of humanity based upon *empirical* judgement - that is judgement *based solely on experience* - such as would be employed by a scientist like Newton. Conversely, he rejected as unworthy of consideration "hypotheses and systems", that is the effort or claim to perceive truths *a priori*, or *without benefit of experience*. To do so was to dismiss the assumptions on which traditional religion was founded. Another unit of the course on T*he Enlightenment*, (Unit 28, *Hume's Essays on Miracles and Providence*) deals with two of his most direct critiques of the religious view. Hume did not altogether deny the possibility of a distant Creator, but he concluded that, since there was no way in which we could ever know anything about him, there was no meaning in our seeking to do so. As to miracles - and we must remember how far the religion of the day was based upon belief in the miracles of the Bible - and the idea of a knowable God, a "particular providence", they were, in terms of empirical judgement, unbelievable.

As we know, even in rational Scotland, Hume's views went too far for him to be offered a university chair. Yet as indicated, perhaps his position is a logical result of promoting the relationship of religion and pure reason. In any case, Hume's contribution to the evolution of human thought is great, not only in the field of pure reason, but perhaps also in a sense, in the religious field as well. It could be said that his work, and the rational mood it promoted, in turn prompted the kind of re-definition of the 'spiritual' viewpoint, and reconsideration of *a priori* modes of thought which, for example, could be said to be a major strand of Romanticism. If this strand is less prominent in Scotland itself, it could be because of the depth of eighteenth century rationalism, and, in turn, the logical emphasis of the Calvinism against which it reacted, yet from which it sprung.

As to Hume's rational morality itself, a section by Nicholas Phillipson entitled "Hume: the Philosopher as Citizen" (*The Enlightenment*, Unit 28), explains his position both as to private morality and public obligation. Hume believed that tolerant and benevolent moral judgements will emerge from the kind of social interaction that encourages the consideration of the other person's point of view, and his *Enquiries and Essays* sought to promote such attitudes:

David Hume, by Louis Carrogis. Scottish National Portrait Gallery

> *... he proposed to discuss the different beliefs men and women held about moral, political and literary matters in such a way that his readers would not only be amused, but would learn to be more tolerant, less dogmatic about their prejudices.* (Phillipson)

Particularly important perhaps in Hume's secular context, was that this formula for personal morality should extend to the public arena through which the nation's position would be increasingly defined, that is to say in politics. Party factionalism was for him as barbarous a religious factionalism, and just as inappropriate in the age of reason:

> *True civic virtue consisted in cultivating a political detachment that would enable men to hold their political prejudices in check and evaluate them in the light of the central problem of learning how best to preserve the rules of justice in a complex, commercially orientated society. In other words, cultivating a conscientious indifference to party political warfare and learning to respect those governments which tried to administer the laws fairly and to preserve the rules of justice was, for Hume, the mark of the virtuous citizen in the modern age.* (Phillipson)

With hindsight, we might well question the viability of Hume's proposals with regard to both public and private morality. But his belief in an essential human benevolence that reason can nurture, was the desirable end inspiring the many illustrious thinkers of his age, just as his experimental method inspired them by defining the means to those ends.

Of the many major figures in philosophy, history and the sciences of Hume's generation and soon after, one other, Adam Smith, demands individual mention. Like Hume, his importance is underlined by his position in the course on *The Enlightenment*, (Units 25-27) and below we again utilise Brown's remarks. A philosopher himself, holding the chairs of Logic, and later Moral Philosophy at Glasgow, Smith again demonstrates the relationship between philosophical theory and social application, his major works being his ethical inquiry entitled *Theory of Moral Sentiments* (1759), together with the bible of the emerging science of political economy, *The Wealth of Nations* (1776). As a student in Glasgow, he encountered both academic excellence and commercial boom. The university was dominated by Francis Hutcheson, himself:

> ... *author of* **An Inquiry into the Original of Our Ideas of Beauty and Virtue** (1725) *and an inspiring lecturer on ethics, aesthetics and political economy, holding views about 'the moral sense', 'natural religion', 'utility', etc., broadly speaking akin to those of Hume and later of Adam Smith himself.*

At the same time:

> *Glasgow was not only a centre for intellectual activity, it was also at this time expanding very rapidly in size and commercial prosperity. One of the main features of the treaty of Union with England was that Scotland should henceforth be allowed to trade on equal terms with England, and as a result of this Glasgow had developed a flourishing trade with the American plantations. The city had become the chief emporium for American tobacco, which (under the 'mercantile system') foreign countries were not allowed to import directly. Thus, some three-quarters of the tobacco from America was transhipped in Glasgow, before distribution in the Mediterranean, the Baltic, and the North Sea. Clydeside merchants grew rich, and sometimes adopted the ostentatious way of life of 'merchant princes'. The topic of trade was on everyone's lips, and the most famous of all these Glasgow merchants, Andrew Cochrane, founded in the 1740's a weekly club to discuss 'the nature and principles of trade in all its branches'. Adam Smith acquired a number of friends among this fraternity, including Cochrane himself, and thus gained an inside knowledge of commercial matters, reflected later in the* **Wealth of Nations**.

Likewise, when visiting his friend David Hume in Edinburgh, he encountered the "rage for agricultural improvement among Scottish landowners", and at the Select Club, that with Hume he helped to found, artistic and philosophical debates mingled with the discussion of agricultural questions. The result of such inter-action, the

Wealth of Nations, was a critique of economic practice, and a definition of how it should properly function in accordance with the theories and principles of Enlightenment.

As to the essence of his thoughts on such matters, we might turn once more to Brown:

> *Smith has gone down in history, and not untruly, as the most famous advocate of free trade and* **laissez-faire**. *He believed that, in the 'advanced' state which Western society had reached in his day, a continual growth in prosperity was possible for all nations. This growth was dependent in a large degree upon the 'division of labour', that is to say the discovery that, whereas a single workman could scarcely perform all the operations necessary to make a single pin during a whole day, ten workmen, by dividing up these operations and each specializing in one, would be able to manufacture 48,000 or more pins during the same day. (I do not mean that it was Smith who first made this discovery, merely that he laid extreme stress upon its importance). And, given the division of labour, a general prosperity, and a continual growth in prosperity, was a natural and inevitable process - only to be impeded by foolish efforts by government to tinker and interfere.*

However, according to Smith, to tinker and interfere was precisely what all European governments fatally did.

Such interference, whereby each country, through laws, taxes, tariffs and customs protected their own trading rights, were called by him the *mercantile system*. This system, which Smith taught to be in fact contrary to general and continual prosperity, was likewise the source of enmity, and indeed war between the major trading nations, who simultaneously debarred the weaker nations from trading, thereby artificially holding them in penury. If post-Union Scotland benefited from British protectionism, pre-Union Scotland had been considerably destabilised, and forced into that Union, by English protectionism, while notoriously, Ireland continued to starve as a result of the crippling restrictions placed on her trade and industry by Westminster.

Conversely, Smith taught that an abandonment of mercantilism for a policy of free trade would not only accord with a "natural and inevitable process" of international prosperity, it would also express the Enlightenment principles of tolerance and benevolence both within and between nations. Montesquieu, a major figure of the early French Enlightenment, recognised that trade ought to promote peace between nations through their interdependence. Brown refers to Montesquieu, and contrasts this with the harsh realities contained in Daniel Defoe's *Plan of English Commerce* (1728). As Brown concludes:

> *It was left to Adam Smith to show how Montesquieu's picture of trade as an engine for peace could be made to come true and how Defoe's cheerful acceptance and glorification of*

slavery and child labour, and further the whole idea of the need for commercial competition between nations could be discredited - not so much on humanitarian, as on rational and scientific, grounds, as being inefficient and unprofitable.

As to this last, and accurate qualification, it could nonetheless be added that to the men of the Enlightenment, science and rationalism was synonymous with humanitarianism. As with Hume, hindsight raises questions about Smith's theories. But again as with Hume and several of their contemporaries, his work constituted a crucial stage in the evolution of human thought.

(iii) Art and Architecture

Earlier in this section, it was suggested that the disjunction between a reprobate world and an absolute religious ideal obliterated the area in which literature had functioned. This is even more obviously the case with painting. The depiction of the sacred, or of the affairs of the reprobate world, were each in their own way sacrilegious, and neither could co-exist with Calvinist Scotland. All that might be done was in the field of portraiture, and what painting there was came in this form. When painting of quality began to appear in Enlightenment Scotland it was likewise in the area of portraiture, an area that also suited the human emphasis of the Enlightenment itself. The first artist of real note is Allan Ramsay, the son of the poet of the same name (see Part II, Section 4). The elder Ramsay encouraged his son's talent and like many Scottish painters thereafter, he spent a good deal of time refining his craft on the Continent, especially in France, and in what his father humourously called 'the seat of the beast beyond the Alps'. His painting is said to most resemble the work of contemporary French artists, an interesting extension of an inter-action between Scotland and France, the other outstanding centre of Enlightenment thought, which was much frequented by the likes of Hume and Smith. Indeed, like them, Ramsay was a friend and correspondent of men like Voltaire and Rousseau. He painted a portrait of the latter for David Hume, as indeed he painted Hume himself around the same time.

Considerable as they certainly are, many regard Ramsay's skills in portraiture to have been surpassed by the major figure of the rising generation, Henry Raeburn. Raeburn's style differs a good deal from Ramsay's. While stark distinctions would be inappropriate, it would be interesting to consider how far these differences reflect changing times. For example, there is a Raeburn portrait of Sir Walter Scott in the Scottish National Portrait Gallery. In comparing Ramsay's portrait of David Hume, (National Library of Scotland) the embodiment of Reason, with Raeburn's rendering of Scott, the 'Wizard of the North', can you see any changes in style that might relate to the move from Enlightenment to Romanticism?

Certainly the influence of Scott, and of Burns, is reflected in the painting of the day. Neither the landscapes of Alexander Naysmith, nor those of his son Patrick could be said to be intensely Romantic. They do however express an unprecedented interest in the natural world and this has its source in the work of Scott and the other great Romantic writers. David Wilkie on the other hand, and a whole school of followers, reflect in historical and domestic genre pieces the desire to give expression to a way of life that was past or rapidly passing that we also find in Burns, Scott, Hogg and Galt. Like the writers Wilkie's paintings are at their most sure in recording the recent past, and his subjects are generally life-asserting, avoiding the mawkish religiosity which is often found in later followers. Moving towards the early Victorian era Scottish painting reflects most of the predilections of the time. The work of David Scott seems to form a bridge between Blake and the Pre-Raphaelites, while William Dyce is more fully under the influence of the latter both in subject matter and in attention to natural detail. As we shall see other influences produced many visual equivalents of the Kailyard. But the course of Scottish art will be taken up again in the next section.

The achievement of Scottish architecture is a major feature of the period under discussion. The work of men such as Sir William Chambers, Robert Mylne, William Craig, Robert Reid, William Playfair and several others could be cited to give an impressive account of Scottish architecture in the Georgian period, and that is before we even mention the remarkable Adam family William, and his sons John, James and of course Robert, whose work is one of the most important influences in the whole history of Western architecture. Most of these men did a great deal of their work outwith Scotland, while some of their Scottish efforts have since been demolished. However, enough remains to bear witness to an originality and assurance in building, that parallels the mood that we have noted elsewhere in Enlightenment Scotland. Country houses on a variety of scales proliferated, the earliest often in the Palladian manner, with later examples seeking a purer classicism. Then there are the somewhat ambiguously termed "Georgian Gothic" buildings of which the most famous illustration in Culzean Castle. However, the single enterprise that provides examples of many of the great architects of the day, and at the same time supplies us with an interesting expression of historical change, is the New Town of Edinburgh. As with the details relating to the country houses, a fuller description of the New Town can be found in the set texts and the further reading. Here, you might consider how the transition from the Scots Baronial castle to the neo-classical elegance of Hopetoun House reflects the wider historical changes. To take a more important example, consider how the old vibrant, overcrowded, chaotic heart of the Scottish capital, itself the crucible of the Enlightenment, was displaced by the product and architectural expression of that Enlightenment, the New Town of Edinburgh.

SCOTLAND AND THE MODERN AGE: QUESTIONS OF IDENTITY

OBJECTIVES

Here we will try to:

⚙— consider the ways in which Scottish writing continued to reflect the factors inherent in the country's historical experience, in combination with the pressures particular to the modern world,

⚙— summarise the course of the non-literary arts in the modern period,

⚙— look at the major re-assessment of Scottish culture that took place in the wake of the Great War, and consider the nature of its continuing influence.

SOME MAJOR THEMES

(i)   Continuing and Contemporary Influences

A glance at the sections in Part I for this period will indicate the profound economic and social changes that the country experienced in the course of the nineteenth century. In many ways this general process that we call the Industrial Revolution was the material expression of the rational theories and experimental methods that set the tone of the preceding century. It is not surprising therefore that a nation so prominent in the process of the Enlightenment should be likewise prominent in the practical manifestation of that process in the following period.

The effect of intense industrialisation had an influence on the contemporary writer wherever it was felt, and we must now look at the response registered by Scottish literature. It should be remembered that the Industrial Revolution was itself preceded by an agricultural revolution that had created the great displaced rural population which would later be absorbed within the factories and mills of industrial Britain. A consciousness that a timeless rural lifestyle, that had in a variety of ways employed most of the population was passing away forever, and a desire to record something of that passing lifestyle, was increasingly a concern of writers in the second half of the eighteenth century. In the case of the Scottish writer, this combined with the long standing erosion of identity consequent upon the Union with England and expressed in the dilution of the Scots language, to render his efforts particularly urgent. Moreover, while everywhere, continuing advances in the natural sciences made for a crisis of faith and redefinition of belief which was to be a feature of the period, the particular nature of the Scottish religious tradition again gave its own tone to the reactions in this country. Thus, the urge to record a way of life that for national and international reasons was rapidly disappearing, is an aspect of the work of Burns, Scott, Hogg and Galt, that is referred to in Part II. But they were also living through such change, and for better and worse, the new also features in their writing - as in Burns' democratic spirit, the respectably 'British' side of Scott's fiction, or the fascination with the practicalities of economic and social change in Galt. Other writers of the period, such as Lockhart, D. M. Moir, and the undervalued Susan Ferrier, variously reflect such matters. However, as the nineteenth century progressed, the accelerating process of change and the increased uncertainty that this produced, saw the tone in which rural life was treated gradually reduced to the sort of sentimentality that we associate with the Kailyard School (see Part II, Section 10). Thus, by mid-century the Scottish novel was for the most part involved in a drift towards blatant nostalgia. This is not without interest, for of course escapism is itself a response to reality, underlining that reality's incompatibility with the past.

Two of the most competent writers in the genre, Margaret Oliphant and George MacDonald, produced their most enduring work on those occasions when they went beyond the kailyard. They are at their most powerful when, as in Oliphant's "Stories of the Seen and Unseen", and MacDonald's *Phantastes*, *The Golden Key* and *Lilith*, they move into the world of fantasy. Of course, this can be taken as just a more rarified form of escapism, but it is indicative of a central dilemma that the period faced, in so far as it at least attempts a "re-awakening of a sense of the noumenal in a time of sceptical naturalism" (R. Hart, *The Scottish Novel*). Another Scot, the historian and philosopher Thomas Carlyle, provided one of the fullest delineations of this dilemma. Many of his works, such as "Signs of the Times", *Past and Present*, and Sartor Resartus discuss the spiritual malaise of a machine age that was tending to reduce the whole of existence to a mechanical definition. If the solutions he proposes, as when he tries to restore spiritual value to the nineteenth century work process, fail to convince, they nonetheless convey something of the romantic writer's consciousness of the inadequacies of his age, and of the burning need for re-assessment. A reaction against mechanism, and against the rationalism from which it sprung, is one of the most striking features of nineteenth century literature. It saw the emergence of various re-definitions of human existence all of which, whether theist or atheist, whether emphasising the spirit or the imagination, sought to return humanity to a context that reason alone failed to recognise. Using the terminology of the preceding section, we have a movement away from pure empiricism, and an assertion of the necessity of an *a priori* dimension, which is the heart of the phenomenon we term Romanticism. Interestingly however, it is not an aspect of Romanticism that finds much expression in the context of Scottish literature.

There may be several reasons for this. The most persuasive *a priori* expressions are poetic in a period when Scottish literature excelled in other fields. It could be argued though, that the answer lies in Scotland's long and continuing inclination towards an empirical view, that the Enlightenment and before that even Calvinism had nurtured. It is interesting that our one major Scottish Romantic poet Lord Byron, is unique in having nothing to do with any form of 'transcendentalism'. Of course, such variety is simply to the greater good of poetry. But in his poetry, if not in his personality, Byron is very much of an eighteenth century temperament. Firmly based in the material world, his best work is urbane, humane and above all funny. But in none of these things is it quintessentially Romantic, and in this perhaps, the author is quintessentially Scottish. In any case, as the century progressed and the contradictions of the modern world became more oppressive, and in the absence of *a priori* solutions, Scottish literature for the most part sought refuge in the past and in the kailyard. But the situation implies an alternative possibility that should be noted. One might face up to the contradictions of material reality, chronicle them, and perhaps try to make sense of them.

The physical and spiritual degradation of millions in the slums that were the basis of the "workshop of the world" is a contradiction that has confounded the modern consciousness well beyond the Victorian period. In that period, the best of Romanticism might be said to have successfully qualified at least the theories that produced the contradiction. Other responses fail to convince, their reaction, as in Scotland, being essentially one of geographical, historical and religious insulation against that which would confound. By contrast it is in the work of two late Victorian Scottish poets that we find, variously, attitudes that anticipate some of the most influential voices of the twentieth century. Living, if not flourishing in London, both John Davidson and James Thomson BV (as distinct from the eighteenth century, author of *The Seasons*) suffered a degree of poverty and a sense of failure which rendered the harsh reality of the modern world inescapable. One result of this is that their poetry draws conclusions as to the nature of that world that are among the most stark and modern statements of the nineteenth century.

In ballads such as "Thirty Bob a Week", Davidson speaks for the debased working poor:

> It's naked child against a hungry wolf
> It's playing bowls upon a splitting wreck;
> It's walking on a string across a gulf
> With millstones fore-and-aft about your neck;
> But the thing is daily done by many and many a one;
> And we fall, face forward, fighting on the deck.

The Dedication to "John Davidson's Testament" finds him at once accepting the implications of a materialist universe, and seeking to make of it a positive, secular credo, in a manner that foreshadows Hugh MacDiarmid:

... there is no Other World; there never was anything that man has meant by Other World; neither spirit, no mystical behind-the veil; nothing not-ourselves that makes for righteousness, no metaphysical abstraction. Time is only matter, which is infinite, which is space, which is eternity; which we are. This is the greatest thing told since the world began. It means an end of the strangling past; an end of our conception of humanity and divinity, of our ideas of good and evil, of our religion, our literature, our art, our polity, it means that which all men have desired in all ages, it means a new beginning; it means that the material forces of mind and imagination can now re-establish the world as if nothing had ever been thought or imagined before; it means that there is nothing greater than man anywhere; it means infinite terror, infinite greatness.

Elsewhere, Davidson's response to the prospect is less confident, at times approaching the despair that found fullest expression in Thomson's works, the most effective of which, *The City of Dreadful Night*, anticipate moods and tones later to be found in Eliot's *Wasteland*:

I find no hint throughout the Universe
Of good or ill, of blessing or of curse;
I find alone Necessity Supreme;
With infinite Mystery, abysmal, dark,
Unlighted ever by the faintest spark
For us the flitting shadow of a dream.

The City of Dreadful Night was written for, and by:

... one desolate, Fate smitten,
Whose faith and hope are dead, and who would die.

Thomson suffered a vagrant's death and Davidson killed himself. If the Kailyarders provide an extreme example of the tendency to insulation and escape that the pressures of the age promoted, Thomson and Davidson registered the most courageous assessments of those pressures, and of their psychological implications, recorded in the nineteenth century. It was not until the twentieth century that the struggle towards a positive response to these dilemmas was fully engaged.

(ii) Art and Architecture in the Modern Period

In the second half of the nineteenth century painting, like literature, expressed the escapism that was an aspect of the period in the production of a good deal of whimsy and nostalgia. Just as important literary commentary on the changing world withered in the course of the century to the formulae of the Kailyarders, so the unsentimental scenes that David Wilkie celebrated were often reduced to the mawkish over the same period by his successors. However, this was less universal in painting than in literature, and indeed there emerged simultaneously the beginnings of a tradition in Scottish art that can at once be seen to relate to European developments, and to evolve a distinctively Scottish flavour.

The first painter who clearly displays such qualities is William McTaggart (1835-1910). At times he comes close to the sentimental genre pieces of his contemporaries. But elsewhere, particularly when the landscape itself comes to dominate the painting, and his impressionistic fascination with light effects is given play, there is a modernity about McTaggart's art that distinguishes him from the others. Though conservatism continued to dominate the artistic establishment, from about 1880 the precedents we see in McTaggart's work were taken up and developed, mainly by that group of painters that known as the Glasgow School. In the work of such artists as George Henry, David Gauld, E.A. Hornel, J. Stuart Park and Andrew Melville (any study of the School will expand the list) we can witness the experimentation and innovation of the time, as well as a certain tone that is particular to the Scottish painters. In other arts too - eg. woodwork, metalwork, furniture - there were exciting developments, and indeed in all these fields, as well as in architecture, Scotland's unique contribution to Art Nouveau is epitomised in the genius at the heart of the Glasgow movement, Charles Rennie Mackintosh (1868-1928).

In the twentieth century Scottish art has continued to reflect national and international traits. The artists known as the Scottish Colourists, S.J. Peploe, Leslie Hunter, F.C.B. Cadell and J.D. Fergusson have on the one hand links with Cezanne and Matisse, and with an exciting use of colour that can be seen in the work of the Glasgow School and before that in McTaggart. Positive links with the Scottish literary revival can be seen in the work of William Johnstone, who, for example, sought a basis for his surrealism in the symbolism of the Pictish standing stones. The vigour of the period is indicated by the inter-action that saw MacDiarmid write a series of poems in response to Johnstone's paintings (a further aspect of such cross-fertilisation is the relationship between the composer Francis George Scott and the major poets of the revival). Scotland has continued to produce accomplished artists up till and including the present. It would be impossible either to describe them all or to justify selection. However, perhaps the brief survey of Scottish art here will indicate some basic aspects of the subject on which you can build yourself.

Architecturally, the Victorian period was revolutionary in the sense that the effects of the Industrial Revolution dictated the tone in proportion to its impact in any given area. Obviously the major cities were chiefly affected, and of these Glasgow and Dundee, the big industrial centres, underwent the more thoroughgoing transformation. There was a great deal of building in Edinburgh and Aberdeen also. Essentially though, this was straightforward expansion. The inordinate population growth in the more industrial cities rapidly turned suburbs into slums which would in turn be raised and rebuilt. Much that was distinctive in Dundee disappeared in this way. In Glasgow, the Georgian elegance of the homes of the eighteenth century tobacco barons was engulfed in the Victorian expansion of the commercial centre, while the residential areas re-grouped in the countryside of Queens Park or Kelvinside. Banks and commercial institutions sought the architect's talents as well as the home-builder and the Church. Coinciding with the Glasgow School of painters, a number of architects in the city responded inventively to such demands. Among these, Alexander 'Greek' Thomson designed buildings with a personal flair that in a sense renders the nickname inappropriate. In the city centre the demand for space and the invention of the elevator combined to push buildings skyward. This, in combination with the ornamental tastes of the period prompted in a variety of architects u turn of the century style which till about twenty years ago conveyed the exciting tenor of a major world city. As to Victorian Gothic, the best example is the re-sited university on Gilmore Hill, almost contemporary with the amazing experiments in modern architecture of Mackintosh, in public building like the Glasgow School of Art, and residential conceptions such as Hill House in Helensburgh.

Edinburgh produced more expressions of the Victorian Gothic sensibility, as for example the enormous St Mary's Episcopal Cathedral (the Episcopalian Church was in general a great patron of the style) or, by contrast, the atmospheric intricacies of the Scottish Portrait Gallery. Elsewhere, buildings in the Renaissance style, such as the Royal Scottish Museum, or the MacEwen Hall, were likewise added to medieval slums of the Old Town and the classical elegance of the New Town, which together formed the essential tone of the city.

As to the country house, the period likewise saw Gothic and Renaissance styles rivalling the classical work of the Georgian period, while a particularly Scottish revival saw the emergence of a more elaborate version of the Scottish Baronial style.

The slums of Edinburgh are mentioned above, as is the even greater problem of life in the industrial centres. Throughout the twentieth century architects have at times produced inspired innovative designs - consider the building that houses the Burrell Collection. But the problem of creating an environment in which a greatly expanded population can live in a civilised, human fashion - a problem exacerbated by the demands of the motor car - is one that the architect and town-planner share with the poets and artists of the modern age. Indeed despite the architect's more direct relationship to the dilemma, it cannot be said to have been resolved on any widespread basis.

(iii) The Twentieth Century: Paths towards the Present

We have seen that doubts about the reality on benevolent progress, and concern about what was being lost in the process are central features in nineteenth century thought. For many, the unimaginable losses inflicted on humanity in the course of

Poet's Pub by Alexander Moffat. Scottish National Portrait Gallery.

the Great War was the ultimate confirmation of these doubts. The consequent dismissal of old assumptions, and the search for means of re-definition, found expression in the seminal statements of Modernism that emerged during the 1920's. This revolution found its voice in Scotland as elsewhere, and here it combined with factors springing from specifically national considerations. As Part II suggests, at the heart of the 'Scottish Renaissance' was Hugh MacDiarmid, and though this must not obscure the participation of several other gifted writers, it is certainly the case that MacDiarmid set the tone of Scottish letters, not only in his own generation, but continuing into the present. The re-assertion of a Scottish context in political, cultural and linguistic terms merged happily with the wider concern for re-definition that called forth the music of Stravinsky, the painting of Picasso, the linguistic experimentation of Joyce and Elliot. The neglected field of Scotland's cultural and linguistic past provided unworked sources of re-definition:

> ... And there's forgotten shibboleths o' the Scots
> Ha'e keys to senses lockit to us yet
> - Coorse words that shamble thro' oor minds like stots,

Syne turn on's muckle een wi doonsin emerauds lit.
    (Gairmscoile)

The intellectual as well as the linguistic commitment to which MacDiarmid re-dedicated Scottish letters has remained a feature of the cultural climate ever since, as has, perhaps, a sympathy with Nationalist, and/or Socialist politics. Encompassing all this might be said to be a turn of mind that centres on a faith in the human intellect, an acceptance of a material definition of existence, and in the merging of the two, a commitment to the possibility of a positive future within a materialist framework such as MacDiarmid's later poetry often contemplates. Of such poetry, the fine contemporary poet, Edwin Morgan has written:

He (MacDiarmid) has never believed that art can be relegated from the general
evolutionary stream (full of hopeful mutations and choppy setbacks as it is) to a backwater
however warm and consolatory of 'permanent' human feelings.
    *(Edwin Morgan, **Hugh MacDiarmid**, Edinburgh 1976)*

Thus, Morgan rightly applauds the integrity of what he elsewhere calls MacDiarmid's "evolutionary credo", and in so far as the contrast is with the mere escapism of such as the Kailyarders, few would question his assessment. However, if any concern for "'permanent' human feelings" is to be dismissed as escapist, we would have to reject a remarkably high percentage of mankind's cultural achievement. The fact is perhaps, that a concern for material reality, such as MacDiarmid, and Morgan express, always will co-exist with speculations as to a further reality that in their own terms at least, seek not escape but deeper truth. Indeed, recognition of this co-existence is necessary to a full account of the twentieth century revival itself.

The alternative view is most fully expressed by Edwin Muir, whose contentious appraisal of the linguistic situation in *On Scott and Scotland,* provides one key text for Part II. We might well disagree with his conclusions there, but his ideas are stimulating, and in his own terms he too is motivated by concern for the survival of Scottish culture, looking to a Scottish 'nationalisation' of the English language, along the lines of the achievement of Yeats and Joyce in Ireland. In any case, his views on linguistic matters form part of a wider concern for the attainment of identity, both in national and in wider human terms. Part II contrasts his position with MacDiarmid's thus:

Muir argues that the regeneration of Scottish culture can result only from unification,
through the repair of the 'dissociation of sensibilities'.

By contrast, we have:

MacDiarmid's espousal in the early twenties of the principle of revolutionary dialectic on
every level -aesthetic, political, intellectual.

The essence of Muir's principle of "unification" or reconciliation lies in the perception of 'permanent' values, in which context the contradictions of existence might be resolved. The last of his *Collected Poems* concludes that he has:

> *...drawn at last from time that takes away*
> *And taking leaves all things in there right place*
> *An image of forever*
> *One and whole.*
>
> *And now that time grows shorter, I perceive*
> *That Plato's is the truest poetry,*
> *And that these shadows*
> *Are cast by the true.*

To recap one last time, this could be termed an *a priori* statement, and the alternative empirical temperament that gave us Hume and the Enlightenment, and that MacDiarmid might be said to have maintained would ask what it does for the human condition in the material reality in which we find ourselves. Conversely, Muir would argue that reality's dilemmas spring from the absence of a spiritual context. At the end of the day, it could be said that between them they express the basic alternative responses to human existence, and that the one is simply incomplete without the other. This view is enhanced if we consider that the two major novelists of the revival stand in a similar relationship to each other, with Grassic Gibbon sharing MacDiarmid's commitment to the material, and Neil Gunn, like Muir, seeking resolution in a wider, spiritual context. More recently, Muir's poetic successor is another Orcadian, George Mackay Brown, and it is clear in the work of both how far the timelessness' of their vision is facilitated by their background. It does not spring so easily perhaps from the urban reality of twentieth century Scotland, as the Glaswegian, Edwin Morgan might point out, and it is this context with which he, and novelists like Alisdair Gray seek to come to terms. Thus, it is perhaps within the framework of these two responses that we can best understand humanity. More particularly, a recognition of folk's shifting relationship between the two positions can greatly assist our understanding of Scotland past and present.

FURTHER READING

There is a substantial literature on the themes discussed here, but in particular we recommend:

D. MacMillan (1990) *Scottish Art 1460-1990*.

D. Macmillan (1994) *Scottish Art in the Twentieth Century*.

J. Purser (1992) *Scotland's Music : A History of the Traditional and Classical Music of Scotland*.